——— • THE • ———
COLLEGE HANDBOOK
— • OF • —
CREATIVE WRITING

◆ THE ◆
COLLEGE HANDBOOK
◆ OF ◆
CREATIVE WRITING

ROBERT DeMARIA
Dowling College

HBJ

HARCOURT BRACE JOVANOVICH

San Diego   New York   Chicago   Austin   Washington, D.C.
London   Sydney   Tokyo   Toronto

PREFACE

I have written this handbook of creative writing because there is virtually nothing of its kind available to teachers and students in university and college writing courses. I hope it will satisfy the need for a concise source of information about writing as a craft and as a career.

Talent cannot be taught, although it can be nurtured. Matters of craft, however, *can* be taught, and learning them will not damage a writer's native ability. This book does not aim to be prescriptive. It does not tell the student what to write or how to write it. Instead it describes how universal writing problems have been dealt with by experienced writers, and it explains how the mistakes commonly made by novice writers can be avoided.

The book is organized to be as practical as possible. It outlines the general principles of writing and then moves on to specific problems that writers encounter. Chapters 1–4 discuss the fundamental elements in a piece of creative writing — theme, setting, characters, and plot. Chapters 5–11 deal with the basic techniques for handling point of view, tone, description, dialogue, time, and imagery. Chapters 12 and 13 go over the mechanics of manuscript preparation and present a brief review of grammar, punctuation, and spelling. Finally, Chapter 14 looks at writing as a career and offers suggestions on such things as marketing, inquiries, and agents.

Throughout the book there are examples of effective writing, a number of which are presented in their entirety. At the end of each chapter there are discussions and writing exercises. In addition, there are several useful glossaries and reference lists, including a Glossary of Literary Terms that follows Chapter 14.

My hope is that this book will prove to be a handy supplement in writing courses without changing the nature of the learning process or the relationship between student-writer and writing teacher.

I would particularly like to thank Robert Karmon of Nassan Community College; Bill Meissner of St. Cloud University; and Thomas Rabbit of the University of Alabama for their helpful comments.

It is impossible, however, to name *all* the people who helped to make this book possible. They include students, colleagues, writers, librarians, and the college department staff at Harcourt Brace Jovanovich. I am grateful to all of them.

CONTENTS

4 PLOT   66

5 POINT OF VIEW   92

INTRODUCTION

This is a handbook that deals with the practical aspects of a writer's craft. A discussion of the fascinating issues that relate to the creative process might easily fill another whole book. Writers are concerned, of course, with both the technical questions of craft and the broader questions of creativity. A brief look at how writers experience the process of writing might serve as a revealing introduction to our subject. These remarks come from *Writers at Work, The Paris Review Interviews:*

> *Writers are witnesses. The reason we need writers is because we need witnesses to this terrifying century.*
>
> E. L. Doctorow

> *When the writing is really working, I think there is something like dreaming going on. I don't know how to draw the line between the conscious management of what you're doing and this state.*
>
> John Hersey

Poetry, after all, milks the unconscious. The unconscious is there to feed it little images, little symbols, the answers, the insights I know not of.

Anne Sexton

Making fake biography, false history, concocting a half-imaginary existence out of the actual drama of my life is my life.

Philip Roth

I feel the story I am writing existed before I existed; I'm just the slob who finds it, and rather clumsily tries to do it, and the characters justice. . . . It is entirely ghostly work; I'm just the medium.

John Irving

I didn't choose poetry; poetry chose me.

Philip Larkin

Being a writer is a condition. You're born with it and stuck with it. You have no choice.

Cynthia Ozick

Some writers are pragmatic, even cynical, about their craft. It's just a way to make a living to them. Most serious writers, however, attach special significance to what they are doing. They see themselves as "witnesses." They experience the mystery of inspiration. Perhaps they feel possessed — John Irving says that writing is "ghostly work." Serious writers feel that writing is drawn from the deep well of the unconscious mind. In short, they attribute to writing, and perhaps to all the arts, the highest kind of importance: the creation of beauty and the discovery of truth.

These are high aspirations, almost as difficult to talk about as to achieve. We cannot pause here to explore all the interesting debates in which critics and scholars are now immersed. Instead, our task in this book is to review the details of the writer's craft. Let us, therefore, pass by this seductive labyrinth and begin with an obvious fact: human beings have a need to create works of art.

Not only do we have the need, we have the desire and the capacity. We have something called *imagination*. We can make up things. We can invent. We can generalize and abstract. Furthermore, we are capable of creating the forms that can give expression to our dreams. When the form and the dream are successfully merged into art we experience that elusive phenomenon known as *beauty*.

Art is a more difficult word to define than *craft*. It is complex and controversial. Let's focus instead on *craft*. That word has a nice, down-to-earth sound to it. After all, even carpenters have a craft to learn.

Carpenters learn their craft as apprentices to the master. Musicians and painters also learn this way. Their training is more obvious than the writer's training. Without the basics a musician or painter can rarely get started. Writers, too, learn their fundamentals from the masters, but it is not usually on-the-job training; it is the more private training of reading and personal consultation. It would be a mistake to assume that all writers begin their careers by re-inventing the wheel. However original their ideas may be, all writers learn the essentials of their craft from what has gone before.

Our discussion of the writer's craft necessarily involves certain basic definitions and concepts. Such definitions may not be very exciting at times, but they are often useful.

CREATIVE WRITING

Creative Writing is a term that has taken hold in academic circles. It has become part of the jargon of education. In college catalogues you will find Creative Writing courses and degree programs in Creative Writing. The meaning of the term is very specific. It is not a value judgment. It does not mean good writing as opposed to bad writing. It means writing that involves the imagination and invention in form and content. It means *fiction, poetry,* and *drama*. The fiction may be long or short. The poetry may take many different forms, and the drama may be for the stage or the movies or television. All creative writing uses made-up materials of one kind or another. Its main function is not merely to convey facts or information. Its main function is to please the reader or audience aesthetically by playing with the imagination. Some creative writing is light and superficially entertaining; some is very profound and can reveal great truths about the human condition.

TRUTH AND FICTION

There is an old saying that "truth is stranger than fiction." It sounds good, as many epigrams do, but it is not altogether accurate. It is only a way of saying that it is sometimes hard to believe the things that really happen in this world. No one can deny that, but some of the things one finds in fiction can be equally incredible. In Kafka's *Metamorphosis*, for instance, a young man wakes up one morning and finds that he has been transformed into a giant cockroach. The human imagination is extremely inventive.

A literary work is often a blend of fact and fiction. A literal account of someone's adventures in Vietnam is not a novel; it is a memoir or part of an autobiography. The same author might be moved by certain experiences in Vietnam to create a work of fiction. In such works the facts can be adjusted to improve the story. Anne Sexton once said: "I don't adhere to literal facts all the time; I make them up whenever needed."

It doesn't take much background reading to discover that writers draw heavily on their own experiences. Young writers are often advised to make use of the materials with which they are most familiar. That's good advice, as long as they are also prepared to violate the truth in favor of a higher truth.

Some instructors like to shock their students by saying that all writers of fiction are "liars" because they make up things, because they do not tell the truth. This is a mildly amusing remark, but it is somewhat misleading. The word "liar" has a pejorative meaning. People lie in order to conceal or deceive. Writers do not make up things in order to conceal. They invent stories in order to reveal things about human nature and experience. We do the same thing when we dream. We represent inner feelings to ourselves in symbolic form. We make up situations and characters and sometimes nightmarish happenings, but these inventions are an expression of some inner truth about ourselves. One might even argue that *fiction is truer than fact*, because sometimes the real truth can only be told by indirection, by the invention of revealing situations.

In introductory workshops students sometimes produce papers that are really essays and not short stories. They are often personal anecdotes about interesting or even horrifying events. I have read endless accounts of automobile accidents, deaths in the family, drug abuse, and various childhood traumas. Some of these personal essays are very well written.

Some of them even contain good raw materials for fiction, but always I must ask: "What's the story?" A personal essay is not a short story. It is bound by the facts and does not allow for invention. What's more, its tone is often clearly autobiographical. Nevertheless, there are times when it is impossible to distinguish between fact and fiction, and it may not be all that important to do so as long as the narrative is dramatic and has form and significance.

PROSE AND POETRY

Prose is any kind of writing that is built essentially out of sentences and paragraphs. Fiction is prose, but so is nonfiction. Poetry, on the other hand, is built essentially with lines, and it involves the manipulation of sounds in order to create verbal music. As in the case of fact and fiction, there is a good deal of overlapping between prose and poetry. Both can have narrative elements. Both can have pleasing rhythms, characters, and conventional punctuation, but poetry relies heavily on special forms, on configurations of lines, and often on rhymes and rhythms. In effect, poetry is a hybrid art form, a cross between prose and music.

DRAMA AND FICTION

The most obvious difference between drama and fiction is that drama is intended for performance, whether the performance is on a stage or on a screen. That difference is sufficient to establish drama and fiction as distinct literary classifications.

There are, however, many similarities between these two major genres. They both involve made-up stories. They both involve characters, plot, dialogue, and description.

One might argue that a play is merely a dramatized story, but that would be an oversimplification. Performance makes an enormous difference. Every medium has its advantages and its limitations. The visual experience is not the same as the reading experience. Actually seeing a drama on stage is not the same as seeing a story in your mind. A performed drama can not escape from its live stage or even from its electronic stage. In fiction, "all the world's a stage." The human imagination has fewer restrictions than any other medium.

Though it is possible to discuss the common denominators in these genres in pretty much the same way, it is necessary to understand the distinctive techniques employed in each genre. There are things that can be done in a play that cannot be done in fiction, and there are things that can be done in fiction that cannot be done in a play.

VARIETY IN THEME AND FORM

We might ask ourselves why there is so much variety in the verbal arts. We have short stories, novellas (short novels), novels, poems, prose poems, plays, poetic plays, scripts for movies and television, docudramas, and something that Truman Capote called "the non-fiction novel" (a journalistic novel based on fact; an example of which is Capote's *In Cold Blood*). The answer is simple: we have a wide range of human experiences and a strong urge to give them some form of expression. The form we choose depends on the experience. The special thrill of a flaming sunset may not require a novel. It might be best expressed in a poem. A complicated family saga covering several generations would be difficult to squeeze into a poem, and might be expressed most effectively in a long novel or television mini-series. A brief amorous encounter might make a good short story. A highly visual adventure requiring special effects might best be treated in a filmscript. There is, of course, much overlapping. Some subjects lend themselves to several forms. For instance, there have been poems as well as short stories about brief amorous encounters, and many a novel has been made into a film. Writers should define their ideas and experiences from the beginning so that they can choose the form that is the most appropriate for the material.

SELECTION

Selection is essential to all the arts. Writing can never duplicate real life in any literal sense. Real life is a lot messier than art. It is more random, less organized, full of accidents and distractions — too full, in fact, of thousands of little details. To report completely all the actions, feelings, and thoughts (conscious and unconscious) of one day in the life of one person would require an enormous volume, much larger than James Joyce's *Ulysses*, which is a seven-hundred-page novel that tries to capture a single day in the lives of some Dubliners.

Human experience is very complex. The brain operates twenty-four hours a day, every day. It is constantly receiving, interpreting, and responding to internal and external stimuli. Even an ordinary person who thinks his or her life is uneventful and boring has moment-to-moment experiences that are impossible to record completely. Think of all the microscopic details that are involved in even the simplest action. Imagine what is involved in getting up and going to work in the morning: the sound of the alarm clock, the sensation of waking into awareness, emerging from the mysterious realm of sleep with all its strange subterranean dramas, the taste in one's mouth, the feeling of warmth or cold, the texture of the bedclothes, rituals in the bathroom, the smell of soap, the sound of water, and so on. Under a microscope every moment, every sensation is expanded: dressing, eating, driving to work, reading the newspaper, meeting people, and so on.

The raw materials of life are overwhelming and without form and meaning when looked at in this way. They are only given form and meaning through a process of selection. The writer does not record experience; he or she creates a work of art from the *selected* and carefully *arranged* details of experience. The writer creates a story, poem, or play. The writer's craft makes it possible to deal with a variety of things: theme, setting, characters, plot, point of view, tone, style, description, dialogue, thoughts, time sequences, images, patterns and forms. These skills are the subjects covered in this handbook.

CHAPTER ONE

THEME

1a
Every literary work must have a point, a *raison d'être*.

(1) A writer can write about almost anything.

There is virtually no limit to what a writer can write about. There are *exterior* events, all those things that happen to people, and there are *interior* events, the things that happen inside a character's head. These raw materials can only be turned into fiction, poetry, and drama if they are given *form* and *significance*. A literary work can deal with complex events that take place over a long period of time or merely with an intense experience that takes place in a moment.

(2) A summary of a literary work cannot convey the full meaning of the whole work.

Non-fiction provides us with a wide range of information and ideas. Literature provides us with imagined human experience. Non-fiction *tells* us something. Literature *shows* us something.

The grammar-school game of "Show and Tell" is often used to clarify the distinction. There is a big difference between being told by a child that he found a dead rat and having him actually produce the ugly corpse from a brown paper bag.

Literature is an art form made from words. It contains ideas, but goes beyond. It is as much art as music or painting, and its ultimate impact is emotional and aesthetic. No description of a literary work can take the place of the whole work, anymore than a comment on music can take the place of the music itself.

(3) We can describe what a literary work is about by examining the subject, the theme, the situation, and the plot.

Since the whole meaning of a literary work can only be found in the whole work, anything short of that is bound to be an abstraction, a classification, or a summary. Some very well known writers have refused to discuss what their work is about. "It stands on its own," they insist. "Just read it."

It is a lot easier to describe what a piece of non-fiction is about. An essay, for instance, has a clear central idea or *theme*, which can usually be stated in a single sentence. Composition students are encouraged, even required, to use such "topic" sentences. An essay on capital punishment, for example, might take as its theme the statement that capital punishment does not deter violent crimes. This theme is developed with evidence and arguments in the full essay. It is a lot more difficult to describe what a novel such as *Crime and Punishment* by Dostoevsky is all about, or even a short story such as "The Lottery" by Shirley Jackson. When we *do* try to describe what a literary work is about we can make use of several kinds of abstractions or summaries. We can describe the *subject*, the *theme*, the *situation*, and the *plot*.

The subject is the broadest classification we can use. A subject is a category, such as war, violence, revenge, compassion, kindness, honor, ambition, and so on. We can say that *Romeo and Juliet* is a play about love, for instance. How exactly it deals with that subject is revealed in the theme, situation, and plot.

The theme of a literary work is the author's central message or the central dramatic impact of the work. In *Romeo and Juliet* the lovers are described as "star-crossed." The theme of the play, therefore, is that some love affairs are destined to end in tragedy.

The situation in a literary work consists of a set of circumstances with which the work begins. For example, the situation in *Romeo and Juliet* is that the families of two young lovers are involved in a bitter feud. Everything that happens subsequently is part of the plot.

The plot is a summary of all the action in a literary work. A plot cannot be a list of random happenings. It must have a shape. The action must begin, rise to a crisis, and then be resolved. In other words, the plot is a summary of coherent and significant action. It is the spring that makes the clock tick.

Subject, theme, situation, and *plot* tell us something about the work, but the whole is greater than the sum of the parts. Therefore, describing what a literary work is about leaves us far short of experiencing it. Of "The Lottery" (1948) we might say the following: It is a short story about tradition (*subject*). It is about how people blindly adhere to their traditions without knowing what they are all about (*theme*). It is set in a typical farming community in which the residents gather for their annual lottery (*situation*). The events unfold in a suspenseful and significant sequence (*plot*). We are not told at first what the nature of the lottery is. The preparations are described in detail, as are the residents of the town. Some of the people are named and followed in greater detail. One of these is Mrs. Hutchinson, who arrives a bit late and joins her family. Another is Mr. Summers, who conducts the lottery. Still another is Old Man Warner, who defends the tradition when Mr. Adams says that "in the north village they're talking of giving up the lottery." Warner reminds them of the old saying: "Lottery in June, corn be heavy soon," and he says: "There's *always* been a lottery." There is a holiday atmosphere in the square, but also a hint of something unpleasant. We wonder, at this point, whether the person chosen will be a winner or a loser. The crowd grows tense as the time approaches for the head of each household to draw a folded piece of paper from the black box. They are called up alphabetically and told not to open their folded slips of paper until everyone has drawn. There is a breathless pause. Then the slips of paper are all opened. Mr. Hutchinson has drawn the marked slip. His wife objects, but the drawing goes on. There are five members in the Hutchinson family, husband, wife, and three children. Each must now draw from a smaller group of papers. Mrs. Hutchinson draws the slip with the black spot on it. A space is cleared around her in the crowd. The townspeople pick up stones, and, in spite of Mrs. Hutchinson's protests, they stone her to death.

This stark summary of the content and theme cannot convey fully the emotional impact and the deeper levels of meaning in this modern classic. It does, however, provide a kind of X ray of the bones, a fleshless description of what the story is about. Much more could be said. On the other hand, one should keep in mind that, ultimately, a literary work is not merely *about* something; it *is* something.

1b

There is such variety in literary themes that it would be impossible to list them completely.

(1) Some great themes have appeared frequently in our literary heritage.

The Greeks were interested in the concept of *hubris*; that is, excessive pride. Hence, the theme that mere human beings should not overreach themselves and try to be god-like.

The classical notion of tragedy is that a good person with a tragic flaw can make an error in judgment that will lead to his or her downfall.

The concept of destiny plays a role in some literary works, in which the theme, invariably, is that a person's fate is inescapable.

The struggle between good and evil is the basis of many works. Good and evil can take many forms, but these forms are usually determined by a cultural or religious context. The influence of ancient Greece and the Judaic-Christian tradition is clear in Western literature. In Shakespeare's *Othello*, Iago is pure evil. His behavior needs no other explanation. He is living evidence of the influence of Satan in the world. In *Billy Budd*, Melville describes the evil that possesses Claggert as "natural depravity." Nothing, therefore, can prevent the clash between Billy and Claggert.

Love is often dealt with as a powerful force in human experience. "Love is not love/ Which alters when it alteration finds," says Shakespeare in one of his best known sonnets (116). Milton's famous remark about love makes a sexual distinction: "Love is of man's life a thing apart; 'tis woman's whole existence." In Hemingway's *A Farewell to Arms*, and in other love stories, love is described as a kind of religion. For Othello it is the very ordering force of the universe. When his love for Desdemona is threatened, he feels on the brink of chaos: "Perdition catch my soul / But I do love thee! And when I love thee not, / Chaos is come again." For some writers love may even go beyond the grave. In her often quoted sonnet that begins "How do I love thee?" Elizabeth Barrett Browning says, "and, if God choose, / I shall but love thee better after death." Love, of course, is a subject that includes more than just the romantic attachments of men and women. It includes familial love and friendship and even, in a broader sense, such things as love of God and country.

"No man is an island," said John Donne. There are many variations on this theme. We cannot isolate ourselves completely from our fellow creatures, nor can we remove ourselves from our own humanity. Exile was a punishment worse than death in the ancient world. The wanderer, the outcast, the outsider, the exile, the stranger — all appear frequently in literature.

(2) Certain major themes have emerged in contemporary literature.

Some of the major themes in contemporary literature are focused on the *self*; others deal with a world that is full of peril, a world that breeds more anger and despair than hope.

Alienation and loneliness are common experiences in a fragmented world. The modern decline in family and community structures has elevated loneliness as a literary subject. The theme haunts the works of modern writers as diverse as Joseph Conrad, T. S. Eliot, Virginia Woolf, and Elizabeth Bowen.

Coming of age in the modern world is extremely confusing. Being young has always been difficult, but in a world in which traditional modes of behavior have been challenged out of existence, the young have to create their own modes of behavior, and, in a sense, they have to create themselves. The result is considerable agony and chaos. Earlier literature rarely dealt with this subject. Today it is a major concern. This is one of the reasons why J. D. Salinger's *Catcher in the Rye* (1951) appears on so many high school reading lists.

Male–female relationships have become very complex since the so-called sexual revolution of the 1960s. Nowhere has the loss of tradition and structure in society caused more confusion than in the relationships between men and women. Romeo and Juliet may have had their problems, but they knew exactly where they stood and what was expected of them. Today's proliferation of paperback romances may be an escapist reaction to the confusion, or even a simplistic way of dealing with the new varieties of interpersonal problems. There are, of course, also many serious and worthwhile literary works on the subject, most of them by women who have been writing with greater freedom in an atmosphere of liberation — writers such as Margaret Atwood, Edna O'Brien, and Erica Jong.

There are many topical themes related to current issues, such as racial tensions, drug and alcohol abuse, abortion, poverty, and the problems of the handicapped. Films made for television feast on such themes.

Related to modern technology there are themes that deal with such things as the abuse of the environment and the dehumanizing of society. Science fiction is full of such themes, but they also show up in other works, such as the film *Network*, which was written by Paddy Chayevsky. Charlie Chaplin's

Modern Times (1936) was an early satirical treatment of technology. The theme here and elsewhere is that the factory system has made humans mere cogs in the wheel and removed from their work any of the old significance and satisfaction.

Disaster themes have become common and reflect our general anxiety. Many of these have been treated in popular movies that make use of sophisticated special effects.

Philosophical confusion has followed in the wake of political and social upheaval and acceleration of scientific speculation. It is difficult to know what to think about anything. The result is often a feeling that nobody cares and that nothing matters, which may explain the blind pursuit of materialism and pleasure.

Concern about the future has led to some dismal prophecies and fantasies, the most famous of which are Aldous Huxley's *Brave New World* and George Orwell's *1984*.

Themes dealing with crime and violence have appeared with increasing frequency, reflecting, perhaps, the frustrations of a world in confusion. Popular works of all kinds exploit these themes, which are often merely excuses for displays of bloodshed and cruelty.

Ic
Clarity in literature is arrived at more through descriptions of experience than through statements of ideas.

In an essay the theme is announced early on and everything that follows supports the theme. In literature the experience is uppermost, and in it the reader discovers a theme.

(1) **Sometimes the theme is obvious and can be clearly stated.**

In this famous poem by Robert Herrick (1591–1674) the theme is stated in the very first line:

TO THE VIRGINS, TO MAKE MUCH OF TIME

Gather ye rosebuds while ye may,
    Old time is still a-flying;
And this same flower that smiles today
    Tomorrow will be dying.

The glorious lamp of heaven, the sun,
    The higher he's a-getting,
The sooner will his race be run,
    And nearer he's to setting.

That age is best which is the first,
    When youth and blood are warmer;
But being spent, the worse, and worst
    Times still succeed the former.

Then be not coy, but use your time,
    And, while ye may, go marry;
For, having lost but once your prime,
    You may forever tarry.

(2) **Sometimes the theme is difficult to express.**

It is not always possible to reduce certain experiences to a purely intellectual statement. The proportions of head and heart in a given work will vary enormously. Symbols may be artistically powerful but are often difficult to interpret. This poem by William Blake (1757–1827) has been the subject of considerable discussion and controversy:

THE SICK ROSE

O rose, thou art sick.
The invisible worm
That flies in the night
In the howling storm

Has found out thy bed
Of crimson joy,
And his dark secret love
Does thy life destroy.

What is this destructive "invisible worm"? Is it some moral failure, some corruption? Or is it more literally a disease?

Id
Significance in literary work varies greatly.

There are many degrees and kinds of significance in literary themes. The broad spectrum ranges from the silliest kind of romance or comic-book adventure to the works of such major literary figures as Herman Melville and Jane Austen. There is enormous variety in literature. Some critics try to draw the line and create criteria for what they call true literature, as opposed to mere entertainment or downright junk. Drawing a precise line is always a bit arbitrary, and not really necessary. What we have is a continuum from the very trivial to the very important. Since the range is very wide, some of the material between these extremes can prove quite interesting without actually being world-shaking. What good fiction, poetry, or drama does for us is to leave us with the feeling that our experience has been expanded vicariously and that perhaps we know something afterward that we did not know before. In other words, good literature has an impact that, in some way, however small, changes the reader. Trivial literary entertainments such as thrillers and romances and television dramas, however, cannot be dismissed with contempt. They have a role to play in the lives of many people, and many of the writers involved find such work a pleasant and profitable form of employment, though significance in such works is clearly minimal. Their aim is to thrill, chill, and titillate. Frank Lloyd Wright once described television as "chewing gum for the eyes." It's an excellent description of that medium and might also apply to most of our light literature. Chewing gum gives you a lot of action but no nutrition. Great literature, on the other hand, is full of emotional, spiritual, and intellectual nourishment.

EXAMPLE 1

THE INVISIBLE MAN
Ric Weinman

The invisible man is the main attraction. They come from all over to see him. Our small town circus has always been popular, but now they come a thousand miles and all they want to see is him.

The invisible man does only one show each night. He says the shows are very exhausting. When asked why he does the shows at all he replies that it is to make people happy.

His show is always the last show of the night. The tent in which the show is held goes quite dark, and the people in the audience, knowing what is to come next, hush their voices to a thick whisper. Suddenly, two bright spot lights are projected on the rear of the stage. In one of them is standing a short, slight, dark-skinned man with black curly hair and a very somber-looking face. In the other spot light is a piece of wooden floor. There stands the invisible man. The crowd cheers.

After a few minutes, the somber-looking man holds up his hands and the crowd falls silent. "The invisible man sends you all his greetings," the somber-looking man usually says. These words, even in his low, gravelly voice, evoke more cheering. He is the invisible man's helper. He is the only one who can hear what the invisible man says. But even he doesn't claim to be able to see the invisible man. No one can do that. He is quite entirely invisible. There is a popular rumor that under a full eclipse of the sun the invisible man will suddenly become visible, but as of yet, no full eclipse of the sun has occurred in our small town to either prove or disprove this for a fact.

The crowd squeezes together like marshmallows, trying to get as close to the stage as possible. Those who stand in the front row are pressed so hard against the chest-high stage that it is often difficult for them to breathe. They all swear it is worth it though, and quite worth the long wait they endured to reach that strategic position. Those who want to be in the front row usually get in line right after the show ends the night before.

A balding, middle-aged man in a rumpled but expensive-looking business suit standing in the front row waves his arm furiously. The somber-looking man points to him. "Do you ever think of joining the State Department?" the middle-aged man asks. There is a short pause in which the whole tent is wrapped in a dense silence. "No," the somber man says. "The invisible man says that he never feels like joining the State Department because he doesn't feel himself to be part of the state. He feels that he is his own state and that his political responsibilities lie within those boundaries." The business man, having been called upon and given an excellent answer, seems to glow with an intense joy. He looks like one who has been blessed.

More hands are in the air. A little girl, perhaps four years old, is called upon. "I'd like to know if you would give me a kiss?" She asks shyly. The crowd is suddenly very tense. The audaciousness of the little girl's request angers them. They feel she is being denigrating. They feel she has no right to make such a request that can only be refused. "The invisible man

| Example **23**

says he will kiss you," the somber man says. The crowd relaxes, both surprised and pleased. "How wonderful of him," someone says. The little girl is lifted onto the stage and sticks her head forward with her eyes closed, her lips curled up in an expectant pout. The crowd becomes very still. "The invisible man says he has kissed you," the somber man says. "He did?" she exclaims, opening her eyes. Suddenly she knows it is true. A beautiful smile lights up her face and the crowd cheers. The little girl is lifted back down.

"To what do you attribute your invisibility?" This question is from a young woman. The crowd groans. It is an often-asked question and the answer is well known to most of those present. Mainly, though, it's the waste of a precious question — the invisible man answers only four questions each night. "The invisible man says that when he was a young boy his father died and his mother became a drunkard. Since there was no one to pay him much attention, he stopped believing he existed. As many wise men know, belief creates reality. Not long afterwards he started to fade from visible existence." Hands fly in the air.

"Does the invisible man think he'll ever meet an invisible woman?" This question from a teenage boy. "Please direct your question to the invisible man, not to me," the somber man says. The boy looks confused for a moment. His mother whispers something in his ear. The boy nods his head and smiles. "Do you think you'll ever meet an invisible woman?" The crowd is excited. They like this question. They anxiously await the answer. "The invisible man says that he does in fact already know an invisible woman but that he is not yet ready to introduce her to the world." For a moment the crowd is so shocked by the answer, there is no break in the silence. Then there is an amazed whisper. And another. And another. Suddenly the whole tent is alive with whispers which flow together and rise and fall like waves of the ocean, like a great tide washing against the shores of incomprehensible time. "An invisible woman." "An invisible woman." "An invisible woman." It sounds something like a chant the old ones used to sing. The somber-looking man holds up his hands but it is some time before the crowd is again silent.

"As you know," he begins slowly, his weak, scratchy voice somehow a perfect match for the rough tent and expectant faces, "before we conclude each night's ceremony we try to see if we can't bring the invisible man into the visible world, even for just the briefest of fleeting moments. If you'll all hold hands as best you can and try to concentrate on the invisible man becoming visible, there's a slight chance that the power of your thoughts will make him solid enough to enable you to catch a quick glimpse of him." By the time he finishes speaking, everyone is already holding hands. A hush falls on the tent and the meditation begins. For five minutes the silence is so intense a man with a slight asthma in the back of the tent can be heard all the way up front by the stage. Finally there is a whisper. "I think I saw him." "I think I saw him, too." "I saw him, I know I did." "I saw him, too. He was about six feet tall and had light-brown hair." "Yes, he had light-brown hair." "Did you see his hair?" "Yes, it was light brown and he was about six feet tall." At least half the people are certain they've glimpsed him and another third thinks they did but are not absolutely sure. They all agree though: he is about six feet tall with light-brown hair. Of this there can be no doubt.

The crowd files out of the tent and disperses into the night. Some of them will dream of him tonight. In their dreams the invisible man may take many forms.

EXERCISES

DISCUSSION

1. What is the theme of Blake's poem "The Sick Rose"?

2. What is the theme of "The Invisible Man" by Ric Weinman (Example 1)? Is this a fantasy in which there really is an invisible man? Is it a story about a circus act intended to entertain the audience? Is it an indictment of religion?

3. Four questions are asked by the audience in "The Invisible Man." What are they? Do they have any special significance?

4. Explain the meaning of the last paragraph in "The Invisible Man."

WRITING

1. Write a short story, poem, or one-act play on one of the following themes:
   a. Growing up involves the loss of innocence.
   b. Individuals often find themselves in conflict with the conventions of their society.
   c. Romantic dreams often become disappointing realities.
   d. "Gather ye rosebuds while ye may . . ."

2. Here is a short poem by Margaret Atwood. It seems to deal with the relationship between two people. Show that you understand what this poem means by expanding it into a longer poem, a short story, or a one-act play.

> you fit into me
> like a hook into an eye
>
> a fish hook
> an open eye
>
> **Margaret Atwood**

CHAPTER
TWO

SETTING

Every literary work has to take place somewhere, even if the setting is only minimally implied, as it often is in poetry.

2a
The variety of settings used for stories, poems, and dramas is virtually endless.

A literary work can be set anywhere, from the inner space of a dream to the outer space of science fiction.

(1) Some settings are merely the landscape of the author's mind.

Most poems refer to specific circumstances with an implied or an actual setting, but some poems seem to be general comments on life or outbursts of emotion. Sometimes these

feelings are even translated into landscape terms, metaphori-
cally, of course, as in a poem by Christina Rossetti called "Cobwebs," which is often grouped with other somber poems such
as "Dead before Death." She may seem to be describing a place
in "Cobwebs," but surely she must be describing her own state
of mind:

> It is a land with neither night nor day,
>> Nor heat nor cold, nor any wind nor rain,
>> Nor hills nor valleys: but one even plain
> Stretches through long unbroken miles away,
> While through the sluggish air a twilight grey
>> Broodeth: no moons or seasons wax and wane,
>> No ebb and flow are there along the main,
> No bud-time, no leaf-falling, there for aye: —
> No ripple on the sea, no shifting sand,
>> No beat of wings to stir the stagnant space:
>> No pulse of life through all the loveless land
> And loveless sea; no trace of days before,
>> No guarded home, no toil-won resting-place,
> No future hope, no fear for evermore.

Some poems that belong in the landscape of the author's
mind may be reveries, memories, or dreams that name no
other setting. Some of these, however, hint at specific incidents, and therefore vaguely suggest a setting in the outside
world. Emily Dickinson's outbursts of emotion provide good
examples. In "Wild Nights" the reverie implies a love affair of
some kind, and the dream-like imagery creates a symbolic
setting.

WILD NIGHTS! WILD NIGHTS!
Emily Dickinson

Wild Nights — Wild Nights!
Were I with thee
Wild Nights should be
Our luxury!

Futile — the Winds —
To a Heart in port —
Done with the Compass —
Done with the Chart!

Rowing in Eden —
Ah, the Sea!
Might I but moor — Tonight —
In Thee!

In this poem we hear the longing of a lonely character, and we might imagine that these thoughts are provoked by a stormy night, and that the narrator is lying awake in bed, a solitary soul in a remote place.

(2) Some external settings are minimal and generic.

Some literary works take place in a setting that is never identified as a specific or real place. It might merely be a living room, a bar, a boat, a castle, a village, a battlefield, or, as in that famous stage direction, "another part of the forest." Fairy tales and folk tales tend to be vague about locations. They often begin: "Once upon a time in a kingdom by the sea . . ." or something to that effect.

Many plays are preoccupied with a human drama or a comic situation and merely specify a single set — a room, a pub, a railroad station. The generic setting for Luigi Pirandello's *Six Characters in Search of an Author* is simply "the stage of a theatre."

The settings in poems are often minimal and unnamed, though they may give rise to significant experiences. In the following poem by Seamus Heaney the setting is merely described as "the slope of the cutting." No country or town is mentioned. It is, in a sense, a generic rural setting. The emphasis is on the young boys and their revelations about the world outside their little place.

THE RAILWAY CHILDREN

When we climbed the slopes of the cutting
We were eye-level with the white cups
Of the telegraph poles and the sizzling wires.

Like lovely freehand they curved for miles
East and miles west beyond us, sagging
Under their burden of swallows.

We were small and thought we knew nothing
Worth knowing. We thought words travelled the wires
In the shiny pouches of raindrops.

Each one seeded full with the light
Of the sky, the gleam of the lines, and ourselves
So infinitesimally scaled

We could stream through the eye of a needle.

In "The Lottery" Shirley Jackson uses a generic small American town as the setting for a shocking and primitive ritual. In Hemingway's "A Clean, Well-Lighted Place" the setting is a generic Hispanic cafe. It doesn't really matter exactly where it is. The vagueness of location in stories such as these tends to give them a universal quality.

(3) Some literary works take place entirely in dreams.

The dream setting can be effective, suggestive, and symbolic. In a dream almost anything can happen. Locations can be realistic or fantastic. The setting can shift suddenly. The subconscious mind is cavalier about such things. The result is often surrealistic.

One of the most famous dream poems is Samuel Taylor Coleridge's *"Kubla Khan: or a Vision in a Dream."* It was actually written immediately after the author woke up from an opium dream.

Students in writing workshops are rather fond of dream settings. Perhaps it unleashes the imagination. Unfortunately, they are equally fond of the alarm clock that wakes up the protagonist at the very peak of the suspense. The sudden discovery by the reader that the whole adventure was merely a dream can prove extremely disappointing.

(4) Some settings are pure fantasy — places in imaginary worlds.

Writers have been using imaginary journeys to imaginary places — past, present, or future — since ancient times. Plato imagines a Spartan utopia in *The Republic.* Dante descends into hell in *The Divine Comedy.* Lewis Carroll's Alice goes down the rabbit hole into a mad, fantastic world. In more recent times we have the *Modern Utopia* of H. G. Wells, the satirical utopia of Aldous Huxley's *Brave New World*, and Charlotte Haldane's *Man's World*, which, like Huxley's novel, rejects a world shaped by science, technology, and materialism. In lighter science fiction, futuristic heroes fight it out with the forces of evil in countless galaxies and solar systems that are largely imaginary.

(5) Most literary works have realistic settings.

Since literature is essentially about human experience, readers find it easy to empathize with realistic characters in realistic settings. A great many writers, using a great variety of styles, have chosen real locations for their works. We think of Jane Austen's little world, of James Joyce's Dublin, and of William Faulkner's South. A reader does not have to be familiar with the specific setting to appreciate the work. There are common denominators in human experience that allow us to identify with characters in England or France or Russia, in rural or urban areas, in New England, in the South, or in the Midwest. That is why we can all read a novel about a dull doctor in a provincial French town who is married to a restless and romantic woman, who becomes involved in a series of love affairs that lead her, eventually, to a tragic end. The novel, of course, is *Madame Bovary* by Gustave Flaubert.

(6) Some realistic settings have fictitious names.

When it comes to selecting a setting and naming it, writers have three choices. They can use:

1. A real place with a real name,
2. A real place with a fictitious name,
3. A fictitious place with a fictitious name.

Setting a story in a real place such as New York and calling it New York is no problem, since anything can happen in New York, and, in any case, nobody knows everything that goes on in such a big city. Setting a story in a very small town, however, and calling it by its real name can cause some problems. In some small towns everybody knows everything that ever happened there. It is difficult to insist that certain events took place and certain characters existed when, in reality, they did not. Some writers avoid this problem by using a fictitious name for a real town. If there is no special reason for choosing a certain location, some writers will simply make up a place, perhaps a typical American small town. It might resemble a lot of towns without actually being modeled after any particular place.

Thomas Hardy used the fictitious name Wessex for Dorset, a real county in England. William Faulkner used the name Yoknapatawpha county for a real region in his home state of Mississippi. On the other hand, Dorothy Parker, Saul Bellow, James Baldwin, and Woody Allen simply call New York by its real name.

2b
The accuracy of your setting depends on its importance to the story.

In some literary works the setting is *incidental*, and the main concern is plot or character. In other works the setting plays a *major role*. In poetry the setting itself is sometimes the *central focus* of the work. William Wordsworth writes about the countryside above Tintern Abbey. Dylan Thomas describes his town in Wales in musical detail. Robert Frost contemplates the walls and woods of his New England landscape.

(1) Some settings require personal and detailed knowledge.

Many writers make use of their hometown or the various places in which they have lived. And why not? These are the places one knows best. In autobiographical works they often play a significant role. It would have been difficult for James Baldwin to write *Go Tell It on the Mountain* if he had not grown up in Harlem. There is a long list of important writers whose works depend heavily on an intimate knowledge of the settings they use. James Joyce had to have an intimate knowledge of Dublin to write *Ulysses*, and William Faulkner could not have written such works as *The Sound and the Fury* and *Absalom! Absalom!* without being a native southerner. Flannery O'Connor also drew on her southern background to write her fiction, including the brilliant novel *Wise Blood*.

(2) Some settings do not require an intimate knowledge of the place.

Many a Hollywood or television script has been set in places never even visited by the writer. Almost any well-known place in the world can be conjured up with stereotypes and stock shots. The Eiffel Tower in Paris, the White House in Washington, Big Ben in London, a crowded market place in Casablanca. Old Hollywood films are especially notorious for creating sets out of stereotypes — the French cafe, the canals of Venice, the imaginary jungles through which Tarzan swung. A high degree of accuracy was not necessary. The central focus of these works was action, adventure, romance, intrigue. Even excellent human dramas made use of these theatrical sets. *Casablanca* did not become one of the most popular movies of all time because of the accuracy with which the place was depicted. It was important because of the love story, the conflict, the illusion of important events, and the incredible number of quotable lines.

(3) Historical fiction and drama depend on careful research.

Though stereotypes are sometimes used in works set in the past, a serious attempt to deal with a historical period should involve a careful and accurate reconstruction of that period. Stock shots of Roman orgies and gladiators may do for junk films and adventures with a comic-book sense of history, but a novel such as *I, Claudius* by Robert Graves requires a much more thorough background.

(4) Don't tell your reader too little or too much about the setting.

The degree of accuracy and the amount of detail you use must depend on the nature of your project. If the setting is very significant, you should know it well and weave details carefully into the fabric of events. If the setting is not very significant, do not burden your reader with unnecessary details. Too much description can get in the way of the story. On the other hand, a reader always likes to know where the action is taking place. Do not be too vague. Try to be convincing without being intrusive.

2c
The significance of the setting varies from genre to genre.

(1) In autobiographical works the setting can tell us something about the author.

A *novel of emergence* is a novel about the early years and young adulthood of a character. Since children are very sensitive to their environment, the setting of such a novel is significant. Charlotte Brontë's *Jane Eyre*, set in Yorkshire, and Charles Dickens' *David Copperfield*, set in London, are such novels. A later example is D. H. Lawrence's *Sons and Lovers*, in which the dismal life of a coal-mining family in Nottingham, figures prominently.

(2) Sometimes the setting itself is the main subject of the work.

One might argue that the main character in Faulkner's *Absalom! Absalom!* is the South itself, and that Thomas Sutphen is merely a symbolic or mythological figure.

There have been many attempts to capture the way of life in a typical small town in America. One of the best is *Our Town*, a play by Thornton Wilder, which is a portrait of a fictional place called Grover's Corners, New Hampshire.

(3) Some settings are used symbolically.

In Conrad's *Heart of Darkness* the journey up the Congo River is hardly treated as a mere travelogue. It is a journey back to the primitive state of man and to certain shadowy and violent regions of the human mind and heart. In Melville's *Moby Dick*, the sea, the whale, and the whaling ship are all treated symbolically. The novel is not just an adventure story; it is an ambitious metaphysical masterpiece. In drama we have the bleak landscape of Samuel Beckett's *Waiting for Godot* or the bare room in Hell in Jean Paul Sartre's play *No Exit*.

(4) Some settings present obstacles that influence or determine the action.

Jungles, deserts, rivers, mountains, and islands all have figured in light or serious literature. Who can forget that steaming delta through which Humphrey Bogart and Katharine Hepburn made their way aboard the *African Queen*, or the desert across which Lawrence of Arabia led his Arab troops to attack the Turks?

Such settings are often difficult enough in themselves, but when visited by natural disasters, as they often are, they provide truly dramatic stages for suspense, heroism, and disaster. At sea there are typhoons. In the mountains there are avalanches. Islands are swept by hurricanes and tidal waves. Forests become blazing infernos.

(5) Some settings are satirical.

Some of the imaginary places in utopian and prophetic literature are designed to criticize contemporary life. Huxley's *Brave New World* is a prime example, as is Samuel Butler's *Erewhon*, in which illness is considered a crime and crime is considered an illness. In a novel called *The Fixed Period*, Anthony Trollope invented an island named Britannula, ruled by a president named Mr. Neverbend.

Satire can be very amusing and significant. In order to use it well you not only have to create a convincing imaginary setting, but you have to have a good understanding of the real place that is being satirized.

EXAMPLE 2

BARCELONA

Alice Adams

In the darkened, uneven cobbled square, in the old quarter of Barcelona, the Barrio Gótico, the middle-aged American couple who walk by appear to be just that: American, middle-aged. The man is tall and bald; his head shines dimly as he and his wife cross the shaft of light from an open doorway. She is smaller, with pale hair; she walks fast to keep up with her husband. She is wearing gold chains, and they, too, shine in the light. She carries a small bag in which there could be — more gold? money? some interesting pills? They pass a young Spaniard lounging in a corner whose face the man for no reason takes note of.

Persis Fox, the woman, is a fairly successful illustrator, beginning to be sought after by New York publishers, but she sees herself as being in most ways a coward, a very fearful person; she is afraid of planes, of high bridges, she is overly worried by the illnesses of children — a rather boring list, as she thinks of it. Some years ago she was afraid that Thad, her husband, who teaches at Harvard, would take off with some student, some dark, sexily athletic type from Texas, possibly. More recently she has been frightened by accounts everywhere of muggings, robberies, rapes. She entirely believes in the likelihood of nuclear war. She can and does lie awake at night with such thoughts, for frozen hours.

However, walking across these darkened cobbles, in the old quarter of Barcelona, toward a restaurant that Cambridge friends have recommended, she is not afraid at all, only interested in what she is seeing: just before the square, an arched and windowed walk up above the alley, now crenellated silhouettes, everywhere blackened old stones. Also, she is hungry, looking forward to the seafood for which this restaurant is famous. And she wishes that Thad would not walk so fast; by now he is about five feet ahead of her, in an alley.

In the next instant, though, before she has seen or heard any person approaching, someone is running past her in the dark — but not past; he is beside her, a tall dark boy, grabbing at her purse, pulling its short strap. Persis' first instinct is to let him have it, not because she is afraid — she is not, still not, afraid — but from a conditioned reflex, instructing her to give people what they want: children, her husband.

In the following second a more primitive response sets in, and shes cries out, "No!" — as she thinks, Kindergarten, some little boy pulling something away. And next thinks, Not kindergarten. Spain. A thief.

He is stronger, and with a sudden sharp tug he wins; he has pulled the bag from her and run off, as Persis still yells, "No!" — and as (amazingly!) she remembers the word for thief. "Ladrón!" she cries out. *"Ladrón!"*

Then suddenly Thad is back (Persis has not exactly thought of him in those seconds), and almost before she has finished saying "He took my bag!" Thad is running toward the square, where the thief went. Thad is running, running — so tall and fast, such a sprint, as though this were a marathon, or Memorial Drive, where he usually runs. He is off into the night, as Persis yells again, *"Ladrón!"* and she starts out after him.

Persis is wearing low boots (thank God), not heels, and she can hear Thad's whistle, something he does with two fingers in his mouth, intensely shrill, useful for summoning children from ski slopes or beaches as night comes on. Persis, also running, follows the sound. She comes at last to a fairly wide, dimly lit street where Thad is standing, breathing hard.

She touches his arm. "Thad —"

Still intent on the chase, he hardly looks at her. He is not doing this for her; it is something between men. He says, "I think he went that way."

"But Thad —"

The street down which he is pointing, and into which he now begins to stride, with Persis just following — this street's darkness is broken at intervals by the steamy yellow windows of shabby restaurants, the narrow open door of a bar. Here and there a few people stand in doorways, watching the progress of the Americans. Thad sticks his head into the restaurants, the bar. "I don't see him," he reports back each time.

Well, of course not. And of course each time Persis is glad — glad that the boy is hidden somewhere. Gone. Safe, as she and Thad are safe.

They reach the end of the block, when from behind them a voice calls out, in English, not loudly, "Lady, this your bag?"

Thad and Persis turn to see a dark, contemptuous young face, a tall boy standing in a doorway. Not, Thad later assures Persis, and later still their friends — not the thief, whom he saw as they first crossed the square, and would recognize. But a friend of his?

The boy kicks his foot at something on the cobbles, which Thad walks over to pick up, and which is Persis' bag.

"I can't believe it!" she cries out, aware of triteness, as Thad hands over the bag to her. But by now, now that everything is over, she is seriously frightened; inwardly she trembles.

"Well, we got it." Thad speaks calmly, but Persis can hear the pride in his voice, along with some nervousness. He is still breathing hard, but he has begun to walk with his purposeful stride again. "The restaurant must be down here," he tells her.

Astoundingly, it is; after a couple of turns they see the name on a red neon sign, the name of the place they have been told about, where they have made a reservation.

The kitchen seems to be in the front room, next to the bar: all steam and steel, noisy clanging. Smoke and people, glasses rattling, crashing. "I really need a drink," Persis tells Thad, as instead they are led back to a room full of tables, people — many Americans, tourists, all loud and chattering.

At their small table, waiting for wine, with his tight New England smile Thad asks, "Aren't you going to check it? See what's still there?"

Curiously, this has not yet occurred to Persis as something to be done; she has simply clutched the bag. Now, as she looks down at the bag on her lap, it seems shabbier, a battered survivor. Obediently she unsnaps the flap. "Oh good, my passport's here," she tells Thad.

"That's great." He is genuinely pleased with himself — and why should he not be, having behaved with such courage? Then he frowns. "He got all your money?"

"Well no, actually there wasn't any money. I keep it in my pocket. Always, when I go to New York, that's what I do."

Why does Thad look so confused just then? A confusion of emotions is spread across his fair, lined face. He is disappointed, somehow? Upset that he ran after a thief who had stolen a bag containing so little? Upset that Persis, who now goes down to New York on publishing business by herself, has tricks for self-preservation?

Sipping wine, and almost instantly dizzy, light in her head, Persis tries to explain herself. "Men are such dopes," she heedlessly starts. "They always think that women carry everything they own in their bags. Thieves think that, I mean. So I just shove money and credit cards into some pocket. There's only makeup in my bags."

"And your passport." Stern, judicious Thad.

"Oh yes, of course," Persis babbles. "That would have been terrible. We could have spent days in offices."

Gratified, sipping at his wine, Thad says, "I wonder why he didn't take it, actually."

Persis does not say, "Because it's hidden inside my address book"—although quite possibly that was the case. Instead, she says what is also surely true: "Because you scared him. The last thing he expected was someone running after him, and that *whistle*."

Thad smiles, and his face settles into a familiar expression: that of a generally secure, intelligent man, a lucky person, for whom things happen more or less as he would expect them to.

Persis is thinking, and not for the first time, how terrible it must be to be a man, how terrifying. Men are always running, chasing something. And if you are rich and successful, like Thad, you have to hunt down anyone who wants to take away your possessions. Or if you're poor, down on your luck, you might be tempted to chase after a shabby bag that holds nothing of any real value, to snatch such a bag from a foreign woman who is wearing false gold chains that shine and glimmer in the dark.

EXERCISES

DISCUSSION

1. Discuss the significance of the setting in "Barcelona" by Alice Adams.

2. Is the old quarter of Barcelona described in sufficient detail in Alice Adams' story? Is it possibly too detailed?

3. Would the overall effect of the story be the same if it took place in a large American city, such as New York?

WRITING

1. Describe your home town or any other place that is familiar to you.

2. Describe life on an imaginary planet called Cronos.

3. Write a film-script that is set in a typical New England or Southern town.

4. Write a short story that takes place in a foreign country that you have never been to.

5. Write a poem about a natural setting, such as a forest, river, desert, beach, or mountain.

6. Write a poem or a story that takes place in a dream.

CHAPTER
THREE

CHARACTERS

3a
Since literature is about human experience, all literary works have characters.

(1) A character is an imaginary person created to play a role in a literary work.

A character is a created human being born in your imagination. The literary imagination involves interpretive imitations of life. Your characters are pictures, shadows, images in a mirror, people sent forth from your imagination to make sense out of the chaos of human experience.

(2) Literary characters are created for a purpose, but real-life people just are what they are.

Fictitious characters exist in the author's mind and on paper. Since they are created for a purpose, they usually have a certain coherence and definition. At simple extremes they are heroes and villains. In most realistic works they are more complex, but the bottom line is that they are "employed." Their employer is the writer, who has a job for them to do in his or her literary project. Living a real life is not the same as being specifically created to play a role in a drama or a novel. Literature is not life; it is *about* life.

(3) Nonhuman characters figure prominently in some forms of literature.

In works such as *Aesop's Fables*, in children's literature, and in animated cartoons we find a lot of animals that can talk. We also find trees that can talk, and rocks, and other things in nature, such as the wind and thunder. Actually, all of these things, when they appear in stories, in poems, in dramas, and movies, are humanized. It is known as *anthropomorphism*, not strictly in the sense that a human form is given to a nonhuman thing, but in the sense that human speech and feelings are attributed to this thing. In general, animals and inanimate objects can only be used in literature if they are given some human characteristics. One can describe a duck in scientific terms or as a farmyard animal that is part of the setting, but that duck is not the same as Donald Duck, who has a clear and definite personality.

(4) How much we have to know about a character depends on the nature of the literary work.

In a long work a character may be presented from the cradle to the grave, but often a literary work is like a view through a keyhole. We see only a portion of a character's life. The rest of the character's life is implied, and there is only the impression that the characters have real lives. In order to create this illusion, the writer has to know more about the characters than is revealed to the reader. Some writers prepare detailed biographical notes on their characters before beginning their play or story, and many a writer has felt that, in a sense, the characters really exist. Flaubert said: "Everything one invents is true, you can be sure of that. Beyond a doubt my poor Bovary is suffering and weeping in twenty French villages at this very moment." Woody Allen toys with this idea in "The Kugelmass Episode," a short story in which the protagonist is able to go back in time and have a love affair with Madame Bovary. Later, Emma is able to walk right out of her novel and the nineteenth century in order to visit her lover in modern New York.

The gimmick is amusing, and certainly there are characters who are so effectively depicted that they become real in the reader's mind, but that does not mean that either the author or the reader knows *everything* about them. In fact, it is not necessary to know everything in order to create the illusion of reality. What is necessary for that illusion is depth of understanding and skillful presentation.

(5) Characters in literature can be presented with the help of a number of literary devices.

The people in fiction are not any different from the people in poetry or drama, but there may be some differences from genre to genre in the devices used to bring them to life. On the other hand, there are certain devices that are common to all the forms of creative writing (see the chapters on *description, dialogue,* and *thoughts*). What we are concerned with here are the broader goals you hope to achieve when you present your characters. Those goals can be discussed in terms of the following questions:

1. What do your characters look like? (appearance)
2. What are your characters thinking? (depth)
3. Why do your characters do what they do? (motivation)
4. How believable are your characters? (plausibility)

The balance of this chapter will deal with these four points.

3b
There is often some literary significance in the appearance of a character.

(1) The appearance of a character is sometimes influenced by literary traditions.

Some of the literary traditions about the appearances of characters seem simplistic today, and even objectionable; nevertheless, the influence of those traditions is sometimes still felt. For instance, there was a time when it was customary in literature, and especially in the theatre, to assume that internal good or evil is reflected in the external qualities of a character. Heroes are attractive, villains are ugly. Richard III was portrayed as a hunchback by Shakespeare. Desdemona, who was innocent and pure, was an unblemished beauty. This tradition influenced the vintage films of the Hollywood era. To a lesser degree that influence continues in all the popular media, but there are more and more exceptions. Now there are even very handsome villains. Even serious works are occasionally touched by this tradition, though in modern times there is more subtlety and flexibility. What's more, the concept of the hero has given ground to the concept of the anti-hero, who is not a villain, but simply an ordinary person. Much of our good literature is no longer about a struggle between a hero and a villain; it is often about a wide variety of people and circumstances. There was a time when the common person was not considered worthy of a central role in any literary work. In modern times literature has become democratized. Central characters are drawn from every segment of society. Willy Loman, for instance, is the pathetic hero of Arthur Miller's *Death of a Salesman*. A very poor and old black woman named Phoenix Jackson is the heroine of Eudora Welty's "A Worn Path."

Though we still have stereotypes in modern writing, we also have unique individuals — a broad range of individuals. The writer has to decide what they look like. Most writers have minds like old attics, in which a lifetime of odds and ends are stored. They tend to be very inquisitive and observant. They walk down a street and notice things: a smile, a glance, a scar, a limp, the face of a young woman, the yellow skin of an old man, the eyes of a child. Writers are scavengers. They are people-watchers, photographers, psychologists, and a lot of other things. A good writer must pay attention to everything he or she encounters — everything! It is from this attic full of fragments that characters are constructed.

Some writers borrow the faces and features of people they know. Often, it's nothing personal, just the need for a model, a need to visualize a character. A *roman à clef*, however, is actually about real people who are presented as thinly disguised fictional characters. This is a special situation.

When writers choose the physical appearance of characters they already have something deeper in mind. They already have a plot or a set of circumstances, and they already have a general feeling for the fictional persons involved. They simply have to flesh out the characters. Their choices will be influenced by the personality of the characters and by the roles they play. Even though stereotypes are not involved, the appearance of the characters must be appropriate. It is, in a way, part of their costumes.

(2) **In some works the physical appearance of a character is only implied or left entirely up to the reader's imagination.**

Hemingway made famous this kind of economy in fiction. In "A Clean, Well-Lighted Place" the opening paragraph introduces us to a man in a cafe. All we are actually told about him is that he is old and deaf, but almost instantly we can picture him. Hemingway uses tone, imagery, and dialogue to help along the reader's imagination:

> It was late and every one had left the cafe except an old man who sat in the shadow the leaves of the trees made against the electric light. In the day time the street was dusty, but at night the dew settled the dust and the old man liked to sit late because he was deaf and now at night it was quiet and he felt the difference. The two waiters inside the cafe knew that the old man was a little drunk, and while he was a good client they knew that if he became too drunk he would leave without paying, so they kept watch on him.

In fairy tales, fables, and folk tales we often get an even sparser description of the appearance of the character. In Somerset Maugham's "Appointment in Samarra" (see Chapter 12) we have a merchant; a servant; and a woman, who is the spectre of death. None of them is described. They don't even have names.

The amount of physical detail provided by the author involves questions of style and is influenced by the form of the work.

3c

Characters in literary works should have a certain depth of development.

(1) Characters can be classified as *flat* or *round*.

Some characters are superficial or two-dimensional; other characters are three-dimensional and more fully created. They are as complex and convincing as real people. *Flat* characters have very little depth and are often stereotypes—the tall, dark, handsome lover in a romance, for instance, and his beautiful, virtuous, and devoted sweetheart. Entertainment literature does not require characters with depth. It needs only stock characters to amuse us or help us wile away our leisure time. It is devoted largely to love, sex, and violence. It needs heroes and villains, and, especially, husbands and wives and lovers with all the romantic agonies humanly imaginable.

(2) The deeper qualities in *round* characters are those qualities that make the character more lifelike and meaningful.

What is it that we want to know about the characters in serious and significant literature? "It is easier to know man in general

than to understand one man in particular," said La Rochefoucauld in 1665. This fascination with the complexity of the individual is age-old. Science and psychology may not have all the
answers. There are subtleties and mysteries. Literature is
sometimes a more effective way to explore human experience.
In his Nobel Prize acceptance speech William Faulkner said
that literature concerns itself with "the eternal problems of the
human heart."

At the greeting-card level human experiences are described in cliches. Love is a valentine message that begins,
"Roses are red, violets are blue." When serious writers such
as Emily Brontë, Gustave Flaubert, or D. H. Lawrence write
about love it is a profound exploration of a complex emotion.
We are still deeply moved by the story of Heathcliff and
Catherine in *Wuthering Heights*, and we still talk about Emma
Bovary's love affair with love, and about Lady Chatterley's
passionate affair with the gamekeeper. If people weren't so
complicated and fascinating we wouldn't go on writing about
them the way we do.

We want to know what they are *really* like, in what ways
they inescapably participate in human nature, and in what ways
they can be distinguished one from another. We want to know
how they feel, what they think, and how they act in a variety of
circumstances.

Even physically no two people are exactly alike. They dif-
fer in many ways: body language, posture, mannerisms, patterns of speech, attitudes, moods, overt desires and hidden
desires, ordinary fears and secret fears, obsessions, neuroses,
ways of seeing things and ways of seeing themselves. Discovering *everything* about a single individual, including ourselves,
is like dropping a stone into a very deep lake and following its

progress to the murky bottom. Sooner or later we lose sight of it because the absolute bottom is not visible.

3d
The behavior of a three-dimensional character has to be logically motivated.

In superficial adventures the good guys are simply good and the bad guys are simply bad. It is the action that counts, not the characters. In more serious literature motivation is very important. It is often more interesting than the action itself. Understanding the motivations of literary characters helps us to understand human nature and ourselves.

When we talk about Hamlet we talk less about the action than we do about the character, his strange behavior, his indecision, his anger, his sexuality. He is, in fact, a character who suddenly finds himself incapable of action. We want to know why. What's wrong with this guy? Does he want to avenge his father's death or not? He accuses his uncle and mother of incest, but perhaps it is he himself who has incestuous longings.

Your characters need not have the classical stature of Hamlet; they can be ordinary people in the grip of some conflict or obsession. Understanding ordinary people is not much easier than understanding Hamlet, and certainly not less significant.

(1) Every action a person commits is motivated.

In Albert Camus' *The Stranger*, motivation is at the very heart of the novel. With minimal provocation Mersault kills a stranger. It is not really self-defense, and, what's more, after shooting him once, Mersault then empties the gun into him. In court Mersault cannot explain his actions and refuses to testify in his own defense. He is called an emotional monster by the prosecutor, and he is sentenced to death. Existentialists see in the incident the philosophical significance of the gratuitous act of violence, but the novel can also be read as a psychological study in repressed violence.

Where there is an effect there is a cause. Whatever you allow your characters to do, make sure that you understand what motivates them and that you make these motives clear to the reader.

3e
Plausible characters are developed with enough depth and logic to make them believable.

(1) Some characters are not plausible because they are fantasy figures and not realistic human beings.

Many such characters appear in science fiction and stories of the supernatural, but some, such as the monster in Mary Shelley's *Frankenstein*, appear in more serious works and have a kind of literary credibility. Conan the Barbarian belongs in a comic book along with Wonderwoman and the Incredible Hulk. A bit more might be said for King Kong, because the movie touches on the theme of beauty and the beast and perhaps the theme of nature versus civilization, but it's hardly profound. Godzilla is ridiculous, but Moby Dick has an interesting and mysterious presence and takes part in a great symbolic work of art. In mythology there are many incredible but meaningful characters, such as Prometheus and Sisyphus. Lewis Carroll's Alice and Jonathan Swift's Gulliver come closer to being believable characters, except for the fact that they experience incredible adventures. *Dr. Jekyll and Mr. Hyde* by Robert Louis Stevenson is a weird tale, but it is also an interesting way of exploring the split personality and perhaps the good and evil in all of us. Flat or round, mythological or ordinary, some characters can achieve universality because they touch on ideas and feelings that can be understood by all people in all ages.

(2) Realistic characters must be believable.

In order to be effective as a writer you must persuade your readers that your fictional characters might very well exist and that, if they did, they would undoubtedly act just the way they do.

When you breathe life into your characters and set them in motion they take over and only do the things that they are capable of doing or would naturally do when confronted with certain situations. You cannot force your characters to do things that they would not naturally do or things that they are incapable of doing. You cannot create a shy girl like Laura in *The Glass Menagerie* and then expect her to seduce a gentleman caller or to shoot someone. You cannot create a character like Ruby in "Ruby Tells All" (Example 9) and have her sneaking off to the barn to read Marcel Proust. Some people get impatient with Hamlet. Why can't he just get it over with, they think. Why can't he just knock off his uncle and assume the throne of Denmark? The problem is that *as a character, he can only do what he can do*. This is not mere fatalism; it is a matter of psychological consistency. In good literature you have to tell the truth. And the truth is that Hamlet is in a state of high confusion, and that Persis Fox in "Barcelona" (Example 2) thinks men are a bit ridiculous, and that the old man in "A Clean, Well-Lighted Place" is in despair, and that Ruby will never be a middle-class suburban housewife.

EXAMPLE 3

THE STRONGER

August Strindberg

CHARACTERS:

MRS. X., *an actress, married*
MISS Y., *an actress, unmarried*
A WAITRESS

SCENE: *The corner of a ladies' cafe. Two little iron tables, a red velvet sofa, several chairs. Enter* MRS. X., *dressed in winter clothes, carrying a Japanese basket on her arm.*

MISS Y.   *sits with a half-empty beer bottle before her, reading an illustrated paper, which she changes later for another.*

MRS. X.   Good afternoon, Amelia. You're sitting here alone on Christmas eve like a poor bachelor!

MISS Y.   (*Looks up, nods, and resumes her reading.*)

MRS. X.   Do you know it really hurts me to see you like this, alone, in a café, and on Christmas eve, too. It makes me feel as I did one time when I saw a bridal party in a Paris restaurant, and the bride sat reading a comic paper, while the groom played billiards with the witnesses. Huh, thought I, with such a beginning, what will follow, and what will be the end? He played billiards on his wedding eve! (MISS Y. *starts to speak*) And she read a comic paper, you mean? Well, they are not altogether the same thing.

(A WAITRESS *enters, places a cup of chocolate before* MRS. X. *and goes out.*)

MRS. X.   You know what, Amelia! I believe you would have done better to have kept him! Do you remember, I was the first to say "Forgive him?" Do you remember that? You would be married now and have a home. Remember that Christmas when you went out to visit your fiancé's parents in the country? How you gloried in the happiness of home life and really longed to quit the theatre forever? Yes, Amelia dear, home is the best of all — next to the theatre — and as for children — well, you don't understand that.

MISS Y.   (*Looks up scornfully.*)

(MRS. X. *sips a few spoonfuls out of the cup, then opens her basket and shows Christmas presents.*)

MRS. X.   Now you shall see what I bought for my piggy-wigs. (*Takes up a doll*) Look at this! This is for Lisa, ha! Do you see how she can roll her eyes and turn her head, eh? And here is Maja's popgun.

(*Loads it and shoots at* MISS Y.)

MISS Y.   (*Makes a startled gesture.*)

MRS. X.   Did I frighten you? Do you think I would like to shoot you, eh? On my soul, if I don't think you did! If you wanted to shoot *me* it wouldn't be so surprising, because I stood in your way — and I know you can never forget that — although I was absolutely innocent. You still believe I intrigued and got you out of the Stora theatre, but I didn't. I didn't do that, although you think so. Well, it doesn't make any difference what I say to you. You still believe I did it. (*Takes up a pair of embroidered slippers*) And these are for my better half. I embroidered them myself — I can't bear tulips, but he wants tulips on everything.

MISS Y.   (*Looks up ironically and curiously.*)

MRS. X.   (*putting a hand in each slipper*)   See what little feet Bob has! What? And you should see what a splendid stride he has! You've never seen him in slippers! (MISS Y. *laughs aloud.*) Look! (*She makes the slippers walk on the table.* MISS Y. *laughs loudly.*) And when he is grumpy he stamps like this with his foot. "What! damn those servants who can never learn to make coffee. Oh, now those creatures haven't trimmed the lamp wick properly!" And then there are draughts on the floor and his feet are cold. "Ugh, how cold it is; the stupid idiots can never keep the fire going." (*She rubs the slippers together, one sole over the other.*)

MISS Y.   (*Shrieks with laughter.*)

MRS. X.   And then he comes home and has to hunt for his slippers which Marie has stuck under the chiffonier — oh, but it's sinful to sit here and make fun of one's husband this way when he is kind and a good little man. You ought to have had such a husband, Amelia. What are you laughing at? What? What? And you see he's true to me. Yes, I'm sure of that, because he told me himself — what are you laughing at? — that when I was touring in Norway that brazen Frederika came and wanted to seduce him! Can you fancy anything so infamous! (*pause*) I'd have torn her eyes out if she had come to see him when I was at home. (*pause*) It was lucky that Bob told me about it himself and that it didn't reach me through gossip. (*pause*) But would you believe it, Frederika wasn't the only one! I don't know why, but the women are crazy about my husband. They must think he has influence about getting them theatrical engagements, because he is connected with the government. Perhaps you were after him yourself. I didn't use to trust you any too much. But now I know he never bothered his head about you, and you always seemed to have a grudge against him someway.

(*Pause. They look at each other in a puzzled way.*)

MRS. X.   Come and see us this evening, Amelia, and show us that you're not put out with us — not put out with me at any rate. I don't know, but I think it would be uncomfortable to have you for an enemy. Perhaps it's because I stood in your way (*more slowly*) or — I really — don't know why — in particular.

(*Pause. MISS Y. stares at MRS. X. curiously.*)

MRS. X. (*thoughtfully*)   Our acquaintance has been so queer. When I saw you for the first time I was afraid of you, so afraid that I didn't dare let you out of my sight; no matter when or where, I always found myself near you — I didn't dare have you for an enemy, so I became your friend. But there was always discord when you came to our house, because I saw that my husband couldn't endure you, and the whole thing seemed as awry to me as an ill-fitting gown — and I did all I could to make him friendly toward you, but with no success until you became engaged. Then came a violent friendship between you, so that it looked all at once as though you both dared show your real feelings only when you were secure — and then — how was it later? I didn't get jealous — strange to say! And I remember at the christening, when you acted as godmother, I made him kiss you — he did so, and you became so confused — as it were; I didn't notice it then — didn't think about it later, either — have never thought about it until — now! (*Rises suddenly.*) Why are you silent? You haven't said a word this whole time, but you have let me go on talking! You have sat there, and your eyes have reeled out of me all these thoughts which lay like raw silk in its cocoon—thoughts—suspicious thoughts, perhaps. Let me see—why did you break your engagement? Why do you never come to our house any more? Why won't you come to see us tonight?

(MISS Y. *appears as if about to speak.*)

MRS. X.   Hush, you needn't speak—I understand it all! It was because—and because—and because! Yes, yes! Now all the accounts balance. That's it. Fie, I won't sit at the same table with you. (*Moves her things to another table.*) That's the reason I had to embroider tulips—which I hate—on his slippers, because you are fond of tulips; that's why (*throws slippers on the floor*) we go to Lake Mälarn in the summer, because you don't like salt water; that's why my boy is named Eskil—because it's your father's name; that's why I wear your colors, read your authors, eat your favorite dishes, drink your drinks—chocolate, for instance; that's why—oh—my God—it's terrible, when I think about it; it's terrible. Everything, everything came from you to me, even your passions. Your soul crept into mine, like a worm into an apple, ate and ate, bored and bored, until nothing was left but the rind and a little black dust within. I wanted to get away from you, but I couldn't; you lay like a snake and charmed me with your black eyes; I felt that when I lifted my wings they only dragged me down; I lay in the water with bound feet, and the stronger I strove to keep up the deeper I worked myself down, down, until I sank to the bottom, where you lay like a giant crab to clutch me in your claws—and there I am lying now.

I hate you, hate you, hate you! And you only sit there silent — silent and indifferent; indifferent whether it's new moon or waning moon, Christmas or New Year's, whether others are happy or unhappy; without power to hate or to love; as quiet as a stork by a rat hole — you couldn't scent your prey and capture it, but you could lie in wait for it! You sit here in your corner of the café — did you know it's called "The Rat Trap" for you? — and read the papers to see if misfortune hasn't befallen someone, to see if someone hasn't been given notice at the theatre, perhaps; you sit here and calculate about your next victim and reckon on your chances of recompense like a pilot in a shipwreck. Poor Amelia, I pity you, nevertheless, because I know you are unhappy, unhappy like one who has been wounded, and angry because you are wounded. I can't be angry with you, no matter how much I want to be — because you come out the weaker one. Yes, all that with Bob doesn't trouble me. What is that to me, after all? And what difference does it make whether I learned to drink chocolate from you or some one else. (*Sips a spoonful from her cup*) Besides, chocolate is very healthful. And if you taught me how to dress — tant mieux! — that has only made me more attractive to my husband; so you lost and I won there. Well, judging by certain signs, I believe you have already lost him; and you certainly intended that I should leave him — do as you did with your fiancé and regret as you now regret; but, you see, I don't do that — we mustn't be too exacting. And why should I take only what no one else wants?

Perhaps, take it all in all, I am at this moment the stronger one. You received nothing from me, but you gave me much. And now I seem like a thief since you have awakened and find I possess what is your loss. How could it be otherwise when everything is worthless and sterile in your hands? You can never keep a man's love with your tulips and your passions — but I can keep it. You can't learn how to live from your authors, as I have learned. You have no little Eskil to cherish, even if your father's name was Eskil. And why are you always silent, silent, silent? I thought that was strength, but perhaps it is because you have nothing to say! Because you never think about anything! (*Rises and picks up slippers.*) Now I'm going home — and take the tulips with me — *your* tulips! You are unable to learn from another; you can't bend — therefore, you broke like a dry stalk. But I won't break! Thank you, Amelia, for all your good lessons. Thanks for teaching my husband how to love. Now I'm going home to love him. (*Goes.*)

EXERCISES

DISCUSSION

1. In Strindberg's play, *The Stronger*, only one of the characters actually speaks (Mrs. X), but there are two other characters involved in the situation — Miss Y (Amelia), who is onstage, and Bob, the husband of Mrs. X, who never actually appears onstage. What do we learn about these characters? How do we learn about them?

2. Which one of the women in this play is "the stronger"? Did Bob once have a love affair with Amelia? Mrs. X describes her husband as "a kind and good little man." Does this reveal anything about their relationship? Why doesn't Amelia speak? Why does she laugh from time to time?

3. The two women onstage are never described. What do you imagine they look like?

WRITING

1. Describe a stereotypical (*flat*) character, such as a lawyer, business person, professor, criminal, private detective, waiter or waitress, librarian, entertainer, or athlete.

2. Write a short story in which there is an incredible character, suitable for science-fiction, fantasy, or the supernatural.

3. Write a story or play in which a character with some *depth* confesses to a very close friend that he or she once did something terrible that has, until now, remained a haunting secret. Make the situation *plausible* and try to convey the *motives* of the character.

4. Write a poem about an interesting stranger that you noticed on the street or on a bus or in the park. Concentrate on *appearance* and what it reveals.

5. Write a brief biography of the old man in Hemingway's "A Clean, Well-Lighted Place."

6. Describe yourself in the third person as though you were talking about a character in a story.

7. Using your imagination and this sonnet by Shakespeare, write a brief scene between the poet and his mistress, revealing as much as you can about the characters.

MY MISTRESS' EYES ARE NOTHING LIKE THE SUN
1609

My mistress' eyes are nothing like the sun;
Coral is far more red than her lips' red;
If snow be white, why then her breasts are dun;
If hairs be wires, black wires grow on her head.

I have seen roses damasked red and white,   5
But no such roses see I in her cheeks;
And in some perfumes is there more delight
Than in the breath that from my mistress reeks.
I love to hear her speak, yet well I know
That music hath a far more pleasing sound;   10
I grant I never saw a goddess go;
My mistress, when she walks, treads on the ground.
And yet, by heaven, I think my love as rare
As any she belied with false compare.

CHAPTER
FOUR

PLOT

4a
Avoid the vague use of the term *plot*.

The term *plot* is often used too vaguely. In order to understand precisely what it means you should understand the meanings of *story, action,* and *plot,* and how these three things are related.

(1) Story usually refers to the whole work.

A story is a work of fiction that includes a *setting* in which *characters* who *talk and think* become involved in *significant action*. It is the whole work, including its special *tone and style* and *point of view*.

In a broader sense, the word *story* can be applied to any narrative, whether it is fiction, nonfiction, drama, or poetry, as long as significant action is involved. We use "story" in such expressions as: The Watergate story, the story of Adam and Eve, the story of Romeo and Juliet.

(2) Action refers to all the things that happen in a story, especially those things that involve the characters.

Action is anything that happens, anything from the incidental to the epic. Since the term is very broad, the following useful distinctions should be made:

INTERNAL AND EXTERNAL ACTION

Internal action is what happens inside a character's mind, consciously or unconsciously. *External action* refers to things that happen outside of the character's mind, things done *by* the character or *to* the character. A dream is an internal event. A hurricane is an external event.

REAL-LIFE ACTION

In real life there are all kinds of actions, from the trivial to the catastrophic. A lot of real-life action is *random*. Some things just happen. A dog barks, the weather turns bad, someone gets sick. Some happenings are more *significant*. There is a major decision to be made, there is a premeditated act of violence, an extremist group plans a military coup.

In real life a lot of things can happen simultaneously. In writing it is difficult to record simultaneous action because writing itself is sequential — one sentence follows another. A writer can only suggest that several things are happening at the same time. On stage or screen this is an easier task.

FICTIONAL ACTION

In literary works all action is *significant*, not random. Every action is carefully selected. In written fiction all action is presented *sequentially*. A writer cannot present two things at exactly the same moment. However, as noted above, simultaneous events can be presented in a performed drama.

There are two kinds of action in fiction: *habitual action* and *unique action*. The routine things that a character does, such as going to work or eating lunch, are *habitual*. The unusual things that occur, such as falling in love or getting lost in a jungle, are *unique*. Fairy tales usually make this distinction clear at the very beginning: "Once upon a time in the land of Anglia there was a miserly king who was in the *habit* of counting his money every day. *One day* he was interrupted by an evil dwarf."

(3) Plot refers to the meaningful arrangement of the significant action in a story.

The plot of a literary work is a summary of the *unique* and significant action in that work. It is an artistically arranged sequence of events that serves as the skeleton for the whole story, which has to be completed or fleshed out by setting, characterization, description, dialogue, style and tone. A good plot usually has the following elements: *conflict, suspense, development, resolution*.

4b

Conflict refers to whatever causes the central dramatic tension in a story.

In literature the term *conflict* has a very broad meaning. In its most obvious sense it suggests a clashing of forces, as in good versus evil, but it also means any problem, external or internal, that a human being experiences and longs to resolve.

Since conflict is an aspect of plot, it is most often discussed in relation to fiction and drama, but it can be frequently applied to poetry as well, even though many poems do not have much of a plot. The following anonymous poem, for instance, written over five hundred years ago, clearly has a conflict but only hints at a plot:

WESTERN WIND

Western wind, when wilt thou blow,
    The small rain down can rain?
Christ, if my love were in my arms
    And I in my bed again!

The author seems to be far from home, perhaps at sea or on some marauding or military adventure. Apparently the coming of the west wind will mean a gentle rain and a homeward journey.

Why does conflict give rise to literature? There is an old saying that it is the sick oyster that produces the pearl, meaning that a grain of sand sets up an irritation, which the oyster tries to deal with by developing a pearl around it. The saying suggests that all artists are driven by some disturbance or problem and that their art is an attempt to relieve the disturbance or resolve the problem. It seems to be the unpleasant destiny of human beings to be plagued by problems and, therefore, to be fascinated by problem-solving. In literature one can find the drama of conflict and resolution rehearsed over and over again.

Since there are many different kinds of conflict, they are sometimes conveniently classified as follows: *people versus people, people versus society, people versus nature,* and *people versus themselves.*

(1) People versus people.

War is the most obvious and massive indication that all too often people cannot live together in peace. It is a fundamental flaw in human nature. Wars have affected so many people in so many horrible ways that it is no wonder so much literature, great and trivial, has dealt with the subject. Homer's *Iliad,* written almost three thousand years ago, deals with the Trojan War. Conflict in war stories is not only physical conflict; it often involves questions of honor, glory, betrayal, and guilt. In Hemingway's *A Farewell to Arms,* for instance, the hero falls in love and deserts the army to flee to Switzerland with his beloved.

Crimes clearly involve people versus people, though sometimes an author concentrates on the sociological implications or on the internal, psychological drama, as in the case of Dostoevsky's *Crime and Punishment* or Stendhal's *The Red and the Black.*

Conflicts between individuals are too numerous to list or classify. People can disagree about almost anything — property, politics, principles, family affairs, and love. In "The Ballad of Reading Gaol," Oscar Wilde says:

> Yet each man kills the thing he loves,
>   By each let this be heard,
> Some do it with a bitter look,
>   Some with a flattering word,

The coward does it with a kiss,
The brave man with a sword!

Oscar Wilde's approach to love may have been rather eccentric, to say the least, but there is no doubt about the frequency with which love conflicts appear in literature, and love tragedies may be more popular than happy tales of love. Romeo and Juliet die. Desdemona is strangled. Madame Bovary and Anna Karenina commit suicide. Heathcliffe hears the ghost of his beloved call his name. Two men kill each other over a woman in Lorca's *Blood Wedding*. And Rhett Butler leaves Scarlet O'Hara with the famous line: "Frankly, my dear, I don't give a damn."

Though love conflicts abound in literature, other conflicts between people appear with considerable frequency. King Lear is betrayed by his two evil daughters. In Conrad's *Victory* a man and a woman living on a remote island are terrorized by three evil men. In the movie *Chinatown* a domineering father seduces his own daughter, who bears his child. In *Citizen Kane* the central figure is in love with money and power and lets no one stand in his way.

(2) People versus society.

Any individual who resists the rules and values of his or her society runs the risk of criticism or even punishment. Benign eccentrics, including artists, are sometimes exceptions. If the rebellion against society is extreme, the individual can expect a very hard time, indeed, whether the rebellion is a question of conscience or a violent crime. A lot of people were arrested in the 1960s because they took part in civil-rights or anti-war demonstrations. In literary works rebels are often portrayed as heroes. Ordinary criminals are usually portrayed as villains. A fairly recently coined expression for a chronic offender is *sociopath*, someone who simply can't get along with society.

Technology and the problems of big cities and sprawling suburbs have created many conflicts between the individual and society. Governments have grown larger. Ordinary people feel helpless against their remote governments. Farmers find it difficult to survive. The family has eroded. There is loneliness in the cities and suburbs. There is racial and ethnic tension. There is polarization between rich and poor. Violence and drug use continue to increase. These subjects appear in serious literature as well as in the routine programs of television and in mass-market paperbacks. The landscape of modern society is not very attractive, except for a few oases of glitter and wealth, which have become a fantasyland on television through such programs as *Dallas, Dynasty,* and *Falcon Crest.*

An early modern example of a literary work about the conflict between the individual and society is Ibsen's *An Enemy of the People*, a play first performed in 1882. The hero is a doctor who discovers that the water in a resort town is polluted. The town's economy depends heavily on its health-giving baths. The mayor and businessmen want to cover up the medical report. The doctor finds himself standing virtually alone against the conventional majority.

The most famous counter-culture work produced by a member of the Beat Generation is Allen Ginsberg's long poem "Howl" (1955), the angry tone of which is apparent from the opening lines. Richard Wright's brilliant novel *Native Son* (1940) is about a black man victimized by a white society. In more recent years this conflict has been the basis of many works from Ralph Ellison's *The Invisible Man* (1952) to Alice Walker's *The Color Purple* (1982).

(3) People versus nature.

By *nature* we usually mean the tangible world around us that is shaped by natural forces, not by humans. We mean the sea, the wilderness, the animal kingdom, and the vastness of outer space. Some people would include the concept of God and destiny, depending on their philosophical persuasions. In literature we find people in conflict with nature in both simplistic and profound works. Disaster and survival stories have exploited all the ancient elements — air, earth, fire, and water. There have been stories of hurricanes, avalanches, towering infernos, and tidal waves. There have been stories of killer ants, killer bees, killer tarantulas, and even killer tomatoes. Beyond such low-level entertainments we find some more interesting efforts, such as *Lifeboat, The Rains Came,* and *The African Queen*. One of the greatest novels on the subject is *Moby Dick*.

(4) People versus themselves.

Sometimes a story focuses on a character's internal conflict. This conflict can be triggered by circumstances or it can be the result of some psychological disorder. Hamlet has a terrible internal conflict. He feels he must avenge his father's death, but he is filled with doubts and other confusing feelings. Lady Macbeth's ambition and sense of guilt drive her mad. In more modern works we find characters struggling with alcoholism (*The Lost Weekend* and *Under the Volcano*) and with the problem of drug addiction. Sheer madness figures in many horror stories and films, of which one of the most famous is Hitchcock's *Psycho*. The most dramatic treatment of the divided self is *The Strange Case of Dr. Jekyll and Mr. Hyde* by Robert Louis Stevenson.

4c
Suspense is a condition created by uncertainty.

Suspense is a state of curiosity, uncertainty, or anxiety about a conflict or problem, the outcome of which cannot as yet be determined. It is a natural human response to certain situations, whether the situations are real or fictitious. In real situations the anxiety is direct. In fiction, it depends on *empathy*, our ability to identify with the feelings of others, including made-up characters. Once the story or drama is over our curiosity disappears, along with our uncertainty and anxiety, whether the ending is tragic or happy. In good literature there is also a residue of wisdom or aesthetic exhilaration. In lighter entertainments there is only a satisfied curiosity. People who gobble up romances and murder mysteries or routine television dramas readily admit that they forget about them almost instantly, as soon as they find out "whodunit" or whether or not a pair of lovers will work out their problems and live happily ever after.

In any literary work that has a plot, suspense begins as soon as the conflict or problem is introduced, which is usually at the very beginning. A ship is wrecked on the shores of a deserted island and only a man and a woman survive. What will happen to them? Three prospectors set out to search for gold in the dangerous Sierra Madre area of Mexico. A mercenary is hired to assassinate a rebel leader in Central America — and so on.

In stories of pure adventure suspense is all important. Suspense follows a formula and can be diagrammed. First there is the *problem*, then there are *complications* that heighten the sense of danger or mystery, sometimes to the point at which our hero is hanging (literally or figuratively) from the edge of a cliff (hence the term *cliffhanger*), and then there is a *resolution*, a happy or unhappy ending. Suspense is an intolerable state that demands a resolution, even an unpleasant one.

In more complex literary works it may not be as easy to find the basic diagram of suspense. There may be ideas or characterizations that rival the suspense in importance, but very often even works of great literary merit are full of suspense. Certainly, we want to know what happens to Ahab and his mad pursuit of the white whale, and, certainly, we want to know what happens to Emma in *Madame Bovary* and what becomes of Willy Loman in *Death of a Salesman*.

4d
Development refers to the events that grow out of a conflict before it is resolved.

(1) Every narrative needs movement.

Creating a conflict is only a starting point in literature. In nature nothing stands still. A wound will either heal or fester. A person on the ledge of a tall building either has to jump or fall or somehow get back inside. However, you can't simply present your problem and then immediately resolve it. You can't say that a person crawled out onto a ledge and then jumped to his or her death. You can't leap from conflict to resolution. That would not only kill your character but all the suspense, and you wouldn't have much of a story. You need *development*. You have to hold the interest of your readers. You have to involve them by exploring the situation and the character more deeply, not merely through exposition but through *action*.

Development often makes up most of the plot. A conflict can be stated in a sentence or a paragraph, and some resolutions are swift and sudden, but what you must do in between is to heighten the reader's curiosity by devising a series of events that reveals the true nature of the situation and leads to a conclusion that, afterward, seems inevitable to the reader.

If there is a "man on the ledge" in your story, the reader wants to know why he is out there. Does he really want to commit suicide or does he just want attention? Perhaps he is a rejected lover who is trying to punish the woman who rejected him. If he is psychologically disturbed, what exactly is his psychological problem? Has he just had a fight with his domineering mother? Is he a paranoid character who feels that everyone is plotting against him? There has to be some sort of *motivation* for his behavior. Furthermore, something has to happen before the resolution. Perhaps the police send for a priest who knows the man. Perhaps they get in touch with his psychiatrist or the woman who rejected him or his mother. Someone tries to talk him down. The police spread a net. A friend crawls out onto the ledge to calm him down. Perhaps the friend slips and almost falls, but is saved by the man who thought he wanted to commit suicide. Saving another person's life may make him realize suddenly that he is needed and that his life has some value and meaning after all.

(2) The sequence of events must develop logically.

When you create a sequence of events in your development you have to be sure that every event has some significance and that these events build toward a climax. One of the most serious mistakes made by amateur writers is to try to reveal everything all at once. Development needs pace. A story or drama is most effective when it is a gradual and ascending revelation. Details of character and setting can be revealed as you go. It is not important to tell us everything about everybody in the first paragraph. It is much more important to indicate the nature of the problem and to set things in motion. Many opening sentences or paragraphs contain a hook to capture the reader's attention. "The invisible man is the main attraction," is the opening of "The Invisible Man" (Example 1). If you spend too much time on your setting and cast of characters at the beginning, especially in a short story, you might confuse or bore your reader.

If your sequence of events is going to build toward a climax, the situation has to grow more intense before it is resolved.

In "Barcelona" (Example 2) we begin with a middle-aged American couple in the darkened streets of a seedy neighborhood in a foreign city. The sense of danger is heightened. Suddenly, a thief snatches the woman's purse. The man chases the thief. He searches restaurants and bars, but to no avail. He is about to give up when a stranger who is not the thief points to the abandoned purse in the street and says, "Lady, this your bag?" In the final scene we explore the reactions of the couple as they recover in a restaurant. The real meaning may be in these reactions, but there would not have been a story without a significant sequence of events.

4e
Every conflict must have a resolution.

(1) The resolution must fit the plot.

You can't drop a completely random ending on your reader, like a concrete block that accidentally falls from a high building. An ending is absurd if it is not a plausible conclusion to a certain sequence of events. You can't select a *conflict* and create *characters* and *develop* a dramatic and cohesive series of events without ending the whole process with a meaningful and believable *resolution*.

The word *resolution* may be misleading to some people. It sounds as though the problem you began with must be solved. That's not the case at all. You are a writer solving an artistic problem. You are not a therapist solving human problems. If all conflicts and problems were solved in that way in literature, every story would end happily. As we know, many do not. The unhappy or tragic ending can often be a more logical resolution artistically than the happy ending.

(2) Some resolutions are clear and simple; others are more complex and subtle.

In light entertainments, in which there are conflicts between good guys and bad guys, or problems between lovers, the usual resolution is that good prevails over evil or, in the case of romance, that love conquers all. In more serious literature a resolution may involve a dramatic change in the main character, a spiritual revelation, a significant decision, an act of violence or of self-destruction.

Though some of the old dramas seem to end with a bang, and some of the more contemporary works seem to end with a whimper, the good ones all have significance. Oedipus plucks out his eyes and Othello strangles Desdemona, but all that happens in "The Invisible Man" (Example 1) is that the circus performance ends with the audience imagining that they actually saw an invisible man; all that happens at the end of "Barcelona" (Example 2) is that Persis Fox has a few thoughts about how difficult it must be to be a man, and about how men don't quite understand women. Modern literature does not require a stage littered with corpses anymore than it requires characters larger than life. Subtle endings involving ordinary people can be just as moving and just as meaningful as the louder events of antiquity. In all cases, however, a resolution is a *literary conclusion*, not a real-life conclusion.

EXAMPLE 4

THE NECKLACE

Guy de Maupassant

She was one of those pretty and charming girls born, as though fate had blundered over her, into a family of artisans. She had no marriage portion, no expectations, no means of getting known, understood, loved, and wedded by a man of wealth and distinction; and she let herself be married off to a little clerk in the Ministry of Education.

Her tastes were simple because she had never been able to afford any other, but she was as unhappy as though she had married beneath her; for women have no caste or class, their beauty, grace, and charm serving them for birth or family. Their natural delicacy, their instinctive elegance, their nimble-ness of wit, are their only mark of rank, and put the slum girl on a level with the highest lady in the land.

She suffered endlessly, feeling herself born for every deli-cacy and luxury. She suffered from the poorness of her house, from its mean walls, worn chairs, and ugly curtains. All these things, of which other women of her class would not even have been aware, tormented and insulted her. The sight of the little Breton girl who came to do the work in her little house aroused heart-broken regrets and hopeless dreams in her mind. She imagined silent antechambers, heavy with Oriental tapestries, lit by torches in lofty bronze sockets, with two tall footmen in knee-breeches sleeping in large armchairs, overcome by the heavy warmth of the stove. She imagined vast saloons hung with antique silks, exquisite pieces of furniture supporting priceless ornaments, and small, charming, perfumed rooms, created just for little parties of intimate friends, men who were famous and sought after, whose homage roused every other woman's envious longings.

When she sat down for dinner at the round table covered with a three-days-old cloth, opposite her husband, who took the cover off the soup-tureen, exclaiming delightedly: "Aha! Scotch broth! What could be better?" she imagined delicate meals, gleaming silver, tapestries peopling the walls with folk of a past age and strange birds in faery forests; she imagined delicate food served in marvelous dishes, murmured gallantries, listened to with an inscrutable smile as one trifled with the rosy flesh of trout or wings of asparagus chicken.

She had no clothes, no jewels, nothing. And these were the only things she loved; she felt that she was made for them. She had longed so eagerly to charm, to be desired, to be wildly attractive and sought after.

She had a rich friend, an old school friend whom she refused to visit, because she suffered so keenly when she returned home. She would weep whole days, with grief, regret, despair, and misery.

One evening her husband came home with an exultant air, holding a large envelope in his hand.

"Here's something for you," he said.

Swiftly she tore the paper and drew out a printed card on which were these words:

"The Minister of Education and Madame Ramponneau request the pleasure of the company of Monsieur and Madame Loisel at the Ministry on the evening of Monday, January the 18th."

Instead of being delighted, as her husband hoped, she flung the invitation petulantly across the table, murmuring:

"What do you want me to do with this?"

"Why, darling, I thought you'd be pleased. You never go out, and this is a great occasion. I had tremendous trouble to get it. Every one wants one; it's very select, and very few go to the clerks. You'll see all the really big people there."

She looked at him out of furious eyes, and said impatiently:

"And what do you suppose I am to wear to such an affair?"

He had not thought about it; he stammered:

"Why, the dress you go to the theatre in. It looks very nice, to me. . . ."

He stopped, stupefied and utterly at a loss when he saw that his wife was beginning to cry. Two large tears ran slowly down from the corners of her eyes towards the corners of her mouth.

"What's the matter with you? What's the matter with you?" he faltered.

But with a violent effort she overcame her grief and replied in a calm voice, wiping her wet cheeks:

"Nothing. Only I haven't a dress and so I can't go to this party. Give your invitation to some friend of yours whose wife will be turned out better than I shall."

He was heart-broken.

"Look here, Mathilde," he persisted. "What would be the cost of a suitable dress, which you could use on other occasions as well, something very simple?"

She thought for several seconds, reckoning up prices and also wondering for how large a sum she could ask without bringing upon herself an immediate refusal and an exclamation of horror from the careful-minded clerk.

At last she replied with some hesitation:

"I don't know exactly, but I think I could do it on four hundred francs."

He grew slightly pale, for this was exactly the amount he had been saving for a gun, intending to get a little shooting next summer on the plain of Nanterre with some friends who went lark-shooting there on Sundays.

Nevertheless he said: "Very well. I'll give you four hundred francs. But try and get a really nice dress with the money."

The day of the party drew near, and Madame Loisel seemed sad, uneasy and anxious. Her dress was ready, however. One evening her husband said to her:

"What's the matter with you? You've been very odd for the last three days."

"I'm utterly miserable at not having any jewels, not a single stone, to wear," she replied. "I shall look like absolutely no one. I would almost rather not go to the party."

"Wear flowers," he said. "They're very smart at this time of the year. For ten francs you could get two or three gorgeous roses."

She was not convinced.

"No . . . there's nothing so humiliating as looking poor in the middle of a lot of rich women."

"How stupid you are!" exclaimed her husband. "Go and see Madame Forestier and ask her to lend you some jewels. You know her quite well enough for that."

She uttered a cry of delight.

"That's true. I never thought of it."

Next day she went to see her friend and told her trouble.

Madame Forestier went to her dressing-table, took up a large box, brought it to Madame Loisel, opened it, and said:

"Choose, my dear."

First she saw some bracelets, then a pearl necklace, then a Venetian cross in gold and gems, of exquisite workmanship. She tried the effect of the jewels before the mirror, hesitating, unable to make her mind to leave them, to give them up. She kept on asking:

"Haven't you anything else?"

"Yes. Look for yourself. I don't know what you would like best."

Suddenly she discovered, in a black satin case, a superb diamond necklace; her heart began to beat covetously. Her hands trembled as she lifted it. She fastened it round her neck, upon her high dress, and remained in ecstasy at sight of herself.

Then, with hesitation, she asked in anguish:

"Could you lend me this, just this alone?"

"Yes, of course."

She flung herself on her friend's breast, embraced her frenziedly, and went away with her treasure.

The day of the party arrived. Madame Loisel was a success. She was the prettiest woman present, elegant, graceful, smiling, and quite above herself with happiness. All the men stared at her, inquired her name, and asked to be introduced to her. All the Under-Secretaries of State were eager to waltz with her. The Minister noticed her.

She danced madly, ecstatically, drunk with pleasure, with no thought for anything, in the triumph of her beauty, in the pride of her success, in a cloud of happiness made up of this universal homage and admiration, of the desires she had aroused, of the completeness of a victory so dear to her feminine heart.

She left about four o'clock in the morning. Since midnight her husband had been dozing in a deserted little room, in company with three other men whose wives were having a good time.

He threw over her shoulders the garments he had brought for them to go home in, modest everyday clothes, whose poverty, clashed with the beauty of the ball-dress. She was conscious of this and was anxious to hurry away, so that she should not be noticed by the other women putting on their costly furs.

Loisel restrained her.

"Wait a little. You'll catch cold in the open. I'm going to fetch a cab.

But she did not listen to him and rapidly descended the staircase. When they were out in the street they could not find a cab; they began to look for one, shouting at the drivers whom they saw passing in the distance.

They walked down towards the Seine, desperate and shivering. At last they found on the quay one of those old night-prowling carriages which are only to be seen in Paris after dark, as though they were ashamed of their shabbiness in the daylight.

It brought them to their door in the Rue des Martyrs, and sadly they walked up to their own apartment. It was the end, for her. As for him, he was thinking that he must be at the office at ten.

She took off the garments in which she had wrapped her shoulders, so as to see herself in all her glory before the mirror. But suddenly she uttered a cry. The necklace was no longer round her neck!

"What's the matter with you?" asked her husband, already half undressed.

She turned towards him in the utmost distress.

"I . . . I . . . I've no longer got Madame Forestier's necklace. . . ."

He started with astonishment.

"What! . . . Impossible!"

They searched in the folds of her dress, in the folds of the coat, in the pockets, everywhere. They could not find it.

"Are you sure that you still had it on when you came away from the ball?" he asked.

"Yes, I touched it in the hall at the Ministry."

"But if you had lost it in the street, we should have heard it fall."

"Yes. Probably we should. Did you take the number of the cab?"

"No. You didn't notice it, did you?"

"No."

They stared at one another, dumbfounded. At last Loisel put on his clothes again.

"I'll go over all the ground we walked," he said, "and see if I can't find it."

And he went out. She remained in her evening clothes, lacking strength to get into bed, huddled on a chair, without volition or power of thought.

Her husband returned about seven. He found nothing.

He went to the police station, to the newspapers, to offer a reward, to the cab companies, everywhere that a ray of hope impelled him.

She waited all day long, in the same state of bewilderment at this fearful catastrophe.

Loisel came home at night, his face lined and pale; he had discovered nothing.

"You must write to your friend," he said, "and tell her that you've broken the clasp of her necklace and are getting it mended. That will give us time to look about us."

She wrote at his dictation.

By the end of the week they had lost all hope.

Loisel, who had aged five years, declared:

"We must see about replacing the diamonds."

Next day they took the box which had held the necklace and went to the jewellers whose name was inside. He consulted his books.

"It was not I who sold this necklace, Madame; I must have merely supplied the clasp.

Then they went from jeweller to jeweller, searching for another necklace like the first, consulting their memories, both ill with remorse and anguish of mind.

In a shop at Palais-Royal they found a string of diamonds which seemed to them exactly like the one they were looking for. It was worth forty thousand francs. They were allowed to have it for thirty-six thousand.

They begged the jeweller not to sell it for three days. And they arranged matters on the understanding that it would be taken back for thirty-four thousand francs, if the first one were found before the end of February.

Loisel possessed eighteen thousand francs left to him by this father. He intended to borrow the rest.

He did borrow it, getting a thousand from one man, five hundred from another, five louis here, three louis there. He gave notes of hand, entered into ruinous agreements, did business with usurers and the whole tribe of money-lenders. He mortgaged the whole remaining years of his existence, risked his signature without even knowing if he could honour it and, appalled at the agonising face of the future, at the black misery about to fall upon him, at the prospect of every possible physical privation and moral torture, he went to get the new necklace and put down upon the jeweller's counter thirty-six thousand francs.

When Madame Loisel took back the necklace to Madame Forestier, the latter said to her in a chilly voice:

"You ought to have brought it back sooner; I might have needed it."

She did not, as her friend had feared, open the case. If she had noticed the substitution, what would she have thought? What would she have said? Would she not have taken her for a thief?

Madame Loisel came to know the ghastly life of abject poverty. From the very first she played her part heroically. This fearful debt must be paid off. She would pay it. The servant was dismissed. They changed their flat; they took a garret under the roof.

She came to know the heavy work of the house, the hateful duties of the kitchen. She washed the plates, wearing out her pink nails on the coarse pottery and the bottoms of pans. She washed the dirty linen, the shirts and dish-clothes, and hung them out to dry on a string; every morning she took the dust-bin down into the street and carried up the water, stopping on each landing to get her breath. And, clad like a poor woman, she went to the fruiterer, to the grocer, to the butcher, a basket on her arm, haggling, insulted, fighting for every wretched halfpenny of her money.

Every month notes had to be paid off, others renewed, time gained.

Her husband worked in the evenings at putting straight a merchant's accounts, and often at night he did copying at two-pence-halfpenny a page.

And this life lasted ten years.

At the end of ten years everything was paid off, everything, the usurer's charges the accumulation of superimposed interest.

Madame Loisel looked old now. She had become like all the other strong, hard, coarse women of poor households. Her hair was badly done, her skirts were awry, her hands were red. She spoke in a shrill voice, and the water slopped all over the floor when she scrubbed it. But sometimes, when her husband was at the office, she sat down by the window and thought of that evening long ago, of the ball at which she had been so beautiful and so much admired.

What would have happened if she had never lost those jewels. Who knows? Who knows? How strange life is, how fickle! How little is needed to ruin or to save!

One Sunday, as she had gone for a walk along the Champs-Élysées to freshen herself after the labours of the week, she caught sight suddenly of a woman who was taking a child out for a walk. It was Madame Forestier, still young, still beautiful, still attractive.

Madame Loisel was conscious of some emotion. Should she speak to her? Yes, certainly. And now that she had paid, she would tell her all. Why not?

She went up to her.

"Good morning, Jeanne."

The other did not recognise her, and was surprised at being thus familiarly addressed by a poor woman.

"But . . . Madame . . ." she stammered. "I don't know . . . you must be making a mistake."

"No . . . I am Mathilde Loisel."

Her friend uttered a cry.

"Oh! . . . my poor Mathilde, how you have changed! . . ."

"Yes, I've had some hard times since I saw you last; and many sorrows . . . and all on your account."

"On my account! . . . How was that?"

"You remember the diamond necklace you lent me for the ball at the Ministry?"

"Yes. Well?"

"Well, I lost it."

"How could you? Why, you brought it back."

"I brought you another one just like it. And for the last ten years we have been paying for it. You realise it wasn't easy for me; we had no money. . . . Well, it's paid for at last, and I'm glad indeed."

Madame Forestier had halted.

"You say you bought a diamond necklace to replace mine?"

"Yes. You hadn't noticed it? They were very much alike."

And she smiled in proud and innocent happiness.

Madame Forestier, deeply moved, took her two hands.

"Oh, my poor Mathilde! But mine was imitation. It was worth at the very most five hundred francs! . . ."

EXERCISES

DISCUSSION

1. Summarize the *plot* of "The Necklace" (Example 4). Is the *sequence of events* significant?

2. Describe the *conflict, suspense, development,* and *resolution* in this story.

3. Is the ironic ending artistically appropriate? Could there have been a happy ending to this story?

WRITING

1. Write a short story involving one of the basic conflicts: *people versus people, people versus society, people versus nature, people versus themselves.*

2. Write a story or play with an ironic ending.

3. Write a one-act play called "Woman on the Ledge," using a room with a window as the set.

4. What kind of a story or poem can you make of the following headline? "Survivors of Shipwreck Accused of Cannibalism."

5. Write at least two resolutions for the following situation: Pamela is engaged to Mark but discovers that she has fallen in love with his older brother Sebastian, who has always resented Mark because their mother favors him. The mother objects to her husband's will, in which Sebastian is the major heir to the family fortune.

CHAPTER
FIVE

POINT OF VIEW

We are all *voyeurs*. The movie or television screen is like a window, as is the stage. The usual point of view in a performed drama is defined by the simple relationship between audience and play. Something happens and the audience watches. Complexities of point of view can also be used within the play, as in the case of the soliloquy, which may allow us to share the private thoughts of one character but not another.

In poetry and fiction we view things through the mind's eye. There is a good deal of variety in that vision, and the writer is allowed considerable flexibility.

There are certain conventional categories for the various possible points of view: *the first person, second person, third person limited,* and *third person omniscient.* There is also the *persona* to consider, the voice that speaks the poem or story.

5a
Persona refers to an invented narrator, often no more than a voice that tells the story.

(1) You must never assume that the speaker of the story or poem is the author.

Even if the work is autobiographical or confessional, the author as artist must choose a voice with which to present the material. In their work some authors have worn many hats and spoken with many different voices. Choosing a *persona* is part of choosing the right style and tone for a particular story or poem. Writing is a performance, not a real-life conversation. It is an artifice, a manipulation of language and form. In a self-portrait the author (or painter) is not only the *subject* but the *creator* of the work of art. In works that are not autobiographical it is easier to see that the voice that speaks the story or poem is not the author's personal voice. It is often the voice of a nameless tale-teller, a disembodied voice, the voice of a non-character, uninvolved in the action, detached and objective. On the other hand, the *persona* is sometimes an invented narrator who does have some degree of involvement in the action, possibly even a central role.

5b
In first person narrative the speaker is a character in the story.

When a narrative is told in the first person (*I, we*), the speaker becomes a character. We hear his or her voice. The voice may belong to a well-defined character or one who reveals little about himself or herself. The narrator may have a major role in the story, or no role at all. These are the major possibilities:

- A narrator who seems to be the author,
- A narrator who is an invented character (major or minor),
- A narrator who heard the story from another person,
- Several narrators, each of whom tells part of the story or his own version of the whole story.

(1) A first-person narrator can seem to be the author.

There are several advantages to using a narrator who seems to be the author. First of all, the reader knows immediately who is talking. Secondly, the story or poem is very convincing, since the author seems to be talking about something he or she knows first-hand. It has some of the effect of non-fiction, even though it may be entirely a fabrication. This point of view is used frequently in personal poetry. In such poetry we can't deny that the authors themselves are speaking to us, but we must keep in mind that they are speaking to us through an art form and that they may be taking a few poetic liberties with the truth in order to give wider significance to their experiences.

(2) A first-person narrator can be an invented character (major or minor).

When an invented character is used, we know that we are not listening to the author's voice but to the voice of someone the author has created. Nevertheless, hearing the narrative from someone who participated in the action, even if it is fictional action, gives the work an air of authenticity. If it is the central character who speaks, we feel that we are in direct touch with the character. Hearing the voice of the narrator helps us to know the person, even to visualize him or her (see "Ruby Tells All," Example 9). The character comes to life instantly. When a minor character is used as narrator the character's role is usually to tell us about the central figures. Their comments as outsiders can often be objective and valuable. *Moby Dick* begins "Call me Ishmael." He's the narrator, but the novel is rarely about *him*.

The main limitation of this use of the first person is that narrators can only tell us what they know and what they think. Some events may be unknown to them or passed on to us second-hand as hearsay. There is also some risk of being bored by hearing only one voice, especially in longer works. This can be avoided by having the narrator report a fair amount of dialogue instead of just summing up what happens.

(3) A first-person narrator may have heard the story from another person.

This device gives the impression that what was told to the narrator was a true story. Similar to this approach is the author (*persona*) who tells us that he or she has found an old manuscript or other documents in which there is an interesting story. The materials may be diaries or letters or newspaper clippings, or anything of that sort that will help in the suspension of disbelief. A good example is Hawthorne's *The Scarlet Letter* (1850).

(4) Several first-person narrators can be used; each of whom tells part of the story or a version of the whole story.

This approach is commonly used in court-room dramas or criminal investigations in which direct testimonies are given in the first person. The reader often has to decide who's lying and who's telling the truth. Sometimes no one is really lying. Certain apparent contradictions may be merely a matter of perception or point of view, as in the movie *Rashomon*.

This technique is also used in complex works such as Faulkner's *Absalom! Absalom!* The multiple point of view allows us to see the central figure, Thomas Sutphen, through the eyes of several characters, and it allows us to understand these participating characters better. In *The Collector* by John Fowles, the story of a kidnapping is told first by the young man who did the deed and then by the young woman he kidnapped.

5c
The second-person point of view invites the reader to identify with one of the characters.

The second person (*you*) was popular for a while some years ago in detective stories, but it seems to have become passé, except perhaps in satires of the genre. For example,

> You are a private eye. You're sitting in your office in San
> Francisco when the phone rings. It is a woman with a voice that

can melt ice-cubes long-distance. You pour yourself another
drink and listen more to her voice than to her problem. . . .

The second person sometimes has the same effect as the
first person. What the narrator is really saying is, "Pretend
that you are me." The narrator could have said as easily, "*I* am
a private eye. . . ." The second person used with the present
tense moves toward the immediacy of a filmscript, and, in fact,
is used in the voice-over scenes of private-eye movies, but,
obviously the second person has its limitations and should be
used with caution.

5d
The third-person narrative employs an "invisible narrator."

The first-person point of view may have the edge in poetry,
but in fiction it is the third person that has traditionally been
more common (*he, she, they*). In very recent fiction, however,
the first person has gained ground. *The Norton Anthology of
Contemporary Fiction* (1988) contains stories that are about
equally divided between the two points of view.

The third-person approach has many variations. There is
usually no identifiable narrator, as in the first person, but the
persona as invisible narrator can tell the story or poem in a
variety of voices and tones, with degrees of objectivity, and
with limited or unlimited knowledge. The four conventional
subdivisions of the third-person point of view are: 1) complete
objectivity; 2) limited objectivity; 3) limited omniscience;
4) complete omniscience.

(1) Complete objectivity refers to the point of view in stories that are written as though seen on a stage or screen.

The completely objective point of view is like the view from a seat in the theater. The author describes only what might be seen and heard from a certain distance. In such an approach there can be no commentary or intrusive analysis. The thoughts of characters cannot be presented directly. We cannot be told anything about the past or circumstances beyond those immediately before us. Everything must be revealed through description, dialogue, action, and, occasionally, voice-over thoughts, monologues, or soliloquies. Fortunately, we can learn a good deal this way, as we know from stage and screen productions. In fiction, examples of pure objectivity are rare. More often we will find substantial objectivity with occasional comments or added information from the narrator. Since the advantage of third-person narration is that it allows the *persona* to comment, pure objectivity seems, at times, unnecessarily limited. One might as well write a play or film script.

(2) Limited objectivity refers to the point of view in stories presented through the eyes of one of the characters.

Though objectivity can be limited in a variety of ways, the most common way is to tell the story in the third person, from the point of view of one of the characters. This means seeing things through the eyes of either the central character or one of the less important characters. The narrator who uses this approach knows only what goes on in the mind of one character.

He or she knows how that character thinks and feels and uses the character to give us impressions of other people in the story. The narrator knows the background of the character, birthplace, childhood, and so on, often commenting on the character and revealing secret fears and desires. These are all limitations on pure objectivity and move toward limited omniscience.

This technique is used in "Barcelona" (Example 2). The narrator comments extensively on Persis Fox, the woman whose purse is stolen. When the incident takes place we see it entirely from her point of view:

> In the next instant, though, before she has seen or heard any person approaching, someone is running past her in the dark — but not past; he is beside her, a tall dark boy, grabbing at her purse, pulling its short strap. Persis' first instinct is to let him have it, not because she is afraid — she is not, still not, afraid — but from a conditioned reflex, instructing her to give people what they want: children, her husband.

The narrator never gets directly into the mind of any of the other characters, including the woman's husband. The narrator's actions and reactions all reach us through Persis Fox.

(3) **Limited omniscience refers to the point of view in stories told by a narrator who has some knowledge but not total knowledge of what is happening.**

The knowledge of the narrator can be limited even if everything is not seen through the eyes of one of the characters. We may be told what several of the characters feel and think without having the impression that the narrator is omniscient. Furthermore, the narrator must reveal whatever he or she knows gradually in order to create suspense. This gives us the feeling that limited discoveries are being made all along. In a mystery story we must not be told whodunit at the very beginning. We must not even feel that the *persona* knows.

(4) **Complete omniscience refers to the point of view in a story told by a narrator who knows everything that is going on in the story.**

The narrator who knows everything seems to be god-like. Such a narrator can never be a character, because all characters have a limited point of view. Such a *persona* is only a voice, a convention in fiction or poetry. The reader, who has suspended disbelief, doesn't even wonder who the narrator is, though he or she may give credit to the author for skillful writing. The omniscient narrator is the author's designated tale-teller and can tell us anything the author decides is worth telling. It is only in this sense that the narrator is god-like and omniscient (of course, nobody really is). Such narrators seem to know everything about the characters, including what they are thinking and anything they've ever done. They can comment and analyze. They know everything about history and geography, all the names of all the people in the character's hometown, and so on. Naturally, they don't tell us all these things. They have to be selective because their goal is to tell us a good story, not to write an encyclopedia. Some writers who use this point of view try to jam too much information into the work and wind up boring the reader with irrelevancies. It is important to remember that only *significant* details count.

5e
Unity and consistency in point of view can be achieved by avoiding accidental shifts.

One of the fundamental responsibilities of the writer is to establish a clear vantage point for the reader. That vantage point has to be established at the very beginning. It can be any of the points of view just described, and once it is established the writer should stick with it. Accidental shifts in point of view can be disturbing and disruptive. They may even be distracting enough to shatter the reader's *suspension of disbelief* (a term that describes the reader's willingness to accept fiction as truth). This does not mean that you can't consciously use multiple points of view if the material lends itself to such an approach. They are sometimes used even in short stories, but they are much more common in novels. The reader can accept any approach that is artistically viable. If, however, you start out writing a story that is *completely objective*, as though seen on a screen or stage, and then you start to make elaborate editorial comments, you may confuse the reader. If you start out in the third person, you shouldn't shift accidentally into the first person. If you want your reader to hear directly the voice of one of your characters, you can use the first person or you can make use of dialogue, internal monologue, and such things as letters and diaries, all of which can be contained within a basically third-person point of view. Whatever you do, make sure that the point of view from which your story is told is absolutely clear.

EXAMPLE 5

THE FOX

Paul Ruffin

From where she was sitting at the kitchen table, her hands deep in the ball of dough in a green bowl, she could see him cross the creek beyond the lower pasture and angle up toward the house. He stopped to lean on the fence that bordered the remains of the summer garden, where the bean poles still stood at odd angles beside the all-but-leafless okra stalks. Drought had brought the garden to an early end as it almost always did.

She was dumping the dough out onto the counter when his shadow mounted the steps and filled the doorway. The screen door squawked open, then slammed to behind him. She did not look around at him.

"There was a fox," he said, sliding a chair back from the table and sitting down, "a red one, in the back field. Near the low-water crossing." He leaned and lifted the coffee pot from the counter and filled the cup that he had already emptied twice that morning before leaving the house. The sun, still morning low, slanted into the small kitchen, brightening what inexpensive things she had scattered across it on table and counter and walls over the thirteen years that they had lived there. Dust specks spun in the rays.

"He had one leg hanging silly to the side and dragging and leaving blood." He looked to see whether she had heard. She kept shaping the ball of dough. "He was so close I could see his eyes. I swear they looked like, like he was blaming me for what trouble he'd been in." He reached over and slid open the box of matches by the stove, one-handedly, lifted one out and struck it across the table top and lit a cigarette. Blue smoke curled up and ribboned in the sun.

She dusted her hands with flour and flattened out the dough, rolled it, and lifted the sheet over a pie plate and dropped it into place. With a paring knife she sliced off the excess, leaving a neat edge around the rim of the plate.

"What you making?" he asked.

"Pie."

"What kind? Something special?"

"No. Just a blueberry pie, from them berries I picked back earlier and froze." She stirred the berries again for good measure and lifted them from the burner.

"His eyes. I can't get over his eyes. They looked like cracked marbles, only black and cold. I was almost afraid he was going to come after me, he looked so mad at the world."

She poured the berries into the dough-lined plate and patted them level with her hand with short little strokes to avoid burning herself, then dropped another sheet of dough over the top. Her hands were stained a deep purple. Using the tines of a fork, she crimped the top shell onto the bottom and ran the knife around the rim again, leaving the pie picture-perfect and ready for baking. She struck three vent slits in the top and slid it into the oven.

"One of them old coon traps likely." He looked at her. "I guess that's what he got into. Hell, I ain't checked them things in years. I left maybe four, five right near where he was.

She dried her berry-stained hands on her apron front, walked to the back door, and looked off toward the smoky morning woods. Crows were zipping in and out of a tree by the creek, cawing, diving in, wheeling up and out, cawing and diving in again. "Owl," she said quietly, "they must be after an owl or something."

"What?" He turned toward her.

"Nothing. I was just talking out loud to myself." She returned to the table and sat down across from him, not because she wanted particularly to be there but because there was no place she could get off to in such a small house where his voice would not find her, rising in insistence until she came. She was not certain that he even cared whether she listened or not. She was just another living thing his voice could drive into or bounce off of — she was something to keep him from talking to himself, which even he must have known was proof positive that he had crossed over into craziness.

"He must have got into one last night, broke his foot or leg, might even have gnawed it off to get out, though I couldn't see the tip of it to be sure." He squinted as smoke coiled about his face. "He crawled under the fence and got off into Mason's corn, what there is of it, not much more than enough to hide a fox, I'd say. Could have been the one that killed them chickens last month, same size, same color. Not likely to get at 'm again."

Their relationship, from her intense hatred of him when they were in grade school together through an infatuation in high school that was consummated in her father's hayloft one Sunday afternoon, had come finally full circle, back to something that she thought at times was hate, at other times mere indifference. If she wished him harm, as she found herself doing some days when he was off in the fields and she was alone in the little house or out in the garden, she was almost happy to

see, once he appeared at the door, that none had come to him.
Those times the hate swung much too quickly to something
like love.

It was the indifference that she nurtured, the cold distance
that she put between herself and him even when he was close
enough that she could see the hardness of his eyes. It was the
calm deadness of indifference that allowed her to continue, day
after day, to endure the hill and house and his voice and, each
night that he rose to it, to accept his heavy roughness as he
drove into her until he shuddered and rolled off onto his side of
the bed.

"You shoulda seen them eyes. Like he was blaming me."

She stared past him, past the dust specks in the beam of
sun that crossed his face, past the dreamlike haziness of the
screen, to the wall of woods where the crows were still zipping
in and out of the tree where she was sure some owl crouched,
or hawk, something wiser or nobler than crows.

"May die from it, may not. Lucky he didn't die in the trap.
He's got something to be glad of there."

And there were the times she was sure that she wished
him dead, gone, so that she could try to find some value again
in her life, some meaning, before she was stooped and gray
and broken like her mother before a merciful onslaught of pneu-
monia took her out of it, leaving her father so alone that even
he, in all his hardness, lasted only another year. She was not
so old now — though you could not tell it looking at her hands
and face, where the wind and sun and contact with all the things
that sting and slash and burn on a farm had done their damage — that she could not smooth over and grow graceful, as her
mother had wanted, had taught her to be. She did not even
have a child to pass her dreams on to, no matter what their

possibilities or impossibilities. She was not even certain that his savage seed, which burned in her like a burst of flame, could beget anything softer than a boy, who would be a copy of him.

"I guess I ought to get the shotgun and go finish him off. If he ain't got too far by now." He flicked his cigarette toward the ashtray and dropped the butt into the last of his coffee. It extinguished with a short hiss.

She walked over to the oven, swung the door down, and checked on the pie. The smell billowed up and out and filled the kitchen.

He slid his chair back and walked into their bedroom, where she heard him fumbling in the closet, getting his gun and shells. He emerged, broke the shotgun open, slipped in two red shells, and stood there watching her bent over the pie. "I don't know how long I'll be gone."

She straightened. The sun had crept along the floor now until the corridor of light from the door was only half as long as it had been. Its reflection off the linoleum gave his face an almost blessed look, like that of the saints in pictures she had seen, but his eyes were still dark and merciless, and the hard lines in his face stood out. He smiled and reached to touch her hand where it lay on the counter. She pulled it away.

"You . . . ," he began, then turned to the door to go.

Watching out of the corner of her eye as his shadow darkened the doorway, paused, and disappeared, she took the pie out of the oven and set it onto a back burner to cool. The house quieted then, dropped so far into silence that she could hear nothing but wind stirring the okra stalks and the distant chatter of crows. She walked to the screen and saw him blend into the woods. A fierce smile on her face, she looked once around the little kitchen and walked over to the stove, where she poised her hand at the edge of the pie and plunged it into the hot, dark center, where it stayed until the burning stopped and there was no feeling left at all.

EXERCISES

DISCUSSION

1. Analyze the point of view from which "The Fox" (Example 5) is told. Is it *objective*? Is it *omniscient*? Is it something in between? Which character do we learn more about? How is this accomplished? Does the *persona* make comments that do not come from either character's point of view?

2. Are there any shifts of point of view in this story? Is there a clear and unified vantage point?

3. Would the story be more successful if it were told by the woman in the first-person?

WRITING

1. Using the *first-person* point of view, write a poem about a childhood experience.

2. Write a short story from a *completely objective* point of view, without the benefit of any commentaries or explanations.

3. Write a story about two former lovers who have not seen each other for several years. Use a *multiple* point of view, telling the story first through the man's eyes, then through the woman's eyes.

4. Write a story or a poem from the *third-person omniscient* point of view.

CHAPTER
SIX

TONE AND STYLE

6a
It is important to understand the terminology usually used in discussions of tone and style.

(1) Tone refers to the feelings, moods, and attitudes that are reflected in the way a work is written.

Although it is difficult to separate *tone* from *style*, we usually think of tone as reflecting the *feelings and attitudes* of the writer. *Tone* is not *content*; it is the particular way in which the content is expressed. The tone of a light literary work might be described, for instance, as facetious, farcical, or whimsical. The tone of a more serious work might be depressing, heavy, or mournful. The tone of a particular work is achieved through certain stylistic devices.

(2) Style refers to writing techniques.

A writer's style can be described in terms of such things as vocabulary, syntax, imagery, figurative language, the handling of dialogue and point of view, and other technical peculiarities.

6b
There is a wealth of variety in the terminology used to discuss tone and style.

Since many students are not accustomed to discussions of tone and style, they do not know what words are available to them. Here, in effect, is a little dictionary of words on which you can draw when you talk about tone and style:

Some Useful Terminology for Discussions of Tone and Style

abstract: Theoretical, without reference to specifics.

absurd: Contrary to logic, but sometimes artistically viable.

affected: Assuming a false manner or attitude to impress others.

ambiguous: Having two or more possible meanings.

analytical: Inclined to examine things by studying their contents or parts.

anecdotal: Involving short narratives of interesting events.

angry: Resentful, enraged.

antique: In the style of an earlier period.

archaic: Current in the past, but now rare (*thee, zounds!*).

austere: Stern, strict, frugal, unornamented.

banal: Pointless and uninteresting.

baroque: Elaborate, grotesque, and ornamental.

bizarre: Unusually strange or odd.

bland: Undisturbing, unemotional, and uninteresting.

bombastic: Pretentious and pompous.

boring: Dull, tedious, and tiresome.

breezy: Quick-paced, but sometimes superficial.

childish: Immature (when applied to adults or to writing).

cinematic: Having the qualities of a motion picture.

classical: Formal, enduring, and standard, adhering to certain traditional methods.

colloquial: Characteristic of ordinary and informal conversation.

comic: Humorous, funny, light (there are many levels of comedy).

concise: Using very few words to express a great deal.

confessional: Characterized by personal admissions of faults. (Used more recently to describe very personal, autobiographical writing.)

contemptuous: Expressing contempt or disdain (as opposed to *contemptible*, which means deserving of contempt).

conventional: Ordinary, usual, conforming to established standards. (Can be applied to language as well as to manners or values.)

convincing: Persuasive, believable, plausible.

convoluted: Very complicated or involved (as in the case of sentences with many qualifiers, phrases, and clauses).

cool: Unaffected by emotions, especially anger or fear. In modern slang there are many shades of meaning: great, really fine, calm, composed.

crepuscular: Having to do with twilight or shadowy areas (as in the darker and more hidden parts of human experience).

cynical: A tendency to believe that all human behavior is selfish and opportunistic. (Iago in *Othello* is a cynical character. Some writers are cynical.)

decadent: Marked by a decay in morals, values, and artistic standards. Deplored by some writers; applauded by others.

dense: Thick, compacted, intense, sometimes to a fault.

depressing: Sad, gloomy (without the redeeming qualities of true tragedy).

detached: Disinterested, unbiased, emotionally disconnected.

derivative: Coming from something or someone else. (When a writer's style is derivative it seems to stem from the style of an earlier writer or group of writers.)

discursive: Moving pointlessly from one subject to another. Rambling.

dispassionate: Free from passion. Uninfluenced by personal feelings.

dream-like: Having the characteristics of a dream. (In literature events are sometimes portrayed as though they are happening in dreams, which often contain symbols and distortions of reality.)

dreary: Depressing, dismal, boring.

earthy: Realistic, rustic, coarse, unrefined, instinctive, animal-like. (Sometimes applied to the language of characters who live close to the earth or soil.)

effeminate: Soft, delicate, unmanly (applied to men and sometimes to the style of male writers).

elegaic: Expressing sorrow or lamentation. (An elegy is a mournful poem, often a lament for the dead.)

elitist: Believing that those who are superior in some way have the right to rule.

emotional: Much given to strong feelings (as opposed to intellectual).

emphatic: Using emphasis or boldness in speech, writing, or action.

ephemeral: Lasting only a short time. (Might be applied to writing that is only briefly significant or fashionable.)

epigrammatical: A tendency to make use of epigrams, which are terse, witty, or pointed sayings ("Any time that is not spent on love is wasted," said Tasso).

epistolary: Involving letters. Epistolary novels are made up mostly or entirely of letters written by the characters.

erudite: Learned, scholarly.

eulogistic: Involving formal praise, in speech or writing, usually in honor of someone who has died.

euphemistic: Involving euphemisms, which are mild, indirect expressions substituted for harsh or offensive ones, as in *passed away*, meaning *died*.

evocative: Having the ability to call forth memories or other responses. (Imagery in literature tends to be evocative.)

experimental: Inclined to try out new techniques or ideas. (Used of writers who break new ground, such as James Joyce.)

expressionistic: Stressing the subjective and symbolic in art and literature. Associated with a specific movement in the arts called expressionism.

facetious: Amusing, but light, unserious, and frivolous.

fashionable: Conforming to whatever the current fashion is in dress, manners, language, or any field of endeavor, including literature.

farcical: Humorous in a light way, as in a farce, a play in which the comedy depends a good deal on the situation, often a ridiculous situation.

fatalistic: Believing that everything that happens is destined, and therefore, out of the hands of the individual. (See "Appointment in Samarra" by W. S. Maugham.)

fatuous: Complacent, foolish, and silly.

feminine: Having the natural or conventional characteristics of a woman.

flamboyant: Conspicuously bold or colorful.

fluid: Flowing smoothly. (Writing with a smooth sequence of sounds might be described as fluid prose.)

gloomy: Sad, dejected, depressed, despondent, shadowy. (Not all serious or tragic materials are presented in a gloomy tone. It is more likely to occur in tales of mystery and the macabre.)

gimmicky: Tricky, sometimes excessively, as in contrived endings.

heavy: Profound or serious. (There are various informal modern meanings: *excellent, difficult, tragic.*)

heroic: Bold, altruistic, like a hero. (In writing *heroics* refers to extravagant language, especially that written during the Restoration.)

honest: Truthful, creditable, unpretentious.

hysterical: Uncontrollably or violently emotional. (It is possible to be hysterical with laughter as well as with fear or rage.)

iconoclastic: Inclined to attack cherished beliefs and traditions.

imagist: Inclined to use free verse and imagery in poetry. (British and American imagist poets flourished between 1900 and 1917.)

impressionistic: Inclined to use subjective impressions rather than objective reality. (Especially associated with a movement in painting.)

incoherent: Without logical connections, as in speech or writing that cannot be understood.

inconsistent: Not holding together or retaining form or adhering to the same principles.

intellectual: Having significant mental ability; a tendency to rely on the mind as opposed to the emotions.

ironic: Characterized by an unexpected turn of events, often the opposite of what was intended. (It was *ironic* that when Oedipus searched for the mysterious cause of the plague he discovered that he himself was the cause.)

irreverent: Showing disrespect for things that are usually respected or revered.

journalistic: Characterized by the kind of language usually used in journalism, sometimes pejoratively called *journalese*.

juvenile: Immature or childish. (A fault in adults, but a standard category in publishing — that is, literature intended for children.)

kitschy: Having little or no value (as art or as literature).

lavish: Using a great or profuse amount of anything, including language.

light: Not profound or serious or important. (Murder mysteries and romances are considered light reading.)

limpid: Clear, transparent, lucid (not to be confused with *limp*).

lyrical: Intense, spontaneous, musical.

macho: Strong and manly. Sometimes used in the same sense as *machismo*, which means having an exaggerated sense of being masculine.

masculine: Having qualities considered to be characteristic of men.

melodramatic: Having the characteristics of melodrama, in which emotions and plot are exaggerated and characterization is shallow.

metaphorical: Making use of metaphors, which are figures of speech, non-literal comparisons ("We recognize that flattery is poison, but its perfume intoxicates us." Marquis De La Grange).

metaphysical: Preoccupied with abstract things, especially the ultimate nature of existence and reality.

minimalist: Inclined to use as few words and details as possible. (A fairly new word used to describe a current trend in literature.)

ministerial: Having the qualities (especially the sound) of a minister or preacher.

modern: Characteristic of recent times. (The modern period in literature is sometimes defined as beginning about 1885 and sometimes later.)

monotonous: Tiresome or dull because of lack of variety.

mournful: Feeling or expressing grief. (Certain literary forms are devoted to the expression of grief, such as elegies and eulogies.)

mundane: Ordinary or common, as in everyday matters. ("His mind was filled with mundane details.")

mystical: Having spiritual or occult qualities or believing in such things. (Some writing is supposed to be divinely or mysteriously inspired, and the writer is supposed to be merely a medium used by a higher power.)

naturalistic: Tending to present things in art and literature as they appear in nature or actuality. (Compare *realistic*.)

nostalgic: Inclined to long for or dwell on things of the past (suggests a certain sentimentality).

objective: Uninfluenced by personal feelings. Seeing things from the outside, not subjectively.

obscure: Unclear, indistinct, hard to understand. (Compare *obscurantism*, which is the deliberate use of obscurity and evasion of clarity.)

obsessive: An abnormal and persistent preoccupation with certain ideas or feelings. Sex, death, money, and power are some popular obsessions.

obvious: Not subtle. Easy to understand. (Some things are too obvious to be worth writing about.)

old-fashioned: In the manner of past styles and customs. Outmoded. (Even language can become old-fashioned. Words such as "swell" are clearly dated.)

ominous: Indicating or threatening evil or danger, as dark clouds indicate that a storm is coming. (*Foreshadowing* is a device in writing that provides hints to the reader that something, usually bad, is going to happen.)

onomatopoetic: Forming or using words that sound like what they mean, such as *crash, hiss, boom*.

paranoid: Feeling unreasonably that others are hostile.

parody: A satirical imitation of something serious, such as the endless comic take-offs on Romeo and Juliet.

passionate: Feeling or expressing intense emotion, enthusiasm, or desire (not limited to amorous emotions or sexual desire).

pedagogical: Inclined to use the art of teaching.

pedantic: Inclined to over-emphasize and show off one's learning.

penetrating: Getting deeply into something, either physically or in a more abstract sense, as in a *penetrating* analysis.

persuasive: Able to get a person to do something or to agree with one by an appeal to reason or other convincing devices.

philosophical: Interested in the study of the basic truths of existence and reality. Also, inclined to have a calm and accepting attitude towards the realities of life.

pious: Having or displaying a reverence for God and religion. Sometimes used pejoratively, when the display is excessive and overly righteous.

poetical: Having the qualities of poetry, such as pleasing rhythms or images. (The prose of some fiction writers, such as Virginia Woolf, has been described as poetical.)

polemical: Involving a controversial argument or disputation.

political: Involved in politics. Sometimes political literature tends to be polemical, intellectual, or satirical. It can also fall to the level of propaganda.

pompous: Displaying one's importance in an exaggerated way. Sometimes a quality in comic characters.

ponderous: Heavy, awkward, and dull.

pragmatic: Preferring practical action and consequences to theory and abstractions.

precious: Being affected in matters of refinement and manners, sometimes ridiculously so. (Some language can be described as *precious*.)

pretentious: Having and displaying an exaggerated view of one's own importance.

primitive: Simple and crude. (Primitivism in the arts tries to make use in a sophisticated way of what seems simple and crude.)

profound: Having penetrating insight, deep.

prurient: Preoccupied with lewd and lustful thoughts.

psychological: Having to do with the human mind and human behavior. (The development of modern psychology influenced literature and produced the so-called psychological novel and a kind of clinical approach to characters, especially including the Freudian approach.)

puerile: Foolish in a childish way.

puritanical: Strict or severe in matters of morality (as in the English Puritans of the sixteenth and seventeenth centuries).

ranting: Talking loudly and violently, raving (sometimes suggesting a mental disturbance).

realistic: Inclined to represent things as they really are (not necessarily as they appear to be). See *naturalistic*.

rebellious: Inclined to defy authority (politically, socially, artistically, or in any other way).

repetitious: Tediously repeating the same thing (such as words or ideas).

rhythmic: Characterized by certain patterns, beats, or accents (as in dancing, music, poetry).

romantic: Having feelings or thoughts of love, but when associated with nineteenth century literature or any such literature it suggests a style that emphasizes freedom of form, imagination, and emotion.

sarcastic: Inclined to use nasty or cutting remarks that can hurt people's feelings.

sardonic: Mocking, taunting, bitter, scornful, sarcastic.

satirical: Using sarcasm and irony, often humorously, to expose human folly. (Satire is a commonly used device in literature that is politically or socially critical.)

scatological: Preoccupied with excrement or obscenity. (Scatological humor is sometimes referred to as bathroom humor.)

self-conscious: Being excessively aware of one's self and embarrassed in the presence of others. (The self-conscious style of some writers can be distracting to the reader.)

sensitive: Unusually responsive and aware. Easily affected by people or things in one's surroundings. Having acute sensibility, the capacity to feel things.

sensuous: Taking pleasure in things that appeal to the senses. (*Sensual* suggests a strong preoccupation with such things, especially sexual pleasures.)

sentimental: Expressing tender feelings, sometimes excessively, hence the phrase "sloppy sentimentality."

shadowy: Partially obscured by the lack of light. (Not to be confused with *shady*, which means of questionable legality. Settings and characters in literature might sometimes be *shadowy*.)

sharp: Precise, biting, or harsh (as applied to words). One can be said to have a sharp tongue, meaning that he says harsh or nasty things.

smooth: Polished and free from difficulties or awkwardness, sometimes excessively to the point of blandness.

snobbish: Impressed with social rank and wealth. (See *elitist*.)

staccato: With clear breaks between notes, words, or phrases (a musical term that is sometimes applied to writing).

stilted: Very formal, sometimes excessively, as in stilted prose.

sophisticated: Worldly and experienced when applied to people, intricate or complex when applied to things. In writing, a sophisticated style may suggest complexity or considerable experience in the craft.

stark: Plain, harsh, complete (as in "stark raving mad"). Simple or bare, when applied to style; sometimes even bleak or grim.

subjective: Relying on one's own inner impressions, as opposed to being objective. (Literature that is presented mainly through the thoughts and feelings of characters is often described as subjective.)

subtle: Delicate in meaning, sometimes elusively so.

superficial: Shallow, trivial, dealing only with the surface of things.

surrealistic: Stressing imagery and the subconscious and sometimes distorting ordinary ideas in order to arrive at artistic truths (a modern movement in art and literature).

symbolic: Using material objects to represent abstract or complex ideas or feelings. (Moby Dick is obviously symbolic.)

syntactical: Referring to syntax or sentence-structure. (Certain authors have very distinctive syntactical characteristics.)

tedious: Tiresome and boring.

terse: Effectively concise. (There are many shades and levels of brevity in literature. Some are effective and some are not.)

tragic: Dreadful, disastrous, fatal. (The classical or Aristotelian definition of tragedy is very specific and involves more than just disaster. It involves a character of high standing and impressive character who has a tragic flaw that brings about his or her downfall.)

trite: Stale, worn out, as in trite expressions.

typographical: Having to do with type or print. (Some

writing   has   a   visual dimension —
its arrangement in print plays a role in the work.)

urbane: Sophisticated, socially polished.

vague: Unclear, indefinite, imprecise, ambiguous.

venomous: Poisonous, malicious.

verbose: Wordy to the point of being unclear.

victorian: Prudish, stuffy, and puritanical (qualities associated with the reign of Queen Victoria).

visual: Pertaining to sight. (Some writers appeal mainly to the sense of sight.)

whimsical: Inclined to be playful, humorous, or fanciful.

witty: Being able to perceive and express ideas and situations in a clever and amusing way.

wordy: Using more words than necessary to say what you have to say.

6c

There are as many varieties of tone and style as there are writers.

The long list of words used to describe tone and style should indicate clearly that there is enormous variety in these aspects of literature. Every author's way of writing is like his or her signature, unique in certain ways, however subtle, and for every work just the right tone must be established if the work is to achieve the desired effect. To establish the right tone the writer has many literary devices with which to work, from manipulation of word choice and syntax to imagery, irony, and satire.

To demonstrate varieties of tone and style let us examine three passages on exactly the same subject and situation, each with a distinct tone and style.

(1) A witty, sardonic tone can be established stylistically by irony, satire, and word-play.

If the city were merely a jungle, we'd all be a lot safer. What goes on in the jungle is a natural process of growth and decay. There is that nasty old food-chain, of course. I mean, some lovely little creatures get eaten up. They, in turn, find something even smaller to eat. Nobody seems to mind, at least not in the way that we do. There is no memory, no guilt, no conscious anxiety — only *flick*! The long tongue of a giant frog hauling in an insect. Then crunch, crunch, wriggle, wriggle, and it's all over. You don't have to make up resumes and look for another job because you have become obsolete or redundant, not to mention fat and bald and mystified by the world of computers. Insects are always employed until the big bullfrog gets them. Instinct tells them what to do. I sometimes wish the city *were* a jungle, instead of what it really is — an obscene marketplace. I'd rather be a frog croaking love songs in a swamp than a terminated advertising executive croaking of anonymity in a three-room apartment cluttered with the cosmetic debris of some stranger who calls herself my wife. So, here I am with my severance check in my pocket. Perhaps I should use it to sever myself from all this nonsense and buy myself a one-way ticket to Tahiti. Gauguin did it. Why can't I?

The *tone* of this passage is lively, witty, satirical, sardonic, sophisticated, and urbane. The narrator may be unhappy with his situation, but he makes his point with humor, even if it is bitter humor. This is achieved by using *stylistic devices* such as:

(a) *Irony:* In the opening sentence, for example, he says, ironically, that the jungle is safer than the city.
(b) *Word choice:* Witty and informal, as in "nasty old food-chain"; onomatopoetical, as in *flick, crunch,* and *wriggle;* sharp and critical, as in *terminated, anonymity, cosmetic debris.*
(c) *Word play:* For example, in the two meanings of *croak* and the play on *severance.*
(d) *Satire:* In his amusing and biting references to the "obscene marketplace," for example, and the business world, and the prejudice against older employees; and his reference to marriage in the sardonic expression, "some stranger who calls herself my wife."

(2) A dreary tone can be established stylistically by imagery, a pattern of word choice, and repetition.

There was a dead rat on the sidewalk when he came out of the bolted vault of his apartment house on the West Side. He looked furtively at the hunched group of winos outside the burnt and boarded *bodega.* In the dull light and sticky summer air they looked like a group of ragged apes, and the city itself seemed like a kind of jungle that required special instincts for survival. Fear was his constant companion — fear of attack, fear of losing his job, fear of displeasing his wife, fear of being laughed at because he was fat and bald, and even the minor terror of stepping in dog dung and having to carry the smell of it with him into the transient grave of the subway, and the more permanent grave of his dreary office on Madison Avenue.

The *tone* of this passage is serious, dreary, and emotional. The dominant feelings are fear and disgust. The atmosphere is gloomy and dangerous. This is achieved by using literary devices such as:

(a) *Imagery, metaphors,* and *similes:* His opening reference to a dead rat sets the tone. The winos are like ragged apes. The city is like a jungle. The subway is a transient grave, and his office is a permanent grave.

(b) *Word choice: furtively, hunched, burnt, boarded, dull, sticky, ragged, survival, dog dung, grave.*

(c) *Repetition:* He repeats the word *fear* five times, and he repeats *grave* in an effective comparison.

(3) An objective, serious tone can be established stylistically by an analytical approach.

He thought of New York as a city that had failed, and he knew that it was just a matter of time before he would have to leave. The rents were too high. The traffic was unbearable. The air was foul. Two thousand people a year were murdered in the city. Over two hundred thousand were hooked on heroin, and over thirty-five thousand were homeless. New York was not a jungle; it was a sociological disaster that offended his sense of order and justice. He hated the polarization of rich and poor. The glass and aluminum functionalism of the towering buildings was as unattractive in its own way as the desolation of the South Bronx.

Though it is still full of negative feelings, the *tone* of this passage is more objective and impersonal than the tone of either the first or second passage. *Stylistically*, this is achieved by an analytical and factual approach.

(a) *Analysis:* The opening sentence contains the broad statement that New York is a city that has failed. It is followed by a series of statements, each of which describes a specific way in which the city has failed — high rents, unbearable traffic, foul air, high crime rate, many drug addicts, many homeless people, polarization of rich and poor, ugly architecture.

(4) Consider these additional examples of variety in tone and style.

The three passages analyzed above are contrived illustrations. Let us now consider a few actual works, some of which are included in this book and some of which are so widely known that they can be considered without being included.

"Barcelona," by Alice Adams (Example 2)

Tone: ominous, psychological, sensitive, and subtle (a familiar modern sound).

Style: cinematic and visual, but also subjective because of the strongly focused point of view. The language level is very contemporary, as is the use of the present tense, which has recently become quite fashionable.

"A Clean, Well-Lighted Place," by Ernest Hemingway

Tone: evocative, dispassionate, sad, and depressing (reflecting a rather grim view of life).

Style: artistically and self-consciously brief and rhythmical to the point of being poetic and imagistic. The stark prose is made up of carefully selected descriptive details and minimalist dialogue, often without tags (*he said/ she said*). His style is very distinctive. It has had a powerful influence on modern fiction.

"The Railway Children," by Seamus Heaney

Tone: nostalgic, wistful, with a childish innocence and a sense of awe and adventure.

Style: lyrical with a narrative element. Selective, sharp, descriptive details, and strong, suggestive word choice, as in "sizzling wires," the "burden of swallows," and the raindrops "seeded full with the light."

"Ruby Tells All," by Miller Williams (Example 9)

Tone: earthy, colloquial, wistful, philosophical (as an attitude of acceptance of life).

Style: Though Ruby speaks in a confessional and autobiographical way, the poem cannot be called "confessional" in the same sense as Sylvia Plath's or Anne Sexton's poetry. There is no end-line pattern, but the lines are measured (blank verse). It is very narrative, almost like prose, except for the line structure and distillation of events into poetic phrases, often enhanced by the earthy language (a style not uncommon in Southern writers).

"Do Not Go Gentle into That Good Night" by Dylan Thomas

Tone: sad and affectionate, a powerful, plaintive exhortation.

Style: a villanelle, which is highly rhymed, using only two rhyming sounds throughout its nineteen lines. A traditional form, but used here with powerful and sometimes unusual phrasing, and with frequent alliteration, which adds up to a poem that is very musical and reflects the ethnic background of the author (the Welsh are famous for their love of music and the lilt in their language).

"Daddy" by Sylvia Plath

Tone: confessional, angry, hostile, violent, desperate, and a little hysterical and paranoid.

Style: melodic, partly because of the skillful use of repetition. Magnificent and sometimes shocking imagery and word choice. (*Confessional* is a term that is sometimes used to describe style as well as tone.)

This analytical approach to tone and style is designed to give you some insight into an aspect of writing that is all too often treated with a good deal of vagueness. In actual practice a writer is not likely to be this analytical or self-conscious. Most writers automatically integrate content, tone, and style. They have an instinct for selecting the appropriate voice, language, attitude, and literary devices. In the act of creation a writer is often like an athlete who unconsciously performs with spectacular grace. After the fact, neither the writer nor the athlete can explain exactly what happened.

EXAMPLE 6

THE TOUCH

Anne Sexton

For months my hand had been sealed off
in a tin box. Nothing was there but subway railings.
Perhaps it is bruised, I thought,
and that is why they have locked it up.
But when I looked in, it lay there quietly.
You could tell time by this, I thought,
like a clock, but for its five knuckles
and the thin underground veins.
It lay there like an unconscious woman
fed by tubes she knew not of.
The hand had collapsed,
a small wood pigeon
that had gone into seclusion.
I turned it over and the palm was old,
its lines traced like fine needlepoint
and stitched up into the fingers.
It was fat and soft and blind in places.
Nothing but vulnerable.

And all this is metaphor.
An ordinary hand — just lonely
for something to touch
that touches back.
The dog won't do it.
Her tail wags in the swamp for a frog.
I'm no better than a case of dog food.
She owns her own hunger.

My sisters won't do it.
They live in school except for buttons
and tears running down like lemonade.
My father won't do it.
He comes with the house and even at night
he lives in a machine made by my mother
and well oiled by his job, his job.

The trouble is
that I'd let my gestures freeze.
The trouble was not
in the kitchen or the tulips
but only in my head, my head.

Then all this became history.
Your hand found mine.
Life rushed to my fingers like a blood clot.

Oh, my carpenter,
the fingers are rebuilt.
They dance with yours.
They dance in the attic and in Vienna.
My hand is alive all over America.
Not even death will stop it,
death shedding her blood.
Nothing will stop it, for this is the kingdom
and the kingdom come.

EXERCISES

DISCUSSION

1. Describe the tone of "The Touch" by Anne Sexton (Example 6). Is there any humor in this poem?

2. By what stylistic devices is the tone achieved?

3. The second stanza of the poem begins: "And all this is metaphor." Explain that statement. Does it refer to just the first stanza or to the whole poem?

4. Is the exhilaration in the final stanza consistent with the tone of the rest of the poem? How is that feeling of exhilaration achieved?

5. Discuss the tone and style of the following poem (see Chapter 11 for poetics):

THE MAN IN THE MERCEDES
Judith Kroll (1971)

The killer will be driving a Mercedes.
Watch for a foreign-looking man,
swarthy and short.

We see him from the back of his head:

a fat neck; disappearing hair;
definitely middle-aged (a career
agent)

The man in the Mercedes appears
in the supermarket. He has come
to do a demonstration
of something that changes hope
into pretzels.

6. Here are the opening passages of two short stories. Discuss the tone and style of each passage. Is there anything in the writing to indicate that the story by Lawrence was

written more than fifty years earlier than the story by Oates?

From "The Man Who Loved Islands" by D. H. Lawrence

FIRST ISLAND

There was a man who loved islands. He was born on one, but it didn't suit him, as there were too many other people on it, besides himself. He wanted an island all of his own; not necessarily to be alone on it, but to make it a world of his own.

An island, if it is big enough, is no better than a continent. It has to be really quite small, before it *feels like* an island; and this story will show how tiny it has to be, before you can presume to fill it with your own personality.

Now circumstances so worked out, that this lover of islands, by the time he was thirty-five, actually acquired an island of his own. He didn't own it as freehold property, but he had a ninety-nine years' lease of it, which, as far as a man and an island are concerned, is as good as everlasting. Since, if you are like Abraham, and want your offspring to be numberless as the sands of the sea-shore, you don't choose an island to start breeding on. Too soon there would be overpopulation, overcrowding, and slum conditions. Which is a horrid thought, for one who loves an island for its insulation. No, an island is a nest which holds one egg, and one only. This egg is the islander himself.

From "By the River" by Joyce Carol Oates

Helen thought: "Am I in love again, some new kind of love? Is that why I'm here?" She was sitting in the waiting room of the Yellow Bus Lines station; she knew the big old room with its dirty tile floor and its solitary telephone booth in the corner and its candy machine and cigarette machine and popcorn machine by heart. Everything was familiar, though she had been gone for five months, even the old woman with the dyed red hair who sold tickets and had been selling them there, behind that counter, for as long as Helen could remember. Years ago, before Helen's marriage, she and her girl friends would be driven into town by someone's father and after they tired of walking around town they would stroll over to the bus station to watch the buses unload. They were anxious to see who was getting off, but few of the passengers who got off stayed in Oriskany — they were just passing through, stopping for a rest and a drink, and their faces seemed to say that they didn't think much of the town. Nor did they seem to think much of the girls from the country who stood around in their colorful dresses and smiled shyly at strangers, not knowing any better: they were taught to be kind to people, to smile first, you never knew who it might be. So now Helen was back in Oriskany, but this time she had come in on a bus herself. Had ridden alone, all the way from the city of Derby, all alone, and was waiting for her father to pick her up so she could go back to her old life without any more fuss.

WRITING

1. Write a poem, the tone of which can be described with one of the following sets of terms:
    a. satirical, sardonic, ironic
    b. elegaic, depressing, metaphysical
    c. metaphorical, symbolic, surrealistic
    d. psychological, ominous, paranoid

2. Write a description of a place that you don't like. Make your negative tone clear in your writing as well as your content.

3. Write a satirical story in which the target of your satire is some aspect of education, politics, or television.

4. Write a short story in the tone and style of the passage by D. H. Lawrence or the passage by Joyce Carol Oates.

CHAPTER
SEVEN

DESCRIPTION

Description should be *selective* and *significant*. It should also appeal to the five senses: seeing, hearing, smelling, tasting, and touching. It is the writer's job to create a kind of fictional reality, to make things seem real. The scientist describes the physical world with cold objectivity. The writer describes the world with physical details to create a work of art. This can best be accomplished by careful observation and skillful abstraction.

7a
Abstractions play an important part in literary descriptions.

To abstract means *to remove*. When you write an abstract (summary) of a report, you single out only the most important points. In abstract art only certain significant forms and colors are used. It is non-representational. In writing, words that are abstract refer to some general quality or condition, not to a specific object. *Beauty*, for instance, is an abstract word. So is *truth*. When John Keats says "beauty is truth" he is making an abstract statement, but when Byron says the following he has someone specific in mind:

> She walks in beauty, like the night
>> Of cloudless climes and starry skies . . .

An abstract statement is a generalization that is arrived at by observing many specific cases. Thus, when you say "There is a charming innocence in children," you are making a general observation about children and not a comment about a specific child. Aphorisms and proverbs are generalizations. For example: "As we grow older we grow both more foolish and wiser at the same time" (La Rochefoucauld, 1665).

So much of human thought and expression involves the use of abstractions that we can't just toss them aside when we write fiction, poetry, and drama. In many workshops, student writers are advised to avoid abstractions. This advice is a bit simplistic. What a writer has to learn to do is to use abstract language when it is appropriate and specific language when it is more effective. Most descriptive passages benefit enormously from the use of specific details that appeal to the senses.

7b
Physical details are an essential part of any description.

The use of physical details allows the reader to experience what is going on in the literary work. Good writers are especially perceptive and sensitive when it comes to such details.

In their work they share their observations and their sensitivity with their readers, and, thereby, provide them with vicarious experiences and insights that otherwise they might not have. That is why great writers are not considered mere entertainers. The contributions they make to their culture are important.

(1) It is important for writers to develop the habit of perception.

Some writers are born with the gift of observation; some have to learn how to look at things. It is possible for a young writer to cultivate the habit of perception. One workshop exercise involves the systematic observation of people from head to toe, and the listing of descriptive details and what they reveal about a person. One example should suffice.

What about a character's hair? What can it reveal? Hair doesn't just have a color; it has a texture, and it is done in a certain style. It also moves as the body moves or as the wind moves through it. Hair is a kind of language. How you wear it is a message to the world, sometimes a sexual message, sometimes even a political message. In the 1960s it was very political. Long hair became a sign of protest and the back-to-nature look. More recently, punk hairdos have announced rebellion. The idea is to be outrageous, even offensive. Such youthful rebellions are almost always against the stodginess and conservatism of the older generation and the establishment. Conscious and constant practice in the observation of details such as these can improve a writer's ability to describe things.

A writer's observations can be subtle or superficial. Good writers tend to have greater depth and originality. Commercial writers tend to rely heavily on stereotypes and clichés.

(2) Seeing

A writer must learn to make use of all the five senses when writing descriptions. The highest of these senses, according to Aristotle, is sight. The popularity of television may be modern evidence of how right he was. In performed dramas, of course, sight is essential, but even in poetry and fiction the visual appeal is often dominant. Notice the number of vivid details in the opening paragraphs of "A Worn Path" by Eudora Welty:

> It was December — a bright frozen day in the early morning. Far out in the country there was an old Negro woman with her head tied in a red rag, coming along a path through the pinewoods. Her name was Phoenix Jackson. She was very old and small and she walked slowly in the dark pine shadows, moving a little from side to side in her steps, with the balanced heaviness and lightness of a pendulum in a grandfather clock. She carried a thin, small cane made from an umbrella, and with this she kept tapping the frozen earth in front of her. This made a grave and persistent noise in the still air, that seemed meditative like the chirping of a solitary little bird.
>
> She wore a dark striped dress reaching down to her shoe tops, and an equally long apron of bleached sugar sacks, with a full pocket: all neat and tidy, but every time she took a step she might have fallen over her shoelaces, which dragged from her unlaced shoes. She looked straight ahead. Her eyes were blue with age. Her skin had a pattern all its own of numberless branching wrinkles and as though a whole little tree stood in the middle of her forehead, but a golden color ran underneath, and the two knobs of her cheeks were illuminated by a yellow burning under the dark. Under the red rag her hair came down on her neck in the frailest of ringlets, still black, and with an odor like copper.

(3) Hearing

The following poem by Wallace Stevens is visually striking, but the strongest sensation is *sound* — the cry of the peacocks:

DOMINATION OF BLACK

At night, by the fire,
The colors of the bushes
And of the fallen leaves,
Repeating themselves,
Turned in the room,
Like the leaves themselves
Turning in the wind.
Yes: but the color of the heavy hemlocks
Came striding.
And I remembered the cry of the peacocks.   10
The colors of their tails
Were like the leaves themselves
Turning in the wind,
In the twilight wind.
They swept over the room,
Just as they flew from the boughs of the hemlocks
Down to the ground.
I heard them cry — the peacocks.
Was it a cry against the twilight
Or against the leaves themselves   20
Turning in the wind,
Turning as the flames
Turned in the fire,
Turning as the tails of the peacocks
Turned in the loud fire,
Loud as the hemlocks
Full of the cry of the peacocks?
Or was it a cry against the hemlocks?

Out of the window,
I saw how the planets gathered   30
Like the leaves themselves
Turning in the wind.
I saw how the night came,
Came striding like the color of the heavy hemlocks.
I felt afraid.
And I remembered the cry of the peacocks.

The mating call of the peacock is a harsh, haunting, unearthly cry. Wallace Stevens tries to describe poetically his reactions to that sound. It is not an easy task. Sounds may be more difficult to describe than sights. Consider, for instance, how difficult it is to describe music. Since the world is full of sounds, writers must learn to include them in the fabric of their work. Who can forget that terrifying line by Emily Dickinson: "I heard a fly buzz — when I died — "? And no one has captured the sound of the sea on a calm night better than Matthew Arnold in "Dover Beach":

The sea is calm tonight.
The tide is full, the moon lies fair
Upon the straits; — on the French coast the light
Gleams and is gone; the cliffs of England stand,
Glimmering and vast, out in the tranquil bay.
Come to the window, sweet is the night-air!
Only, from the long line of spray
Where the sea meets the moon-blanched land,
Listen! you hear the grating roar
Of pebbles which the waves draw back, and fling,
At their return, up the high strand,
Begin, and cease, and then again begin,
With tremulous cadence slow, and bring
The eternal note of sadness in.

(4) Smelling

A novel by Tom Robbins called *Jitterbug Perfume* (1984) is preoccupied with the sense of smell, as its title might indicate. In the following scene the ultimate fragrance actually causes a riot:

> Somebody had supplied beer, cases of it, and many in the crowd had lost their reason in it. About seven o'clock, as much of Seattle was finishing its dinner, a dense, hot, rustic odor swept through the street, and as if it had one mind, one nose, the crowd spontaneously panicked. Something snapped in it, and it rushed the gate, tearing it from its hinges and throwing the guards aside.
>
> Disturbed and anxious, pursued by the smell, the people ripped loose the fairy door knocker and streamed into the mansion, where they raced from room to room, looking for the divine magic that had been denied them. And when they found nothing — no gurgling test tubes or sparking coils, no vials of purple elixirs or leatherbound books bursting with esoteric information, no files, even, that they might plunder; when they found merely a posh modern residence lacking so much as a hint of scientific activity and occupied only by a red-faced man who'd been skipping and leaping about in a bizarre dance, and a young girl playing with potted plants, then they truly panicked.

In an earlier scene one of the characters discusses the importance of fragrance in the human experience:

> Bunny: "Scent is the last sense to leave a dying person. After sight, hearing, and even touch are gone, the dying hold on to their sense of smell. Does that sharpen your appreciation of the arena in which we perfumers perform?
>
> "Fragrance is a conduit for our earliest memories, on the one hand; on the other, it may accompany us as we enter the next life. In between, it creates mood, stimulates fantasy,

shapes thought, and modifies behavior. It is our strongest link to the past, our closest fellow traveler to the future. Prehistory, history, and the afterworld, all are its domain. Fragrance may well be the signature of eternity."

There are times in *Jitterbug Perfume* when Tom Robbins gets carried away, but there is no doubt that the sense of smell is extremely important. We all know how effectively a hunting dog can follow a scent, but we are less aware of many of the subtle effects that fragrances and odors have on people. Experiments have shown that newborn babies can pick out their own mothers from a group through their sense of smell. One theory about sexual attraction claims that what is called "chemistry" between people is largely determined by smell. The popularity of perfume is further evidence that we may not be as far removed from other animals as we think. A good writer can make good use of the sense of smell in the descriptions that bring human experience to life. One of Shakespeare's most powerful lines can be found in the final couplet of Sonnet 94:

> For sweetest things turn sourest by their deeds;
> Lilies that fester smell far worse than weeds.

(5) Tasting

In this well-known poem by Delmore Schwartz the sense of taste is very effectively used:

THE HEAVY BEAR WHO GOES WITH ME

"The withness of the body" — WHITEHEAD

The heavy bear who goes with me,
A manifold honey to smear his face,
Clumsy and lumbering here and there,

The central ton of every place,
The hungry beating brutish one
In love with candy, anger, and sleep,
Crazy factotum, dishevelling all,
Climbs the building, kicks the football,
Boxes his brother in the hate-ridden city.

Breathing at my side, that heavy animal,   10
That heavy bear who sleeps with me,
Howls in his sleep for a world of sugar,
A sweetness intimate as the water's clasp,
Howls in his sleep because the tight-rope
Trembles and shows the darkness beneath.
— The strutting show-off is terrified,
Dressed in his dress-suit, bulging his pants,
Trembles to think that his quivering meat
Must finally wince to nothing at all.

That inescapable animal walks with me,   20
Has followed me since the black womb held,
Moves where I move, distorting my gesture,
A caricature, a swollen shadow,
A stupid clown of the spirit's motive,
Perplexes and affronts with his own darkness,
The secret life of belly and bone,
Opaque, too near, my private, yet unknown,
Stretches to embrace the very dear
With whom I would walk without him near,
Touches her grossly, although a word   30
Would bare my heart and make me clear,
Stumbles, flounders, and strives to be fed
Dragging me with him in his mouthing care,
Amid the hundred million of his kind,
The scrimmage of appetite everywhere.

This poem is as much about appetite and taste as *Jitterbug Perfume* is about the sense of smell. It ends with "The scrimmage of appetite everywhere." The bear with which the author identifies has a passion for honey, is "in love with candy," "howls in his sleep for a world of sugar," "strives to be fed." The bear is the clumsy beast inside the poet, his double, his other self, perhaps the animal part of all of us. The bear is always there, all appetite and desire. The poet cannot even free himself from the creature to talk in a civilized way to the one he loves.

The sense of taste is closely related to the sense of smell, not only in our physiology, but in our literature. Descriptions of food require both. In some works such descriptions are convincing enough to make the reader's mouth water—in "A Child's Christmas in Wales," for instance, by Dylan Thomas. And there is no more famous celebration of wine and the pleasures of life than "The Rubáiyát of Omar Khayyám," in which we find this well-known stanza:

> A Book of Verses underneath the Bough,
> A Jug of Wine, a Loaf of Bread—and Thou
> Beside me singing in the Wilderness—
> Oh, Wilderness were Paradise enow!

(6) Touching

There are obviously some things that we cannot fully understand without touching them. Just as the understanding of color requires the ability to see, the understanding of such things as heat and cold, and of physical contacts such as sex, requires the ability to feel. So important is the sense of touch to an infant that without it normal development is not possible. A famous experiment involving rhesus monkeys has proven this. Removed from physical contact with their mothers or some substitute they grow up to be incurably neurotic.

One of the sensations that writers have often tried to describe is the kiss. There are many famous passages that deal with this act, but perhaps none is more famous than the following passage from Christopher Marlowe's *Doctor Faustus*:

> Was this the face that launched a thousand ships,
> And burnt the topless towers of Ilium?
> Sweet Helen, make me immortal with a kiss.
> Her lips suck forth my soul: see where it flies.
> Come, Helen, come, give me my soul again.
> Here will I dwell, for heaven is in those lips,
> And all is dross that is not Helena.

While Tom Robbins argued that the sense of smell was the most fundamental of the human senses, August Coppola makes a strong case for the sense of touch, a field in which he has done a great deal of research. His interest is clearly reflected in his novel *The Intimacy* (Grove Press, 1978):

> He went to the faculty lounge to rest. Then took lunch in the commons. He didn't know what had happened. It was like amnesia; he remembered nothing of those few seconds, only his hand after. He reached out at the table, not looking, and took hold of a soup spoon by his plate. His thumb fit into the depression of the backside at the top of the handle, his fingers playing lightly over the molded pattern. The curves, the cut lines, the bevels. It was an eerie sensation. Somehow the shape seemed to be teasing him, as if alive, beckoning him to touch one part, then another, always shifting elusively beneath his fingertips, cool, smooth, rounded, like the chalk. There was an excitement, something unspoken, a kind of mute urgency. He

looked down at the spoon, turning it over: the pattern was an ugly little cherub face with swollen cheeks and sunken eyes, more like some primitive deity. He closed his eyes, turning the spoon over again, letting his fingers move along the underside. The sensation was suddenly frozen; he could distinguish the cheeks, the hollows for eyes, the beveled mouth — the "face" — just as he had seen it. But the other feeling that had called out to him was gone, as though two separate worlds existed, one of sight, the other of touch.

He bit his lip. It was still terrifying, that blackout, like something unknown there, waiting. And then perhaps — his mind began functioning — it was the birth of some new idea that had come so quickly it had left him mentally breathless before he could capture it. He held the spoon tight in his hand, then let it bang against the plate. The thought struck him: the ultimate reality was still touch, solidity, something to grasp hold of, yet everything in our lives seemed to be based on sight, the things we believe about ourselves, or try to appear as, our language, racial prejudice, class distinction, law and order.

He picked up the spoon, turning it over in his hand. He wondered what life would be like if known only through touch, what it would reveal, what kinds of thoughts and feelings it would give rise to. It was so simple. He couldn't imagine our existence without touch, and yet so little was known about it. He remembered the works he had read of Helen Keller. All that was talked about was the attempt to be sighted, how to turn the handicap into a compensation for the normal world, fitting back in. Never the mysteries of that dark existence she had felt — on its own terms — the things for which there were no names, no words.

The idea intrigued him, helping him to relax, to ease the pain of those few moments. He wondered if there could be a beauty there, if such a primordial beauty did exist, one that might evaporate if brought to light, or seem ugly, as did the little face on the spoon. As a new art form perhaps. Combining sensations of touch to create a new dimension of life, or a new sense of reality, or beauty that might well transport or change or re-shape or release one from all the ugliness one already felt to be real. Just as music could blend sounds to move people, and painting or film change how we see the world. It suddenly seemed to mean a lot to him. It seemed so obvious now. The oldest of all man's senses, and yet never used like that before. Why? What was really there?

(7) Using all five senses can produce a powerful effect.

"Digging" by Seamus Heaney is such an earthy poem that we can find it in every one of the five senses, beginning with the feeling of the pen in the author's hand moving to "the clean rasping sound" of the spade, to the sight of his father digging in the potato fields, to the taste of the milk and "the cold smell of potato mould." This appeal to the senses draws us into the experience. It is, understandably, one of Seamus Heaney's best known poems.

DIGGING

Between my finger and my thumb
The squat pen rests; snug as a gun.

Under my window, a clean rasping sound
When the spade sinks into gravelly ground:
My father, digging. I look down

Till his straining rump among the flowerbeds
Bends low, comes up twenty years away
Stooping in rhythm through potato drills
Where he was digging.

The coarse boot nestled on the lug, the shaft
Against the inside knee was levered firmly.
He rooted out tall tops, buried the bright edge deep
To scatter new potatoes that we picked
Loving their cool hardness in our hands.

By God, the old man could handle a spade.
Just like his old man.

My grandfather cut more turf in a day
Than any other man on Toner's bog.
Once I carried him milk in a bottle
Corked sloppily with paper. He straightened up
To drink it, then fell to right away

Nicking and slicing neatly, heaving sods
Over his shoulder, going down and down
For the good turf. Digging.

The cold smell of potato mould, the squelch and slap
Of soggy peat, the curt cuts of an edge
Through living roots awaken in my head.
But I've no spade to follow men like them.

Between my finger and my thumb
The squat pen rests.
I'll dig with it.

7c
Selectivity is necessary in description.

A description that is literally complete is an impossibility. Even
if it were possible it would not be desirable. We don't have to
know everything about a character who appears in a literary
work, and we don't have to know everything about the setting.

Any attempt to be all-inclusive is bound to result in nothing but clutter and confusion.

(1) Select significant details.

Not all descriptive details are of equal value. We must select those things that have some meaning within the context of the work. When we introduce a character, for instance, it may or may not matter how tall he or she is. If it doesn't matter, what's the point of mentioning it? Of course, if height has some bearing on the situation, then it *is* significant. The same is true of other details, such as age, weight, eyecolor, hair, general appearance, and ethnic background.

All too often a student writer will introduce a character as though the details were taken from his driver's license: "John Sherman was twenty-two years old, five feet eight, and had blue eyes and blond hair." This is certainly information, but it may not be significant information. What the reader wants to know is something about his defining qualities, something that brings him to life as an individual, not as a list of statistics.

In the opening paragraph of "Barcelona" (Example 2) we are introduced to Thad and Persis Fox. The first thing we are told is that they are a "middle-aged American couple." The details that follow are carefully selected to reveal something significant about the characters and the situation in which they find themselves. "The man is tall and bald; his head shines dimly as he and his wife cross the shaft of light from an open doorway. She is smaller, with pale hair; she walks fast to keep up with her husband. She is wearing gold chains, and they, too, shine in the light. She carries a small bag in which there could be — more gold? money? some interesting pills?"

The characters here are not described in isolation; they are described in a setting, "the old quarter of Barcelona." The details of that setting are also carefully selected. There is a great deal more that we could be told about both the couple and the Barrio Gotico of Barcelona, but nothing is included that does not contribute to the story. The gold chains that Persis wears are important because in such a neighborhood she might attract thieves, and the bag she carries is important because it is about to be stolen.

In the second paragraph we are given a thumb-nail sketch of Persis, with the emphasis on her somewhat neurotic nature. This is important, because the main focus of the story will be her reaction to the incident. In the next paragraph we are given some more details about the dark, cobbled streets of the old quarter. These details are significant because they create a sense of danger.

(2) Some writers are more selective than others.

As in the visual arts, the degree of selectivity is partly a matter of style. Some fiction writers are almost as selective as poets, who tend to distill their descriptions into significant and evocative images. Other writers use techniques that require more details and tend to be more analytical than poetic. Conciseness in itself is not necessarily a virtue. It can even be carried too far or become an affectation. Minimalism doesn't always work, and selectivity must not be confused with mere brevity or sparseness. Stylistically, writers like Hemingway and Faulkner are worlds apart. Hemingway is well known for his descriptive economy, and Faulkner is famous for his verbal profusion, but neither of them won the Nobel Prize for wasting words.

7d

Language choice is as important as choosing the correct details.

Good description involves not only selecting the right details, but using the right words. Some writers and critics have even gone so far as to insist that finding the precise word (*le mot juste*) is what good writing is all about. This notion is associated especially with Flaubert, for whom writing was sometimes an agonizingly slow process, because he was such a perfectionist. There may be more to great writing than effective word choice, but it is certainly one of the essentials, especially when it comes to description.

(1) Many factors are involved in effective language.

Choosing the right words depends on such things as the sound of the words, the shades of meaning, and the images the words evoke (see Chapter 11). The use of figures of speech can also add to descriptive effectiveness. As an example, we can use the opening paragraphs of William Faulkner's short story, "A Rose for Emily."

> When Miss Emily Grierson died, our whole town went to her funeral: the men through a sort of respectful affection for a fallen monument, the women mostly out of curiosity to see the inside of her house, which no one save an old manservant — a combined gardener and cook — had seen in at least ten years.
>
>   It was a big, squarish frame house that had once been white, decorated with cupolas and spires and scrolled balconies in the heavily lightsome style of the seventies, set on what had once been our most select street. But garages and cotton gins had encroached and obliterated even the august names of that

neighborhood; only Miss Emily's house was left, lifting its stubborn and coquettish decay above the cotton wagons and the gasoline pumps — an eyesore among eyesores. And now Miss Emily had gone to join the representatives of those august names where they lay in the cedar-bemused cemetery among the ranked and anonymous graves of Union and Confederate soldiers who fell at the battle of Jefferson.

The men in the town thought of Emily as "a fallen monument." This expression conjures up a number of images. She represents the old South, but perhaps has some of the coldness or deadness of a monument. Decay and nostalgia are both suggested here. Her house is built in "the heavily lightsome style of the seventies." *Lightsome* is a literary word that means *lighthearted.* The house was, therefore, heavily decorated, but expressed the lighthearted spirit of the times. Miss Emily's house was the last one left on the street from the grand old days. It is described as "lifting its stubborn and coquettish decay above the cotton wagons and the gasoline pumps." *Stubborn* and *coquettish* suggest a Southern belle, a vivid piece of personification. The cemetery where she lies is described as "cedar-bemused," which may sound odd but somehow feels appropriate. Certainly, "ranked and anonymous graves" is a very effective way to describe the burial place of soldiers, in this case, soldiers who fell in the Civil War. There is a kind of cumulative consistency of word choice in this passage that is linked with the theme of the decay of the old South and the ugliness that replaced it.

EXAMPLE 7

GRISHA

Anton Chekhov

Grisha, a chubby little boy born only two years and eight months ago, was out walking on the boulevard with his nurse. He wore a long, padded snowsuit, a large cap with a furry knob, a muffler, and wool-lined galoshes. He felt stuffy and hot, and, in addition, the waxing sun of April was beating directly into his face and making his eyelids smart.

Every inch of his awkward little figure, with its timid, uncertain steps, bespoke a boundless perplexity.

Until that day the only universe known to Grisha had been square. In one corner of it stood his crib, in another stood Nurse's trunk, in the third was a chair, and in the fourth a little icon-lamp. If you looked under the bed you saw a doll with one arm and a drum; behind Nurse's trunk were a great many various objects: a few empty spools, some scraps of paper, a box without a lid, and a broken jumping-jack. In this world, besides Nurse and Grisha, there often appeared Mama and the cat. Mama looked like a doll, and the cat looked like Papa's fur coat, only the fur coat did not have eyes and a tail. From the world which was called the nursery a door led to a place where people dined and drank tea. There stood Grisha's high-chair and there hung the clock made only in order to wag its pendulum and strike. From the dining-room one could pass into another room with big red chairs; there, on the floor, glowered a dark stain for which people still shook their forefingers at

Grisha. Still farther beyond lay another room, where one was not allowed to go, and in which one sometimes caught glimpses of Papa, a very mysterious person! The functions of Mama and Nurse were obvious: they dressed Grisha, fed him, and put him to bed; but why Papa should be there was incomprehensible. Aunty was also a puzzling person. She appeared and disappeared. Where did she go? More than once Grisha had looked for her under the bed, behind the trunk, and under the sofa, but she was not to be found.

In the new world where he now found himself, where the sun dazzled one's eyes, there were so many Papas and Mammas and Aunties that one scarcely knew which one to run to. But the funniest and oddest things of all were the horses. Grisha stared at their moving legs and could not understand them at all. He looked up at Nurse, hoping that she might help him to solve the riddle, but she answered nothing.

Suddenly he heard a terrible noise. Straight toward him down the street came a squad of soldiers marching in step, with red faces and sticks under their arms. Grisha's blood ran cold with terror and he looked up anxiously at his nurse to inquire if this were not dangerous. But Nursie neither ran away nor cried, so he decided it must be safe. He followed the soldiers with his eyes and began marching in step with them.

Across the street ran two big, long-nosed cats, their tails sticking straight up into the air and their tongues lolling out of their mouths. Grisha felt that he, too, ought to run, and he started off in pursuit.

"Stop, stop!" cried Nursie, seizing him roughly by the shoulder. "Where are you going? Who told you to be naughty?"

But there sat a sort of nurse with a basket of oranges in her lap. As Grisha passed her he silently took one.

"Don't do that!" cried his fellow wayfarer, slapping his hand and snatching the orange away from him. "Little stupid!"

Next, Grisha would gladly have picked up some of the slivers of glass that rattled under his feet and glittered like icon-lamps, but he was afraid that his hand might be slapped again.

"Good-day!" Grisha heard a loud, hoarse voice say over his very ear, and, looking up, he caught sight of a tall person with shiny buttons.

To his great joy this man shook hands with Nursie; they stood together and entered into conversation. The sunlight, the rumbling of the vehicles, the horses, the shiny buttons, all struck Grisha as so amazingly new and yet unterrifying, that his heart overflowed with delight and he began to laugh.

"Come! Come!" he cried to the man with the shiny buttons, pulling his coat tails.

"Where to?" asked the man.

"Come!" Grisha insisted. He would have liked to say that it would be nice to take Papa and Mamma and the cat along, too, but somehow his tongue would not obey him.

In a few minutes Nurse turned off the boulevard and led Grisha into a large courtyard where the snow still lay on the ground. The man with shiny buttons followed them. Carefully avoiding the puddles and lumps of snow, they picked their way across the courtyard, mounted a dark, grimy staircase, and entered a room where the air was heavy with smoke and a strong smell of cooking. A woman was standing over a stove frying chops. This cook and Nurse embraced one another, and, sitting down on a bench with the man, began talking in low voices. Bundled up as he was, Grisha felt unbearably hot.

"What does this mean?" he asked himself, gazing about.

He saw a dingy ceiling, a two-pronged oven fork, and a stove with a huge oven mouth gaping at him.

"Ma-a-m-ma!" he wailed.

"Now! Now!" his nurse called to him. "Be good!"

The cook set a bottle, two glasses, and a pie on the table. The two women and the man with the shiny buttons touched glasses and each had several drinks. The man embraced alternately the cook and the nurse. Then all three began to sing softly.

Grisha stretched his hand toward the pie, and they gave him a piece. He ate it and watched his nurse drinking. He wanted to drink, too.

"Give, Nursie! Give!" he begged.

The cook gave him a drink out of her glass. He screwed up his eyes, frowned, and coughed for a long time after that, beating the air with his hands, while the cook watched him and laughed.

When he reached home, Grisha explained to Mama, the walls, and his crib where he had been and what he had seen. He told it less with his tongue than with his hands and his face; he showed how the sun had shone, how the horses had trotted, how the terrible oven had gaped at him, and how the cook had drunk.

That evening he could not possibly go to sleep. The soldiers with their sticks, the great cats, the horses, the bits of glass, the basket of oranges, the shiny buttons, all this lay piled on his brain and oppressed him. He tossed from side to side, chattering to himself, and finally, unable longer to endure his excitement, he burst into tears.

"Why, he has fever!" cried Mama, laying the palm of her hand on his forehead. "What can be the reason?"

"The stove!" wept Grisha. "Go away, stove!"

"He has eaten something that has disagreed with him," Mama concluded.

And, shaken by his impressions of a new life apprehended for the first time, Grisha was given a spoonful of castor-oil by Mama.

EXERCISES

DISCUSSION

1. Though "Grisha" (Example 7) is told in the third-person, Chekhov limits the point of view mainly to that of a little boy less than three-years-old. How does this affect his use of description?

2. Compare the use of abstractions and the use of physical details in this story. Find some examples of *selectivity*.

3. Are the five senses appealed to in the descriptive passages? Find some examples.

4. How is the language used to create the feeling that we are seeing things through the eyes of a small child?

WRITING

1. Write a story in which a person from a small town visits a big city for the first time and has a strange, wonderful, or frightening adventure. Emphasize descriptive details. Include as many references to as many of the five senses as possible.

2. Write a poem that is about a special person or a special place. Use carefully chosen words and figures of speech.

3. Describe a nightmare, real or fictitious, in vivid detail.

4. Imagine that your car has broken down in a storm on a lonely road and that you have found shelter in an abandoned old house that is believed to be haunted. With the heightened awareness that comes with fear, describe the experience.

5. Describe some of your earliest childhood memories or impressions. What details were especially imprinted on your mind? What sights or sounds or other sensations can trigger these memories?

6. Describe the eyes of two very different people in as much detail as possible. Choose contrasting characters — two men, two women, a pair of lovers, a loser and a winner, a madman and a poet, a hunter and a bird-watcher, a criminal and a victim, and so on.

7. Visit the zoo and describe some of the animals. Rely on observation, not memory or stereotypes.

CHAPTER
EIGHT

DIALOGUE

What characters say to each other can reveal an enormous amount of information. Dialogue can tell us what characters are like, what they think, and what others think of them. It can reveal current action, as well as action that has taken place in the past or might take place in the future. It can also tell us about things that are going on off stage.

Dialogue is clearly the main ingredient in traditional stage plays. Almost all the information we get comes through dialogue. In film and television dramas dialogue is also very important, but technology has expanded the visual dimension. More action is possible, and location changes can be instantaneous.

Dialogue gives fiction the same kind of immediacy characters might have on a stage or screen. In poetry, dialogue is used less frequently, possibly because most poems are brief and are told to us as though the poet is the speaker (*persona*), and also because poetry tends to be less narrative than fiction.

Like description, dialogue must be *selective, significant,* and involve careful *word choice*. Conversations should not be mere recordings of real-life exchanges, because they would be much too long and include too many irrelevancies. Only the most significant things uttered by the characters should be included, and the phrasing should be worked out carefully.

To some extent, the amount and kind of dialogue depends on the author's style. Some writers lean heavily on direct dialogue; others prefer indirect dialogue and elaborate commentaries. Subjective writers depend more on the thoughts and feelings of their characters. Objective writers are more inclined to depend on what the characters actually say.

8a
There is a standard form in which dialogue is written.

(1) All spoken material is placed between quotation marks.

> "Will you marry me?" said Donna, who was pacing angrily across the floor of the penthouse livingroom.
> "You know how I feel about marriage," Mark said.

(2) Each time the speaker changes, a new paragraph is required.

> "Aren't you interested in how I feel?" said Donna.
> "Of course, I am," said Mark.

(3) **The first word inside the quotation marks begins with a capital letter.**

If the statement is interrupted by a tag that identifies the speaker and then is continued as part of a sentence that was started before the tag, then no capital is used in the continuation.

> "I come from a very conventional family," she said. "They happen to believe in marriage."
> "When we first met," he said, "you told me you didn't get along with your family."

(4) **A colon should be used before a piece of dialogue, but these days many writers settle for a comma.**

> She stopped pacing and looked at him with narrowed eyes. Finally, she said: "Do you know what I think? I think you're too self-centered to get married?"

(5) **At the end of a quoted piece of dialogue various punctuation marks can be used.**

A comma is most common and is used whether the dialogue is part of a sentence that will be continued or is a whole sentence followed by a tag. A period is not used at the end of a quotation if a tag follows, but is used if there is no tag. Question marks and exclamation points are used when appropriate, but the tag that follows does not begin with a capital.

> "Good grief!" he said. "Look who's talking about self-centeredness. What do you think marriage is all about?"
> "What do *you* think it's all about?"

"Possessiveness!" he said with a cruel smile. "When women get married, it's not an act of generosity on their part, believe me."

(6) **If there is descriptive material that attends the dialogue, either before or after what is spoken, it appears in the same paragraph.**

She backed away from him as though he were a dangerous stranger. "You know," she said, "in time I could learn to despise you." She picked up her coat and scarf, as though she were preparing to leave.

He made no effort to stop her. "The trouble with you," he said, "is that you want all the advantages of a modern relationship and all the security of an old-fashioned marriage." He went to the door and held it open for her. "You can't have it both ways. The choice is yours."

8b
Tags tell us who is speaking.

Sometimes tags are included; sometimes they are omitted, as long as we already know who the speaker is.

(1) Tags can be very simple.

The simplest tags are *I said, he said, she said*. Some modern writers rarely use anything else and try to use as few tags as possible. The effect of this practice is to reduce these tags almost to the level of mere punctuation, so that the reader can focus completely on what the characters are saying. Hemingway was one of the earliest, and perhaps the best, of the writers who used this technique. Here is a sample from *A Farewell to Arms*. The characters are Catherine Barkley, an English nurse, and Lieutenant Frederick Henry, an American volunteer in the Italian army in World War I. They are in a hotel room in Milan:

> "It's a fine room," Catherine said. "It's a lovely room. We should have stayed here all the time we've been in Milan."
>
> "It's a funny room. But it's nice."
>
> "Vice is a wonderful thing," Catherine said. "The people who go in for it seem to have good taste about it. The red plush is really fine. It's just the thing. And the mirrors are very attractive."
>
> "You're a lovely girl."
>
> "I don't know how a room like this would be for waking up in the morning. But it's really a splendid room." I poured another glass of St. Estephe.
>
> "I wish we could do something really sinful," Catherine said. "Everything we do seems so innocent and simple. I can't believe we do anything wrong."
>
> "You're a grand girl."
>
> "I only feel hungry. I get terribly hungry."
>
> "You're a fine simple girl," I said.
>
> "I am a simple girl. No one ever understood it except you."

(2) Tags can be varied and elaborate.

Earlier literature was more formal, and dialogue tags tended to be more complicated. In some modern writers they still are more complicated than *he said/she said*. These writers tend to vary the verb, as in *he shouted, she whispered, he whined, she cried*. Such variety is more a matter of style than necessity. One should not use old-fashioned expressions, cliches, or clumsy tags just for the sake of variety. A simple tag is better than *he expostulated* or *she blurted out*. A question in dialogue can be followed by *he said*, though often *he asked* is used.

Tags can be elaborated by adding adverbs to them, so that the way the words are spoken is described, as in: "I love you," *he said passionately*. You have to be very careful when you do this, since such elaborations can often sound ridiculous:

> "Don't touch me," she blurted out uncontrollably.
> "I need you," he growled savagely.

The best policy is to allow the dialogue to speak for itself and to avoid attracting too much attention to the tags.

8c
Indirect dialogue is a description or summary of what was said.

Sometimes we learn what a character says indirectly, without the benefit of direct quotations. The narrator can describe or summarize what a character said. No quotation marks are used for indirect discourse, since the exact wording of the character's remarks is not used:

> *Indirect:* John told Mary that he was going to Europe.
> *Direct:* "I am going to Europe," John said to Mary.

A summarized conversation can give the reader a concise, general idea of what the characters have talked about. The whole conversation might not be worth recording word for word, especially if it is long and without enormous significance:

> *Indirect:* John and Mary spent the whole afternoon talking about the museums and art gallerys they had visited in Europe.

Be careful to avoid shifts from indirect to direct discourse:

> *Shift:* What Mary wanted to know from John was "When are you going to Europe?"
> *Use:* What Mary wanted to know from John was when he was going to Europe. (indirect)
> *Or:* "When are you going to Europe?" Mary asked John. (direct)

8d
Direct dialogue requires the use of quotation marks.

When we use the word dialogue we usually mean direct discourse, which has to be in quotation marks and tagged according to the conventions described in 8a and 8b.

(1) Some writers depend heavily on dialogue.

Writers who use a cinematic approach to fiction tend to reduce the action to stage directions and to let the characters speak for themselves. The approach is objective. There is little editorializing and little attempt to get directly into the minds of the characters. What you see (and hear) is what you get.

(2) Dialogue is usually blended with action, commentary, and indirect discourse.

Most writers do not limit themselves to just one device. Their main objective is to recreate experience in whatever way they can. Fiction limited to dialogue and stage directions is sometimes a genuine experiment in pure objectivity, but it can also be just an exercise or even an affectation, perhaps inspired by a current fad.

There is enormous variety in fiction. Some approaches use no dialogue at all, some are pure stream of consciousness, some are all commentary and analysis, but most are a blend of some sort, which does not mean that they are without consistency or distinctiveness of style.

(3) Dialogue can be used in poetry.

Since poetry can have a narrative element, it can use the usual techniques of narration, including dialogue. However, since the work is basically cast in the form of a poem, the narration is contained within that form. This means that it has certain limitations placed on it. If the narration breaks out of the poetic structure, it is liable to become a short story or simply to confuse the basic artistic concept. On the other hand, fragments of narration can be contained within a poetic whole and in themselves need not be completed in the usual way that stories are. Here is a poem by Stephen Crane that contains dialogue:

IN A LONELY PLACE

In a lonely place,
I encountered a sage
Who sat, all still,
Regarding a newspaper.
He accosted me:
"Sir, what is this?"
Then I saw that I was greater,

Aye, greater than this sage.
I answered him at once:
"Old, old man, it is the wisdom of the age."
The sage looked upon me with admiration.

8e
Accents involve distinctive modes of pronunciation.

Language is in a constant state of evolution. Regional conditions, such as isolation or the influx of immigrants can give rise
to differences in pronunciation and to some strictly regional
vocabulary. These differences produce an *accent*. There are
many such accents in American English, among them the New
York accent, the Southern and Western accents, and a variety
of foreign accents.

When a variation of a language undergoes more extensive
changes in its grammar as well as in its vocabulary, we have
what is known as a *dialect*. Many European countries, such as
Italy and Great Britain and Spain, have distinct dialects. In less
industrialized parts of the world there are enormous numbers
of dialects because conditions in these places have not been
conducive to standardizing the language.

When a dialect becomes truly distinct from its mother
language or blends with other languages to form a mode of
speech that outsiders do not understand, we have a whole new
language, such as Gullah in the Carolinas or Creole of Haiti.

In the United States we have few genuine dialects. We are
usually confronted, as writers, with a variety of regional or

foreign accents. If we are to make our dialogue realistic, we have to learn how to capture these peculiarities of speech. We also have to learn how to present foreign characters who are, supposedly, speaking their own language.

(1) A character can seem to be speaking a foreign language even though the story is written in English.

When characters who speak a foreign language appear in a story written in English, their dialogue can be written in their own language (with or without a translation) or in correct English, but with occasional hints of foreign syntax or idioms or even an occasional foreign word. Hemingway does this extremely well. In *A Farewell to Arms*, this is how Lieutenant Henry's Italian friend speaks:

> "One of those shot by the carabinieri is from my town," Passini said. "He was a big smart tall boy to be in the granatieri. Always in Rome. Always with the girls. Always with the carabinieri." He laughed. "Now they have a guard outside his house with a bayonet and nobody can come to see his mother and father and sisters and his father loses his civil rights and cannot even vote. They are all without law to protect them. Anybody can take their property."

In the movies it used to be a Hollywood convention to present foreign characters who are speaking their own language as characters speaking English with a foreign accent. This sometimes ludicrous device is not recommended for fiction or poetry, and is not used much anymore even in movies or television.

(2) A foreign character or a regional character often speaks English with an accent.

An author can try to capture an accent phonetically by trying to write it down exactly as the character pronounces it. Mark Twain does this extensively, especially in *Huckleberry Finn*. In the following passage, Jim is telling Huck's fortune:

> "Yo' ole father doan' know yit what he's a-gwyne to do. Sometimes he spec he'll go 'way, en den ag'in he spec he'll stay. De bes' way is to res' easy en let de ole man take his own way. Dey's two angels hoverin' roun' 'bout him. One uv 'em is white en shiny, en t'other one is black. De white one gits him to go right a little while, den de black one sails in en bust it all up. A body can't tell yit which one gwyne to fetch him at de las'. But you is all right. You gwyne to have considable trouble in yo' life, en considable joy. Sometimes you gwyne to git hurt, en sometimes you gwyne to git sick; but every time you's gwyne to git well ag'in. Dey's two gals flyin' 'bout you in yo' life. One uv 'em's light en t'other one is dark. One is rich en t'other is po'. You gwyne to marry de po' one fust en de rich one by en by. You wants to keep 'way fum de water as much as you kin, en don't run no resk, 'kase it's down in de bills dat you's gwyne to git hung."

It is also possible to capture an accent without altering the spelling, but merely by providing token hints through intonation or vocabulary. Saul Bellow and Woody Allen manage this very well when their characters have a New York accent. A striking contrast to the way Mark Twain handles Jim's dialogue can be found in the way Alice Walker handles the speech of her black characters, who are, of course, more modern. Also, Mark Twain was using some stereotypes of black speech with a bit of comic exaggeration. In any case, the narrator of "Everyday Use" by Alice Walker shows few traces of an accent:

> In real life I am a large, big-boned woman with rough, man-working hands. In the winter I wear flannel nightgowns to bed and overalls during the day. I can kill and clean a hog as mercilessly as a man. My fat keeps me hot in zero weather. I can work outside all day, breaking ice to get water for washing; I can eat pork liver cooked over the open fire minutes after it comes steaming from the hog. One winter I knocked a bull calf straight in the brain between the eyes with a sledge hammer and had the meat hung up to chill before nightfall.

This passage could have been spoken by anyone. It is mainly the context that suggests a regional sound.

EXAMPLE 8

THANK YOU, M'AM
Langston Hughes

She was a large woman with a large purse that had everything in it but a hammer and nails. It had a long strap, and she carried it, slung across her shoulder. It was about eleven o'clock at night, dark, and she was walking alone, when a boy ran up behind her and tried to snatch her purse. The strap broke with the sudden single tug the boy gave it from behind. But the boy's weight and the weight of the purse combined caused him to lose his balance. Instead of taking off full blast as he had hoped, the boy fell on his back on the sidewalk and his legs flew up. The large woman simply turned around and kicked him right square in his blue-jeaned sitter. Then she reached down, picked the boy up by his shirt front, and shook him until his teeth rattled.

After that the woman said, "Pick up my pocketbook, boy, and give it here."

She still held him tightly. But she bent down enough to permit him to stoop and pick up her purse. Then she said, "Now ain't you ashamed of yourself?"

Firmly gripped by his shirt front, the boy said, "Yes'm."

The woman said, "What did you want to do it for?"

The boy said, "I didn't aim to."

She said, "You a lie!"

By that time two or three people passed, stopped, turned to look, and some stood watching.

"If I turn you loose, will you run?" asked the woman.

"Yes'm," said the boy.

"Then I won't turn you loose," said the woman. She did not release him.

"Lady, I'm sorry," whispered the boy.

"Um-hum! Your face is dirty. I got a great mind to wash your face for you. Ain't you got nobody home to tell you to wash your face?"

"No'm," said the boy.

"Then it will get washed this evening," said the large woman, starting up the street, dragging the frightened boy behind her.

He looked as if he were fourteen or fifteen, frail and willow-wild, in tennis shoes and blue jeans.

The woman said, "You ought to be my son. I would teach you right from wrong. Least I can do right now is to wash your face. Are you hungry?"

"No'm," said the being-dragged boy. "I just want you to turn me loose."

"Was I bothering *you* when I turned that corner?" asked the woman.

"No'm."

"But you put yourself in contact with *me*," said the woman. "If you think that that contact is not going to last awhile, you got another thought coming. When I get through with you, sir, you are going to remember Mrs. Luella Bates Washington Jones."

Sweat popped out on the boy's face and he began to struggle. Mrs. Jones stopped, jerked him around in front of her, put a half nelson about his neck, and continued to drag him up the street. When she got to her door, she dragged the boy inside, down a hall, and into a large kitchenette-furnished room at the rear of the house. She switched on the light and left the door open. The boy could hear other roomers laughing and talking in the large house. Some of their doors were open, too, so he knew he and the woman were not alone. The woman still had him by the neck in the middle of her room.

She said, "What is your name?"

"Roger," answered the boy.

"Then, Roger, you go to that sink and wash your face," said the woman, whereupon she turned him loose—at last. Roger looked at the door—looked at the woman—looked at the door—*and went to the sink*.

"Let the water run until it gets warm," she said. "Here's a clean towel."

"You gonna take me to jail?" asked the boy, bending over the sink.

"Not with that face, I would not take you nowhere," said the woman. "Here I am trying to get home to cook me a bite to eat, and you snatch my pocketbook! Maybe you ain't been to your supper either, late as it be. Have you?"

"There's nobody home at my house," said the boy.

"Then we'll eat," said the woman. "I believe you're hungry—or been hungry—to try to snatch my pocketbook!"

"I want a pair of blue suede shoes," said the boy.

"Well, you didn't have to snatch *my* pocketbook to get some suede shoes," said Mrs. Luella Bates Washington Jones. "You could of asked me."

"M'am?"

The water dripping from his face, the boy looked at her. There was a long pause. A very long pause. After he had dried his face, and not knowing what else to do, dried it again, the boy turned around, wondering what next. The door was open.

He could make a dash for it down the hall. He could, run, run, run, *run!*

The woman was sitting on the daybed. After a while she said, "I were young once and I wanted things I could not get."

There was another long pause. The boy's mouth opened. Then he frowned, not knowing he frowned.

The woman said, "Um-hum! You thought I was going to say *but*, didn't you? You thought I was going to say, *but I didn't snatch people's pocketbooks*. Well, I wasn't going to say that." Pause. Silence. "I have done things, too, which I would not tell you, son — neither tell God, if He didn't already know. Everybody's got something in common. So you set down while I fix us something to eat. You might run that comb through your hair so you will look presentable."

In another corner of the room behind a screen was a gas plate and an icebox. Mrs. Jones got up and went behind the screen. The woman did not watch the boy to see if he was going to run now, nor did she watch her purse, which she left behind her on the daybed. But the boy took care to sit on the far side of the room, away from the purse, where he thought she could easily see him out of the corner of her eye if she wanted to. He did not trust the woman *not* to trust him. And he did not want to be mistrusted now.

"Do you need somebody to go to the store," asked the boy, "maybe to get some milk or something?"

"Don't believe I do," said the woman, "unless you just want sweet milk yourself. I was going to make cocoa out of this canned milk I got here."

"That will be fine," said the boy.

She heated some lima beans and ham she had in the icebox, made the cocoa, and set the table. The woman did not *ask* the boy anything about where he lived, or his folks, or anything else that would embarrass him. Instead, as they ate, she told him about her job in a hotel beauty shop that stayed open late, what the work was like, and how all kinds of women came in and out, blondes, redheads, and Spanish. Then she cut him a half of her ten-cent cake.

"Eat some more, son," she said.

When they were finished eating, she got up and said, "Now here, take this ten dollars and buy yourself some blue suede shoes. And next time, do not make the mistake of latching onto *my* pocketbook *nor nobody else's* — because shoes got by devilish ways will burn your feet. I got to get my rest now. But from here on in, son, I hope you will behave yourself."

She led him down the hall to the front door and opened it. "Good night! Behave yourself, boy!" she said, looking out into the street as he went down the steps.

The boy wanted to say something other than, "Thank you, m'am," to Mrs. Luella Bates Washington Jones, but although his lips moved, he couldn't even say that as he turned at the foot of the barren stoop and looked up at the large woman in the door. Then she shut the door.

EXERCISES

DISCUSSION

1. In "Thank you, M'am" (Example 8) Langston Hughes depends heavily on dialogue to make his point. What is his point? In what ways is the dialogue effective in revealing character and theme?

2. Is the dialogue form conventional? Comment on the use of tags.

3. How is the accent handled? Compare the approach of Langston Hughes with those of Mark Twain and Alice Walker (8e).

WRITING

1. Write a short story that is made up largely of dialogue.

2. Write a one-act play in which some of the characters have a regional or foreign accent.

3. Write a poem that makes use of some dialogue.

4. Write a story in which an American, an Englishman, and a Frenchman are taken hostage. One of the terrorists speaks a bit of English; his comrades speak only a non-European language. Imagine a resolution in which one of the hostages is killed and the other two escape.

5. Write a simple parable or folktale in which all of the dialogue is indirect.

CHAPTER
NINE

THOUGHTS

Revealing the thoughts of the characters in a literary work is one of the fundamental concerns of the serious writer. Even the routine thoughts of two-dimensional characters have to be expressed in some fashion or other. There are several ways to accomplish this. *In poetry* it is often the authors who tell us directly what they think about this or that, and the material is often personal and autobiographical. *In drama* the characters reveal their thoughts by talking to each other or by thinking out loud, as in a soliloquy or a cinematic *voice over*. Even facial expressions, especially in *close-ups*, can hint at what is going on in a character's mind.

In fiction the problem is often more complex. Characters can reveal themselves in dialogue or in a first-person narration. It is also possible for narrators using the third-person point of view to tell us what is going on in a character's mind. They can do this by presenting the character's thoughts *directly* or *indirectly* in some organized way, or they can try to capture more fully the complex processes of the human mind, before language gives more grammatical coherence to thought. Hence, we have three approaches: a) *indirect*, b) *direct*, c) *stream of consciousness*.

9a
Indirect thought means a description or summary of what a character thinks.

Though indirect descriptions of the thoughts of a character occur most commonly in the third person, they can also appear in the first-person point of view. For instance:

> I was thinking about what I would do in case the airplane was hijacked by terrorists. (Indirect)

> What will I do in case the airplane is hijacked by terrorists? I thought. (Direct)

Dialogue, strictly speaking, is something that is said aloud, as opposed to thoughts, which are in the mind of the character, even though they may be phrased in a similar way. The above examples put into dialogue might appear as follows:

> I asked the pilot what I should do in case the airplane was hijacked by terrorists. (Indirect)

> "What should I do if the airplane is hijacked by terrorists?" I asked the pilot. (Direct)

The same statements can be put into the third-person in the following way:

> He was thinking about what he would do in case the airplane was hijacked by terrorists. (Indirect)

> What will I do in case the airplane is hijacked by terrorists? he thought. (Direct)

There is a good illustration of *indirect* thought in "Barcelona" (Example 2). The author describes what Persis is thinking in the final paragraph:

> Persis is thinking, and not for the first time, how terrible it must be to be a man, how terrifying. Men are always running, chasing something. And if you are rich and successful, like Thad, you have to hunt down anyone who wants to take away your possessions. Or if you're poor, down on your luck, you might be tempted to chase after a shabby bag that holds nothing of any real value, to snatch such a bag from a foreign woman who is wearing false gold chains that shine and glimmer in the dark.

9b
Direct thought literally occurs in the character's mind.

(1) Direct thoughts often sound like dialogue.

The difference is that they are not spoken aloud. It is as if the character is speaking to himself. Most writers do not place such thoughts in quotation marks. In Hemingway's "A Clean, Well-Lighted Place," two waiters in a Spanish café argue about an old man who is their last customer and refuses to leave. The young waiter is eager to get home to his wife. The older waiter, like the old man, does not seem to have much to live for. Finally, they close the place. We follow the older waiter and we are told what he is thinking:

> "Goodnight," said the younger waiter.

"Good night," the other said. Turning off the electric light he continued the conversation with himself. It is the light of course but it is necessary that the place be clean and pleasant. You do not want music. Certainly you do not want music. Nor can you stand before a bar with dignity although that is all that is provided for these hours.

Up to this point, it seems as though the character is, indeed, talking to himself, but suddenly there is a shift back into the *indirect* approach:

What did he fear? It was not fear or dread. It was a nothing that he knew too well. It was all a nothing and a man was nothing too. It was only that and light was all it needed and a certain cleanness and order. Some lived in it and never felt it but he knew it all was nada y pues nada. [nothing and then nothing]

(2) Some writers put the direct thoughts of their characters in italics.

Usage here is divided. Some users of italics reserve them for stream-of-consciousness passages; some use them for any directly expressed thoughts. The following passage from William Styron's *Set this House on Fire* is described as a thought, but it is also described as a kind of haunting memory. There are obviously thin lines between conscious thoughts, unconscious thoughts, memories, reveries, and daydreams.

A brisk wind blew toward the sea, cooling Cass' brow. For a moment he closed his eyes, the flowers' crushed scent and summer light and ruined hut commingling in one long fluid hot surge of remembrance and desire. *Siete stato molto gentile con me*, he thought. *What a thing for her to say. You have been very kind to me. As if when I kissed her, and the kiss was over, and we were standing there in the field all body and groin and belly made one and wet mouths parted this was the only thing left to say. Which meant of course I'm a virgin and maybe we shouldn't but you have been very nice to me. So—So maybe I should have took her then, with gentleness and anguish and love, right there in that field last evening when I felt her full young breasts heavy in my hands and the wild way she pressed against me and her breath hot against my cheek. . . . Siete stato molto gentile con me . . . Cass . . . Cahssio . . .*

9c
Stream of consciousness is a literary technique used to capture the random, uncensored workings of the human mind.

The intense interest in psychology in the early decades of the twentieth century stirred the curiosity and imagination of the literary world. After all, Freud and Jung and others were talking about how the human mind worked, a subject with which writers have always been preoccupied. Discussions of the subconscious levels of thought led writers to explorations of techniques that might give expression to these thoughts, which were, apparently, more primitive than language itself.

(1) **Some writers try to capture inner thoughts through conventional language.**

Though our deepest thoughts may not occur as well-made sentences, some writers try to give the reader a sense of what is going on by using traditional syntax and certain devices that suggest the subconscious mind at work. In Virginia Woolf's *Mrs. Dalloway*, Clarissa enters a flower shop. Her reaction is described in the third person, but the reader feels drawn directly into the character's mind.

There were flowers: delphiniums, sweet peas, bunches of lilac; and carnations, masses of carnations. There were roses; there were irises. Ah yes — so she breathed in the earthy garden sweet smell as she stood talking to Miss Pym who owed her help, and thought her kind, for kind she had been years ago; very kind, but she looked older, this year, turning her head from side to side among the irises and roses and nodding tufts of lilac with her eyes half closed, snuffing in, after the street uproar, the delicious scent, the exquisite coolness. And then, opening her eyes, how fresh like frilled linen clean from a laundry laid in wicker trays the roses looked; and dark and prim the red carnations, holding their heads up; and all the sweet peas spreading in their bowls, tinged violet, snow white, pale — as if it were the evening and girls in muslin frocks came out to pick sweet peas and roses after the superb summer's day, with its almost blue-black sky, its delphiniums, its carnations, its arum lilies was over; and it was the moment between six and seven when every flower — roses, carnations, irises, lilac — glows; white, violet, red, deep orange; every flower seems to burn by itself, softly, purely in the misty beds; and how she loved the grey-white moths spinning in and out, over the cherry pie, over the evening primroses!

And as she began to go with Miss Pym from jar to jar, choosing, nonsense, nonsense, she said to herself, more and more gently, as if this beauty, this scent, this colour, and Miss Pym liking her, trusting her, were a wave which she let flow over her and surmount that hatred, that monster, surmount it all; and it lifted her up and up when — oh! a pistol shot in the street outside!

"Dear, those motor cars," said Miss Pym, going to the window to look, and coming back and smiling apologetically with her hands full of sweet peas, as if those motor cars, those tyres of motor cars, were all *her* fault.

(2) Some writers violate the conventions of language to try to get at the inner thoughts of a character.

James Joyce's *Ulysses* was a bold exploration of the inner workings of the human mind. In Molly Bloom's famous internal monologue, which is forty-five pages long and unpunctuated, we are allowed to eavesdrop on her private meanderings, which are full of free associations and uncensored memories:

> I wonder what shes got like now after living with that dotty husband of hers she had her face beginning to look drawn and run down the last time I saw her she must have been just after a row with him because I saw on the moment she was edging to draw down a conversation about husbands and talk about him to run him down what was it she told me O yes that sometimes he used to go to bed with his muddy boots on when the maggot takes him just imagine having to get into bed with a thing like that that might murder you any moment what a man well its not the one way everyone goes mad Poldy anyway whatever he does always wipes his feet on the mat when he comes in wet or shine and always blacks his own boots too and he always takes off his hat when he comes up in the street like that and now hes going about in his slippers to look for £10000 for a postcard up up O Sweetheart May wouldnt a thing like that simply bore you stiff to extinction actually too stupid even to take his boots off now what could you make of a man like that Id rather die 20 times over than marry another of their sex of course hed never find another woman like me to put up with him the way I do

know me come sleep with me yes and he knows that too at the bottom of his heart take that Mrs Maybrick that poisoned her husband for what I wonder in love with some other man yet it was found out on her wasnt she the downright villain to go and do a thing like that of course some men can be dreadfully aggravating drive you mad and always the worst word in the world what do they ask us to marry them for if were so bad as all that comes to yes because they cant get on without us white Arsenic she put in his tea off flypaper wasnt it I wonder why they call it that if I asked him hed say its from the Greek leave us as wise as we were before she must have been madly in love with the other fellow to run the chance of being hanged O she didnt care if that was her nature what could she do besides theyre not brutes enough to go and hang a woman surely are they

Devices such as these can give us some idea of what is going on in a character's mind, but it is probably impossible to capture in writing the entire phenomenon of human thought.

EXAMPLE 9

RUBY TELLS ALL

Miller Williams

When I was told, as Delta children were,
that crops don't grow unless you sweat at night,
I thought that it was my own sweat they meant.
I have never felt as important again
as on those early mornings, waking up,   5
my body slick, the moon full on the fields.
That was before air conditioning.
Farm girls sleep cool now and wake up dry,
but still the cotton overflows the fields.
We lose everything that's grand and foolish;   10
it all becomes something else. One by one,
butterflies turn into caterpillars
and we grow up, or more or less we do,
and, Lord, we do lie then. We lie so much
the truth has a false ring and it's hard to tell.   15

I wouldn't take crap off anybody
if I just knew that I was getting crap
in time not to take it. I could have won
a small one now and then if I was smarter,
but I've poured coffee here too many years   20
for men who rolled in in Peterbilts,
and I have gotten into bed with some
if they could talk and seemed to be in pain.

I never asked for anything myself;
giving is more blessed and leaves you free.   25
There was a man, married and fond of whiskey.
Given the limitations of men, he loved me.
Lord, we laid concern upon our bodies
but then he left. Everything has its time.
We used to dance. He made me feel the way   30
a human wants to feel and fears to.
He was a slow man and didn't expect.
I would get off work and find him waiting.
We'd have a drink or two and kiss awhile.
Then a bird-loud morning late one April   35
we woke up naked. We had made a child.
She's grown up now and gone though god knows where.
She ought to write, for I do love her dearly
who raised her carefully and dressed her well.
Everything has its time. For thirty years   40
I never had a thought about time.
Now, turning through newspapers, I pause
to see if anyone who passed away
was younger than I am. If one was
I feel hollow for a little while   45
but then it passes. Nothing matters enough
to stay bent down about. You have to see
that some things matter slightly and some don't.
Dying matters a little. So does pain.
So does being old. Men do not.   50
Men live by negatives, like don't give up,
don't be a coward, don't call me a liar,
don't ever tell me don't. If I could live
two hundred years and had to be a man
I'd take my grave. What's a man but a match,   55
a little stick to start a fire with?

My daughter knows this, if she's alive.
What could I tell her now, to bring her close,
something she doesn't know, if we met somewhere?
Maybe that I think about her father,   60
maybe that my fingers hurt at night,
maybe that against appearances
there is love, constancy, and kindness,
that I have dresses I have never worn.

EXERCISES

DISCUSSION

1. In "Ruby Tells All" (Example 9) Miller Williams uses a very
   direct device for revealing the thoughts of the main character. What is it? Are we supposed to assume that Ruby is
   writing these things, saying them, or just thinking them?
   Is this a monologue, a soliloquy, or just a narrative in the
   first-person?

2. What are some of the more important thoughts that pass
   through Ruby's mind when she thinks about her life or life
   in general?

WRITING

1. Using a different character, write a poem in the style of
   "Ruby Tells All."

2. Write a story that uses indirect descriptions of what your
   characters are thinking.

3. Write a stream-of-consciousness monologue made up entirely of the unpunctuated, free-association thoughts of one

person, as in the passage from Joyce's *Ulysses* (9c). Such meanderings of the mind are usually set in motion by some occurrence, often something quite simple or even trivial. Consider the following as possible starting points:

a. An old man is sitting on a park bench. Across a pond on a stone bridge he sees two young lovers kiss. He hears their laughter, and his mind wanders back to his youth.

b. An attractive middle-aged woman is listening to a piece of classical music that she associates with the poor young man she refused to marry because her parents persuaded her to choose the wealthy suitor who is now her husband.

c. A car backfires and startles a Vietnam veteran, whose thoughts return to his violent experiences in the war.

4. Write a scene in which a man and a woman are having a disagreement about their personal relationship. Use a combination of dialogue and thoughts. Reveal what both characters are thinking, aside from what they are actually saying.

5. A young woman is lying in bed. Beside her on the nightstand there is a bottle of pills. She is contemplating suicide. What runs through her mind?

6. A sailor is the sole survivor of a disaster at sea. He drifts in a raft under the hot sun and begins to hallucinate. Can you describe his state of mind?

CHAPTER
TEN

TIME

When readers begin a literary work they want to know: (1) what is happening; (2) to whom it is happening; (3) where it is happening; and (4) when it is happening. This is all fundamental information that orients readers, so that they can follow the story or drama or poem. In the simple fairy-tale opening we are given all this information in a swift and general way: "Once upon a time in the land of Sumeria there lived a king who had three daughters and no sons." Since many fairy tales and folk tales take place in some indefinite and remote past and in an equally remote or imaginary land, it is not necessary to go into any greater detail about *where* and *when*. More realistic and more modern stories usually take place in more definite places and in periods of time that are more precisely defined. When the artistic situation calls for it, a writer should be able to: (1) establish clearly the *period* in which the work takes place; (2) describe the *immediate action* as it unfolds; (3) look back at *past actions* that preceded the immediate action; (4) indicate the *duration* of the action; and (5) use *transitions* to make clear how much time has passed between major scenes and to introduce flashbacks.

10a

The period of a literary work should be established with appropriate clarity.

(1) A literary work can be set in any time period.

The period can be historically specific or merely within the scope of human conjecture, including the very remote past and the very distant future. For example, consider a movie called *One Million B.C.*, made first in 1939 and then remade in 1966. There are novels such as *The Time Machine* by H. G. Wells and *Last and First Men* by Olaf Stapledon that take us as far into the future as we can possibly imagine. Between these extremes there are endless possibilities.

There are many popular historical periods. For example, the remote past of the Old Testament, used in such novels as Thomas Mann's *Joseph and his Brothers*; the less remote past of the New Testament, used in such works as *The Robe* by Lloyd C. Douglas; ancient Rome, the setting for such novels as Robert Graves' *I, Claudius*; The Renaissance, which is the background for Shakespeare's *Romeo and Juliet*; the early American colonies, which Hawthorne used so well in *The Scarlet Letter*; and the Civil War period, made memorable in Margaret Mitchell's *Gone with the Wind*.

(2) It is sometimes difficult to draw a clear line between what is considered historical and what is considered contemporary.

For older writers who lived through the war years, World War II may seem contemporary. For younger writers who were born twenty years after the war was over, it all seems a matter of history, as does the Vietnam War. In general, we think of contemporary times as those that are part of the experience of people who are now alive. But the present keeps slipping away into the past, and, finally, it is buried along with the last eye-witnesses and becomes history.

(3) It is difficult to bring history back to life.

Though many a good writer has been able to make history live again, in some sense it is always dead, and it is therefore difficult for the living to identify with times that are past. The truly important business of literature seems to be to interpret the experiences of one's own times. Most readers prefer a contemporary setting, though there remains a certain fascination with historical fiction, and young writers should not be discouraged from trying their hand at re-creating an earlier period than their own. Sometimes the past is merely romanticized; sometimes it is re-created accurately. It is important in serious historical fiction to be accurate, but not to swamp the plot with history and lose track of the story.

(4) If you choose a contemporary period, be specific about the time involved.

Unless a specific time is indicated in a literary work, the reader will probably assume that the period is "today," or approximately the year in which the work is written. However, since the term *contemporary* can cover several decades, it may be important to know exactly what the period is, especially if the drama is linked with social or political events. Each modern period is associated with certain events, styles, and ideas. The

1950s were marked by conformity, McCarthyism, short hair and tailfins on cars. The 1960s involved a dramatic social revolution — civil rights and anti-war demonstrations, new music, and long hair. The 1970s settled once again into conservatism after the Watergate scandal, and developed into the era of self-concern, materialism and yuppyism in the 1980s. It is not enough to name a date. The details in the work have to be consistent with that date.

10b
Present action should be distinguished from past action.

(1) Present action refers to what happens in the main time frame established for the story.

There may be flashbacks or other references to prior action, but these are distinguished from the present action. The basic tense chosen by the writer has nothing to do with present action. In most stories the past tense is used, but even if the present tense is used we know that the events have already taken place and that the writer is only trying to make them sound more immediate. When he says, for instance, "I jump into my car and drive like a madman to the nearest farmhouse," we don't assume that he is writing as he drives.

In Paul Ruffin's "The Fox" (Example 5), the main time frame is very simple. A woman in a rural setting is baking a pie in the kitchen. Her husband comes in and says he saw a fox with a wounded leg, possibly from a trap he had once set for coons. He goes on in detail about the incident as she continues her work, but she is thinking about how much she hates this man. It is clear that there is a parallel between the wounded fox and the trapped woman. All this is *present time*. Then there is a break and we hear about their past in two paragraphs that are inserted outside the main time frame of the action. We return to the main action. The man gets his shotgun and says he's going out to finish off the fox. The woman, who has tried to protect herself from this man with cold indifference, remains in the kitchen. Suddenly, she plunges her hand into the center of the hot pie and leaves it there "until the burning stopped and there was no feeling left at all."

(2) In all action some things have to be *omitted*,
     some have to be *summarized*, and some have to
     be *dramatized*.

Any sequence of events in real life can involve hundreds of details. In a literary work it is impossible to include everything, and it is impossible to dramatize everything that *is* included. Some action has to be summarized, especially in works that cover a lot of events over a long period of time. A summarized action is one that is simply *told* to the reader and not acted out. In "The Fox," for instance, we are *told*: "Their relationship, from her intense hatred of him when they were in grade school together through an infatuation in high school that was consummated in her father's hayloft one Sunday afternoon, had come finally full circle, back to something that she thought at times was hate, at other times mere indifference." In contrast to this summarized action, we have the shocking ending of the story, which is dramatized action.

10c
Past action refers to anything that has already taken place prior to the main time-frame of the literary work.

(1) Most past action is summarized.

The easiest and most concise way to bring past events into the current action of a literary work is to make a brief summarized reference to it. This can be done in several ways:

1. The omniscient narrator can simply tell us what happened;
2. Past events can be referred to in dialogue;
3. A character can recall past events in a monologue or soliloquy; and
4. A character can think about the past.

(2) Past action can be dramatized in a flashback.

Most literary works with a plot have a chronological order. They start at the beginning and end at the end. Occasionally, however, the events are not revealed in a chronological order. This does not necessarily upset the main time frame. Sometimes, it is more effective to tell a story by beginning at the end or in the middle.

A *flashback* is a dramatized incident that has already taken place prior to the current sequence of events that constitutes the story, play, or narrative poem. Usually, a flashback is a subjective device, something we witness through the mind of one of the characters in a vivid reverie, memory, or dream. In the movie *Casablanca* Rick's dialogue dissolves into a flashback to happier days in Paris, when he and Ilsa were first in love, and when the Germans were marching into the city. The scene is dramatized and is wonderfully romantic. But things did not work out, and suddenly we are back in Casablanca, back within the framework of *present action*.

The flashback technique has often been used in films, partly because it is easy to accomplish. All one needs is a simple transition. On stage, it is not often used, because the live theater lacks the technology available to film and television. In fiction, it is used, but requires a good deal of skill to avoid confusion and the awkwardness of moving back and forth in time. It is even used in poetry. In "Digging" by Seamus Heaney (Chapter 7) the poet's mind rushes back twenty years to a scene from his boyhood, when he hears his father digging in the garden.

10d
Duration refers to the amount of time that passes in the whole work or any part of it.

Writers must not only indicate *when* the action takes place, they must also indicate *how long* it lasts.

(1) There is a difference between objective and subjective time.

There are, in a sense, two different kinds of time: (1) *objective time*, the sort that ticks away on a clock in what we call "the real world," and (2) *subjective time*, a strictly human experience of duration. We have all waited for minutes that seemed like hours when something important was at stake, and we have all heard the old cliché that time passes quickly when you're having fun.

Subjective writers have always been fascinated with the discrepancy between external and internal time, with the idea that a moment that ticks away on a clock can actually be expanded almost infinitely in a person's mind. In a story called "Moments of Being" by Virginia Woolf, all that happens is that a rose pinned to Fanny Wilmot's dress falls to the floor. Fanny looks for the pin on the floor, finds it and pins the rose back in place. What goes through her mind in that moment takes eight pages to describe.

(2) How can a writer indicate duration?

The handling of *subjective time* is closely linked to those techniques by which writers reveal the thoughts of their characters (see Chapter 9). *Objective time* can be indicated in many ways. In drama, whether on stage or screen, time passes in a given scene pretty much as it does in real life, if it is a fairly realistic drama. Between scenes any amount of time is liable to pass.

In fiction, the duration of the action can be indicated, first of all, in some simple, direct way. For instance, the narrator can tell us that John and Mary spent an hour together, or that the flight to London took six hours. Novels that use a diary form usually indicate the date at the beginning of each section. Epistolary novels usually include dates on the letters. Many of the indicators of duration in an ordinary first-person or third-person narrative are woven into the story in an incidental way without being intrusive. In strictly chronological narratives it is easier to keep duration clear. In narratives that move back and forth in time, things can sometimes get confused.

10e

Transitions are devices for linking episodes.

(1) Transitions are usually used between dramatized scenes.

Since literary works have to be selective and often consist of a sequence of important scenes, there must be transitions to guide the reader from one scene to another. The transition must indicate two important things: how much *time* has elapsed since the last major scene, and *where* the new scene is located. These items are always included in a playscript, but, unfortunately, the audience does not usually have a copy of the script. The information has to be indicated in the set, the action, or the dialogue. A character might glance at his watch and say to his wife: "It's eleven o'clock. Where have you been for the last six hours?" Some transitions in drama are purely technical and can be indicated by lighting or by a curtain. Daylight dims to darkness. Dawn blossoms beyond shaded windows. In crude theatrical productions and early films, it was not uncommon to be shown a literal notice on a card or on the screen: "Two years later," or whatever information was required.

(2) Transitions in fiction can be frequent and varied.

Without the benefit of stage or screen devices, fiction has to rely on the written word. This sometimes makes things easier and sometimes more difficult. A writer can always begin a new scene by saying: "The next day Mary was up by six and ready to leave for New York by seven." On the other hand, there are usually more scenes in fiction, and sometimes there are elaborate transitions full of explanations and summarized action. For instance: "Mary spent the next six months looking after her dying father in a dreary farmhouse in Vermont, an experience that plunged her into a profound depression that did not end with his death. It was not until she met John in April that she began to recover from the ordeal. She was sitting on a bench in Washington Square Park . . ."

In fiction, as in films, transitions are necessary to introduce flashbacks. Some of these have become conventional, even trite. Since the flashback is a dramatized memory of something in the past, we have to make the transition through the point of view of the character, who might stare into a mirror or into a lake, who might look through a photo album or at the portrait of a woman (as in the film *Laura*), or listen to a special piece of music and fall into a reverie. In the movies the lake can shimmer, the camera can go out of focus, the music can fade in or out. Comparable things can be used in fiction, but they have to be described instead of staged. Above all, it is important to make a clear distinction between a flashback and current action. There has to be a transition at both ends. Flashbacks often end abruptly — someone calling the character's name, a knock at the door, the telephone ringing, some kind of intrusion from present reality. Flashbacks should be used with caution. They should not be used too frequently and they should not be too long. The material should be especially significant in some way. Usually incidental information about the past can be introduced more effectively through summarized action that is either part of the persona's narrative or contained in the dialogue.

EXAMPLE 10

AN OCCURRENCE AT OWL CREEK BRIDGE
Ambrose Bierce

I

A man stood upon a railroad bridge in northern Alabama, look-ing down into the swift water twenty feet below. The man's hands were behind his back, the wrists bound with a cord. A rope closely encircled his neck. It was attached to a stout cross-timber above his head and the slack fell to the level of his knees. Some loose boards laid upon the sleepers supporting the met-als of the railway supplied a footing for him and his execution-ers — two private soldiers of the Federal army, directed by a sergeant who in civil life may have been a deputy sheriff. At a short remove upon the same temporary platform was an officer in the uniform of his rank, armed. He was a captain. A sentinel at each end of the bridge stood with his rifle in the position known as "support," that is to say, vertical in front of the left shoulder, the hammer resting on the forearm thrown straight across the chest — a formal and unnatural position, enforcing an erect carriage of the body. It did not appear to be the duty of these two men to know what was occurring at the center of the bridge; they merely blockaded the two ends of the foot planking that traversed it.

Beyond one of the sentinels nobody was in sight; the rail-road ran straight away into a forest for a hundred yards, then, curving, was lost to view. Doubtless there was an outpost farther along. The other bank of the stream was open ground — a gentle acclivity topped with a stockade of vertical tree trunks, loopholed for rifles, with a single embrasure through which protruded the muzzle of a brass cannon commanding the bridge. Midway of the slope between bridge and fort were the spectators — a single company of infantry in line, at "parade rest," the butts of the rifles on the ground, the barrels inclining slightly backward against the right shoulder, the hands crossed upon the stock. A lieutenant stood at the right of the line, the point of his sword upon the ground, his left hand resting upon his right. Excepting the group of four at the center of the bridge, not a man moved. The company faced the bridge, staring stonily, motionless. The sentinels, facing the banks of the stream, might have been statues to adorn the bridge. The captain stood with folded arms, silent, observing the work of his subordinates, but making no sign. Death is a dignitary who when he comes announced is to be received with formal manifestations of respect, even by those most familiar with him. In the code of military etiquette silence and fixity are forms of deference.

The man who was engaged in being hanged was apparently about thirty-five years of age. He was a civilian, if one might judge from his habit, which was that of a planter. His features were good — a straight nose, firm mouth, broad forehead, from which his long, dark hair was combed straight back, falling behind his ears to the collar of his well-fitting frock coat. He wore a mustache and pointed beard, but no whiskers; his eyes were large and dark gray, and had a kindly expression which one would hardly have expected in one whose neck was in the hemp. Evidently this was no vulgar assassin. The liberal military code makes provision for hanging many kinds of persons, and gentlemen are not excluded.

The preparations being complete, the two private soldiers stepped aside and each drew away the plank upon which he had been standing. The sergeant turned to the captain, saluted and placed himself immediately behind that officer, who in turn moved apart one pace. These movements left the condemned man and the sergeant standing on the two ends of the same plank, which spanned three of the crossties of the bridge. The end upon which the civilian stood almost, but not quite, reached a fourth. This plank had been held in place by the weight of the captain; it was now held by that of the sergeant. At a signal from the former the latter would step aside, the plank would tilt and the condemned man go down between two ties. The arrangement commended itself to his judgment as simple and effective. His face had not been covered nor his eyes bandaged. He looked a moment at his "unsteadfast footing," then let his gaze wander to the swirling water of the stream racing madly beneath his feet. A piece of dancing driftwood caught his attention and his eyes followed it down the current. How slowly it appeared to move! What a sluggish stream!

He closed his eyes in order to fix his last thoughts upon his wife and children. The water, touched to gold by the early sun, the brooding mists under the banks at some distance down the stream, the fort, the soldiers, the piece of drift—all had distracted him. And now he became conscious of a new disturbance. Striking through the thought of his dear ones was a sound which he could neither ignore nor understand, a sharp, distinct, metallic percussion like the stroke of a blacksmith's hammer upon the anvil; it had the same ringing quality. He wondered what it was, and whether immeasurably distant or near by—it seemed both. Its recurrence was regular, but as slow as the tolling of a death knell. He awaited each stroke with impatience and — he knew not why — apprehension. The intervals of silence grew progressively longer; the delays became maddening. With their greater infrequency the sounds increased in strength and sharpness. They hurt his ear like the thrust of a knife; he feared he would shriek. What he heard was the ticking of his watch.

He unclosed his eyes and saw again the water below him. "If I could free my hands," he thought, "I might throw off the noose and spring into the stream. By diving I could evade the bullets and, swimming vigorously, reach the bank, take to the woods and get away home. My home, thank God, is as yet outside their lines; my wife and little ones are still beyond the invader's farthest advance."

As these thoughts, which have here to be set down in words, were flashed into the doomed man's brain rather than evolved from it the captain nodded to the sergeant. The sergeant stepped aside.

II

Peyton Farquhar was a well-to-do planter, of an old and highly respected Alabama family. Being a slave owner and like other slave owners a politician he was naturally an original secessionist and ardently devoted to the Southern cause. Circumstances of an imperious nature, which it is unnecessary to relate here, had prevented him from taking service with the gallant army that had fought the disastrous campaigns ending with the fall of Corinth, and he chafed under the inglorious restraint, longing for the release of his energies, the larger life of the soldier, the opportunity for distinction. That opportunity, he felt, would come, as it comes to all in war time. Meanwhile he did what he could. No service was too humble for him to perform in aid of the South, no adventure too perilous for him to undertake if consistent with the character of a civilian who was at heart a soldier, and who in good faith and without too much qualification assented to at least a part of the frankly villainous dictum that all is fair in love and war.

One evening while Farquhar and his wife were sitting on a rustic bench near the entrance to his grounds, a gray-clad soldier rode up to the gate and asked for a drink of water. Mrs. Farquhar was only too happy to serve him with her own white hands. While she was fetching the water her husband approached the dusty horseman and inquired eagerly for news from the front.

"The Yanks are repairing the railroads," said the man, "and are getting ready for another advance. They have reached the Owl Creek bridge, put it in order and built a stockade on the north bank. The commandant has issued an order, which is posted everywhere, declaring that any civilian caught interfering with the railroad, its bridges, tunnels or trains will be summarily hanged. I saw the order."

"How far is it to the Owl Creek bridge?" Farquhar asked.

"About thirty miles."

"Is there no force on this side the creek?"

"Only a picket post half a mile out, on the railroad, and a single sentinel at this end of the bridge."

"Suppose a man—a civilian and student of hanging—should elude the picket post and perhaps get the better of the sentinel," said Farquhar, smiling, "what could he accomplish?"

The soldier reflected. "I was there a month ago," he replied. "I observed that the flood of last winter had lodged a great quantity of driftwood against the wooden pier at this end of the bridge. It is now dry and would burn like tow."

The lady had now brought the water, which the soldier drank. He thanked her ceremoniously, bowed to her husband and rode away. An hour later, after nightfall, he repassed the plantation, going northward in the direction from which he had come. He was a Federal scout.

III

As Peyton Farquhar fell straight downward through the bridge he lost consciousness and was as one already dead. From this stage he was awakened — ages later, it seemed to him — by the pain of a sharp pressure upon his throat, followed by a sense of suffocation. Keen, poignant agonies seemed to shoot from his neck downward through every fiber of his body and limbs. These pains appeared to flash along well-defined lines of ramification and to beat with an inconceivably rapid periodicity. They seemed like streams of pulsating fire heating him to an intolerable temperature. As to his head, he was conscious of nothing but a feeling of fullness — of congestion. These sensations were unaccompanied by thought. The intellectual part of his nature was already effaced; he had power only to feel, and feeling was torment. He was conscious of motion. Encompassed in a luminous cloud, of which he was now merely the fiery heart, without material substance, he swung through unthinkable arcs of oscillation, like a vast pendulum. Then all at once, with terrible suddenness, the light about him shot upward with the noise of a loud plash; a frightful roaring was in his ears, and all was cold and dark. The power of thought was restored; he knew that the rope had broken and he had fallen into the stream. There was no additional strangulation; the noose about his neck was already suffocating him and kept the water from his lungs. To die of hanging at the bottom of a river! — the idea seemed to him ludicrous. He opened his eyes in the darkness and saw above him a gleam of light, but how distant, how inaccessible! He was still sinking, for the light became fainter and fainter until it was a mere glimmer. Then it began to grow and brighten, and he knew that he was rising toward the surface — knew it with reluctance, for he was now very comfortable. "To be hanged and drowned," he thought, "that is not so bad; but I do not wish to be shot. No; I will not be shot; that is not fair."

He was not conscious of an effort, but a sharp pain his wrist appraised him that he was trying to free his hands. He gave the struggle his attention, as an idler might observe the feat of a juggler, without interest in the outcome. What splendid effort! — what magnificent, what superhuman strength! Ah, that was a fine endeavor! Bravo! The cord fell away; his arms parted and floated upward, the hands dimly seen on each side in the growing light. He watched them with a new interest as first one and then the other pounced upon the noose at his neck. They tore it away and thrust it fiercely aside, its undulations resembling those of a water snake. "Put it back, put it back!" He thought he shouted these words to his hands, for the undoing of the noose had been succeeded by the direct pang that he had yet experienced. His neck ached horribly; his brain was on fire; his heart, which had been fluttering faintly, gave a great leap, trying to force itself out at his mouth. His whole body was racked and wrenched with an insupportable anguish! But his disobedient hands gave no heed to the command. They beat the water vigorously with quick, downward strokes, forcing him to the surface. He felt his head emerge; his eyes were blinded by the sunlight; his chest expanded convulsively, and with a supreme and crowning agony his lungs engulfed a great draught of air, which instantly he expelled in a shriek!

He was now in full possession of his physical senses. They were, indeed, preternaturally keen and alert. Something in the awful disturbance of his organic system had so exalted and refined them that they made record of things never before perceived. He felt the ripples upon his face and heard their separate sounds as they struck. He looked at the forest on the bank of the stream, saw the individual trees, the leaves and the veining of each leaf — saw the very insects upon them: the locusts, the brilliant-bodied flies, the gray spiders stretching their webs from twig to twig. He noted that prismatic colors in all the dewdrops upon a million blades of grass. The humming of the gnats that danced above the eddies of the stream, the beating of the dragonflies' wings, the strokes of the waterspiders' legs, like oars which had lifted their boat — all these made audible music. A fish slid along beneath his eyes and he heard the rush of its body parting the water.

He had come to the surface facing down the stream; in a moment the visible world seemed to wheel slowly round, himself the pivotal point, and he saw the bridge, the fort, the soldiers upon the bridge, the captain, the sergeant, the two privates, his executioners. They were in silhouette against the blue sky. They shouted and gesticulated, pointing at him. The captain had drawn his pistol, but did not fire; the others were unarmed. Their movements were grotesque and horrible, their forms gigantic.

Suddenly he heard a sharp report and something struck the water smartly within a few inches of his head, spattering his face with spray. He heard a second report, and saw one of the sentinels with his rifle at his shoulder, a light cloud of blue smoke rising from the muzzle. The man in the water saw the eye of the man on the bridge gazing into his own through the sights of the rifle. He observed that it was a gray eye and remembered having read that gray eyes were keenest, and that all famous marksmen had them. Nevertheless, this one had missed.

A counter-swirl had caught Farquhar and turned him half round; he was again looking into the forest on the bank opposite the fort. The sound of a clear, high voice in a monotonous singsong now rang out behind him and came across the water with a distinctness that pierced and subdued all other sounds, even the beating of the ripples in his ears. Although no soldier, he had frequented camps enough to know the dread significance of that deliberate, drawling, aspirated chant; the lieutenant on shore was taking a part in the morning's work. How coldly and pitilessly — with what an even, calm intonation, presaging, and enforcing tranquility in the men — with what accurately measured intervals fell those cruel words:

"Attention, company! . . . Shoulder arms! . . . Ready! . . . Aim! . . . Fire!"

Farquhar dived — dived as deeply as he could. The water roared in his ears like the voice of Niagara, yet he heard the dulled thunder of the volley and, rising again toward the surface, met shining bits of metal, singularly flattened, oscillating slowly downward. Some of them touched him on the face and hands, then fell away, continuing their descent. One lodged between his collar and neck; it was uncomfortably warm and he snatched it out.

As he rose to the surface, gasping for breath, he saw that he had been a long time under water; he was perceptibly farther downstream — nearer to safety. The soldiers had almost finished reloading; the metal ramrods flashed all at once in the sunshine as they were drawn from the barrels, turned in the air, and thrust into their sockets. The two sentinels fired again, independently and ineffectually.

The hunted man saw all this over his shoulder; he was now swimming vigorously with the current. His brain was as energetic as his arms and legs; he thought with the rapidity of lightning.

"The officer," he reasoned, "will not make that martinet's error a second time. It is as easy to dodge a volley as a single shot. He has probably already given the command to fire at will. God help me, I cannot dodge them all!"

An appalling plash within two yards of him was followed by a loud, rushing sound, diminuendo, which seemed to travel back through the air to the fort and died in an explosion which stirred the very river to its deeps! A rising sheet of water curved over him, fell down upon him, blinded him, strangled him! The cannon had taken a hand in the game. As he shook his head free from the commotion of the smitten water he heard the deflected shot humming through the air ahead, and in an instant it was cracking and smashing the branches in the forest beyond.

"They will not do that again," he thought; "the next time they will use a charge of grape. I must keep my eye upon the gun; the smoke will apprise me — the report arrives too late; it lags behind the missile. That is a good gun."

Suddenly he felt himself whirled round and round — spinning like a top. The water, the banks, the forests, the now distant bridge, fort and men — all were commingled and blurred. Objects were represented by their colors only;

circular horizontal streaks of color — that was all he saw. He had been caught in a vortex and was being whirled on with a velocity of advance and gyration that made him giddy and sick. In a few moments he was flung upon the gravel at the foot of the left bank of the stream — the southern bank — and behind a projecting point which concealed him from his enemies. The sudden arrest of his motion, the abrasion of one of his hands on the gravel, restored him, and he wept with delight. He dug his fingers into the sand, threw it over himself in handfuls and audibly blessed it. It looked like diamonds, rubies, emeralds; he could think of nothing beautiful which it did not resemble. The trees upon the bank were giant garden plants; he noted a definite order in their arrangement, inhaled the fragrance of their blooms. A strange, roseate light shone through the spaces among their trunks and the wind made in their branches the music of aeolian harps. He had no wish to perfect his escape — was content to remain in that enchanting spot until retaken.

A whiz and rattle of grapeshot among the branches high above his head roused him from his dream. The baffled cannoneer had fired him a random farewell. He sprang to his feet, rushed up the sloping bank, and plunged into the forest.

All that day he traveled, laying his course by the rounding sun. The forest seemed interminable; nowhere did he discover a break in it, not even a woodman's road. He had not known that he lived in so wild a region. There was something uncanny in the revelation.

By nightfall he was fatigued, footsore, famishing. The thought of his wife and children urged him on. At last he found a road which led him in what he knew to be the right direction. It was as wide and straight as a city street, yet it seemed untraveled. No fields bordered it, no dwelling anywhere. Not so much as the barking of a dog suggested human habitation. The black bodies of the trees formed a straight wall on both sides, terminating on the horizon in a point, like a diagram in a lesson in perspective. Overhead, as he looked up through this rift in the wood, shone great golden stars looking unfamiliar and grouped in strange constellations. He was sure they were arranged in some order which had a secret and malign significance. The wood on either side was full of singular noises, among which — once, twice, and again — he distinctly heard whispers in an unknown tongue.

His neck was in pain and lifting his hand to it he found it horribly swollen. He knew that it had a circle of black where the rope had bruised it. His eyes felt congested; he could no longer close them. His tongue was swollen with thirst; he relieved its fever by thrusting it forward from between his teeth into the cold air. How softly the turf had carpeted the untraveled avenue — he could no longer feel the roadway beneath his feet!

Doubtless, despite his suffering, he had fallen asleep while walking, for now he sees another scene — perhaps he has merely recovered from a delirium. He stands at the gate of his own home. All is as he left it, and all bright and beautiful in the morning sunshine. He must have traveled the entire night. As he pushes upon the gate and passes up the wide white walk, he sees a flutter of female garments; his wife, looking fresh and cool and sweet, steps down from the veranda to meet him. At the bottom of the steps she stands waiting, with a smile of ineffable joy, an attitude of matchless grace and dignity. Ah, how beautiful she is! He springs forward with extended arms. As he is about to clasp her he feels a stunning blow upon the back of the neck; a blinding white light blazes all about him with a sound like the shock of a cannon—then all is darkness and silence!

Peyton Farquhar was dead; his body, with a broken neck, swung gently from side to side beneath the timbers of the Owl Creek bridge.

1891

EXERCISES

DISCUSSION

1. In "An Occurrence at Owl Creek Bridge" (Example 10), Ambrose Bierce uses *present action, past action, objective time,* and *subjective time.* Find specific examples of these approaches to time.

2. This story is divided into three numbered parts. Do they correspond to any periods of time?

3. Are the transitions clear in this story? Can you identify them?

WRITING

1. Write a short story in which an incident that occurs in a few moments is expanded through a *subjective sense of time.*

2. Write a short story that contains at least one *flashback.*

3. Write a poem in which events that occurred over a long period of time are condensed into a concise summary.

4. Write a one-act play with an historical setting (for instance, a lonely encounter between a Confederate and a Union soldier in the Civil War).

5. A young man sits beside his unconscious and terminally ill father in a hospital. They have never gotten along well, and the young man had to be persuaded by his mother to make this visit. Create a *flashback* that will help to explain the bad relationship, but also describe the *present* feelings of the young man.

6. A young woman who ran away from home at sixteen and was disowned by her parents is now on her way back in a limousine to visit them in their working class factory town. Capture *past events* while she is on the road. Then describe *present events*, her arrival, and her confrontation with her parents. What will happen?

CHAPTER
ELEVEN

IMAGES AND SOUNDS

Words are the medium of the art of writing. A piece of writing, therefore, is limited to the effects the words can achieve. Fortunately, words can do a great deal. For example, with words writers can convey ideas, create images, and create sounds and patterns of sounds. Writers do not necessarily do these things separately. In a single powerful passage a writer can accomplish all three. Consider the *ideas, images* and *sounds* in this poem by Shakespeare (from *The Tempest*):

> Full fathom five thy father lies;
>> Of his bones are coral made;
> Those are pearls that were his eyes;
>> Nothing of him that doth fade,
> But doth suffer a sea change

Into something rich and strange.
Sea nymphs hourly ring his knell:
      Ding-dong.
Hark! now I hear them — Ding-dong bell.

Language is always associated with ideas, but in the literary re-creation of human experience images and sounds are very important, especially in poetry. A consideration of *imagery* can be conveniently divided into three categories: (1) metaphors and similes; (2) allusions; and (3) symbols. *Sounds* in literature can be considered in the following categories: (1) rhyme; (2) rhythm; and (3) patterns and form.

Imagery is a broad term that encompasses all kinds of pictures in the mind and all the literary devices that put them there. Images tend to be visual, but, as in dreams, they appeal to all the senses. Literal description can create images in our minds. Often, however, description contains certain literary devices that are specifically designed to evoke images.

11a
Metaphors and similes make non-literal comparisons.

Some comparisons cannot be taken literally. If you say "Terry looks like Donna," you are making a *literal* comparison. If you say "Terry looks like a beautiful blossom," you are *not* making a *literal* comparison, but you are evoking an *image* that will help to describe Terry. Non-literal comparisons are also called figures of speech. Obviously, a person is not literally a flower, but a person and a flower might both have a certain attractive quality that makes the comparison possible.

(1) A simile says that one thing is *like* another (non-literally).

Similes and metaphors both evoke images. The only difference is that a simile uses the words "as" or "like" ("Terry is as beautiful as a blossom"), and a metaphor says that one thing *is* another ("Terry is a beautiful blossom").

A simile can be a simple comparison, as in Robert Burns' famous line: "Oh, my love is like a red, red, rose . . ." A simile can also be extended and elaborate, perhaps even the basis of a whole poem. In "Sonnet 97" Shakespeare uses an elaborate simile, which compares the absence of the lover from his loved one to a winter:

> How like a winter hath my absence been
> From thee, the pleasure of the fleeting year!
> What freezings have I felt, what dark days seen!
> What old December's bareness everywhere!
> And yet this time removed was summer's time,
> The teeming autumn, big with rich increase,
> Bearing the wanton burthen of the prime,
> Like widowed wombs after their lord's decease;
> Yet this abundant issue seemed to me
> But hope of orphans and unfathered fruit;
> For summer and his pleasures wait on thee,
> And, thou away, the very birds are mute;
> Or, if they sing, 'tis with so dull a cheer
> That leaves look pale, dreading the winter's near.

(2) **A metaphor asserts the identity of the
things compared.**

At times it may strengthen a comparison to leave out *like* or *as*
and simply say that, figuratively speaking, one thing *is* another,
as in "War is hell!" At other times a simile might be more
suitable.

A metaphor can be incidental or it can be elaborate. In
"Ode to a Nightingale" Keats uses the phrase "the viewless
wings of Poesy." A more modern poet, Eamon Grennan, makes
use of more elaborate metaphors in the following poem:

LYING LOW

The dead rabbit's
Raspberry belly
Gapes like a mouth;

Bees and gilded flies
Make the pulpy flesh
Hum and squirm:

O love, they sing
In their nail-file voices,
We are becoming one another.

His head intact, tranquil,
As if he's dreaming
The mesmerised love of strangers

Who inhabit the red tent
Of his ribs, the radiant
Open house of his heart.

(3) Personification means giving human qualities to ideas and things.

There is a natural tendency in literature to translate abstractions and inanimate objects into human terms, because those are the terms we can all experience. Hence, the breeze *whispers*, we are *stalked* by death, ideas *leap* into our minds, the peacock *struts*, and the lion is a *king*.

(4) Metaphors and similes appear in prose as well as poetry.

Though we associate imagery with poetry, there are many fiction writers who make frequent use of it. Here is the opening of *Jitterbug Perfume* by Tom Robbins:

> The beet is the most intense of vegetables. The radish, admittedly, is more feverish, but the fire of the radish is a cold fire, the fire of discontent not of passion. Tomatoes are lusty enough, yet there runs through tomatoes an undercurrent of frivolity. Beets are deadly serious.
>
> Slavic peoples get their physical characteristics from potatoes, their smoldering inquietude from radishes, their seriousness from beets.
>
> The beet is the melancholy vegetable, the one most willing to suffer. You can't squeeze blood out of a *turnip* . . .
>
> The beet is the murderer returned to the scene of the crime. The beet is what happens when the cherry finishes with the carrot. The beet is the ancient ancestor of the autumn moon, bearded, buried, all but fossilized; the dark green sails of the grounded moon-boat stitched with veins of primordial plasma; the kite string that once connected the moon to the Earth now a muddy whisker drilling desperately for rubies.

The beet was Rasputin's favorite vegetable. You could see it in his eyes.

11b
Allusions depend upon a common body of knowledge.

(1) An allusion is a reference to a specific person, place, or thing.

Allusions are often used in similes or metaphors, as in, "Like Sisyphus, he found his work endless and futile." (In Greek mythology Sisyphus was punished in Hades by having to roll a marble block uphill forever, only to have it roll down again as soon as it reached the top.) Allusions expand a writer's ability to use non-literal comparisons and to evoke images. They are drawn from a common body of knowledge in a given culture. Unless they have broad recognition they might be too specialized or obscure to be effective. Many allusions are drawn from Greek mythology, the Bible, familiar literature, well-known events and figures in history, and popular culture, including movies, music, cartoons, and even television commercials. For instance:

- His team-mates called him the Jolly Green Giant.
- Maria had a Mickey Mouse face and a Donald Duck voice.
- Her life was like Schubert's unfinished symphony.
- She was the Marilyn Monroe of the 1980s.
- Like Paul Revere, he tried to warn the public.

- He was a real Huck Finn in his youth.
- He met his Waterloo at Watergate.

(2) Some allusions are extended and elaborate.

In Sylvia Plath's "Daddy" there is an extended allusion to Naziism, to the Holocaust, Aryanism, and German military equipment. She is referring to her father in the following lines, which contain only some of these references:

> I have always been scared of *you*.
> With your Luftwaffe, your gobbledygoo.
> And your neat moustache
> And your Aryan eye, bright blue.
> Panzer-man, panzer-man, O You —
>
> Not God but a swastika
> So black no sky could squeak through.
> Every woman adores a Fascist,
> The boot in the face, the brute
> Brute heart of a brute like you.

11c
Symbols are tangible representations of things that are complex, general, or abstract.

A symbol, whether it appears in literature or anywhere else, is something tangible that stands for something abstract, or something very specific that stands for something very general. Flags are symbols of the countries they represent. The Statue of Liberty symbolizes the democratic ideal. The cross represents the crucifixion and perhaps the whole Christian faith. In a sense, all of language is symbolic, since it is a system of signs that refer to things in the real world. What concerns us for the moment is how symbols function in literature.

(1) There is a connection between symbols in dreams and symbols in literature.

Both dreams and literature use symbols to give expression to feelings that come from the subconscious mind, and both depend, to some extent, on certain basic ways of representing these hidden feelings. In other words, there is a kind of dream language that is also used in literature. There is a private dimension in dreams, however. The same objects may have different connotations for different people. On the other hand, because we all share human nature and some kind of social context, there are certain consistencies in the language of dreams.

(2) In literature, symbols must have some public meaning.

Without a shared context of meaning there wouldn't be any communication between the writer and the reader. Edgar Allan Poe's raven was not exclusively his own nightmare. The raven, the crow, and the owl have long been associated with death. The Indians of the Northwest say that when you hear the owl call your name you will die. In the Freudian system, objects of an appropriate shape, such as towers or guns, are considered phallic symbols; and objects such as houses and staircases and caves refer to the female, often the mother.

(3) Symbols are not comparisons in the same way that metaphors, similes, and allusions are.

Symbols are objects or actions or even people that actually appear in a literary work and bring with them certain connotations.

One of our most famous literary symbols is Melville's white whale, called Moby Dick. It is impossible to read this novel as just another fishing story, in which the big one got away, but what does it all mean? What does the white whale stand for? Is he good or evil? Is he the inscrutable, God-like mystery, that power in the universe that is not to be questioned? He is called Job's whale. Job's problem was that he questioned God's treatment of him, instead of accepting with absolute humility whatever seemed to be God's will. The debate about this famous symbol goes on, but the drama is magnificent and moving. Some important and fundamental truth has been captured here, even if we can't force it into more ordinary language. That is precisely what symbols are for. They accomplish things that ordinary language cannot.

Another well-known symbol is to be found in Virginia Woolf's *To the Lighthouse*. The setting of the novel is the summer house of Mr. and Mrs. Ramsay, somewhere on the British coast, probably in the Hebrides. Offshore, there is a lighthouse with three beams of light. Every summer the Ramsay family and their guests gather at the house. There are artists, poets, and professors. And there are the children. There is much talk of sailing to the lighthouse. It seems at times mysterious and unreachable. An elusive, distant source of light, it is a tangible and suggestive symbol of many things. It suggests something mystical, something beyond human grasp or comprehension, perhaps death or eternity or a cold indifferent universe. Mrs. Ramsay finds it comforting at times, and, at other times, terrifying. Mr. Ramsay is afraid that logic will never get him to the lighthouse, to ultimate truth. Lily, the painter friend of Mrs. Ramsay, can complete her painting only when, after many years, Mr. Ramsay and his children finally sail to the lighthouse. At the moment they land, she has a kind of vision.

In Joseph Conrad's *Victory*, set in the East Indies, the hero runs off to a deserted island with a woman. He is a disenchanted European. She is a lost soul, playing in a hotel orchestra in one of those exotic places Conrad was so fond of (now Malaysia or Indonesia). Their love affair on this deserted island suggests the Garden of Eden. It is a return to purity and innocence, before the Fall. But evil lurks in the wings. A satanic figure, Mr. Jones, imagines that there is a treasure on the island and arrives there to get it. He is accompanied by two henchmen, Ricardo the killer and Pedro the brute. The struggle is full of suspense, but, the ending is, inevitably, tragic.

There has been much discussion of the Marabar Caves in E. M. Forster's *A Passage to India*. This excerpt will serve as a good illustration of how a symbol is described:

> They are dark caves. Even when they open towards the sun, very little light penetrates down the entrance tunnel into the circular chamber. There is little to see, and no eye to see it, until the visitor arrives for his five minutes, and strikes a match. Immediately another flame rises in the depths of the rock and moves towards the surface like an imprisoned spirit: the walls of the circular chamber have been most marvellously polished. The two flames approach and strive to unite, but

cannot, because one of them breathes air, the other stone. A mirror inlaid with lovely colours divides the lovers, delicate stars of pink and grey interpose, exquisite nebulae, shadings fainter than the tail of a comet or the midday moon, all the evanescent life of the granite, only here visible. Fists and fingers thrust above the advancing soil — here at last is their skin, finer than any covering acquired by the animals, smoother than windless water, more voluptuous than love. The radiance increases, the flames touch one another, kiss, expire. The cave is dark again, like all the caves.

Symbols expand human expression and make it possible to grasp certain complexities that cannot be described in a literal fashion.

The Scarlet Letter by Nathaniel Hawthorne is full of symbolism. The novel takes place in Puritan seventeenth-century Massachusetts. Hester Prynne bears an illegitimate child and is branded with an embroidered letter "A" as her punishment. The A is for adultery, since she has a husband, even though he has been away long enough to be considered dead. She refuses to name her lover, who is Arthur Dimmesdale, a young minister. The whole fabric of the novel is made of symbols. The scarlet letter itself is open to many interpretations. Is Hester ashamed of it or proud of it? Does it stand for her sin or her rebellion? She names her daughter Pearl, because she was purchased at such a dear price. Chillingworth, the secretly returned husband, is a satanic figure who seeks revenge. Dimmesdale is a saintly figure, whom Chillingworth tried to destroy with guilt. Much of the symbolism deals with the struggle between good and evil and the struggle between nature and the repressive forces of religion and society.

One of the most effective symbols in drama can be found in Tennessee Williams' *The Glass Menagerie*. Laura, a fragile character, has a collection of equally fragile glass animals, one of which is a unicorn. Laura's attachment to the unicorn indicates her preference for fantasy and her rejection of reality. The unicorn in some cultures has also symbolized virginity, the Virgin Mary, and even Christ. In any case, when Jim, the "gentleman caller," accidentally knocks over the unicorn and it falls to the floor, the horn breaks off. Laura calls it a blessing in disguise, because now the unicorn will look like all the other horses. In other words, the loss of the unicorn's horn symbolizes Laura's return to reality. After her encounter with Jim she will no longer feel unattractive and "freakish," as she puts it, because of her limp and sensitivity. She will feel less different from other people.

(4) Allegory is related to symbolism.

In allegorical works, characters and objects usually represent something more complex than they themselves appear to be. For instance, the rose has been a popular symbol in Western literature. It has been used mostly as a symbol of love, as in the medieval poem "The Romance of the Rose." In this allegory, a lover is admitted to a beautiful park by Idleness. The whole thing takes place in a dream. In the park the lover finds such characters as Pleasure, Delight, Cupid, and, finally, the Rose. After he kisses the Rose, he is driven away by other allegorical figures, such as Danger, Shame, Scandal, and Jealousy. Two French authors were involved and the poem is much too long to summarize completely. It is a classical allegory and it clearly contains symbolic elements.

11d
Rhyme involves an arrangement of similar sounds.

We usually associate the manipulation of sounds with poetry, but it occurs, of course, in all of literature. The language in the plays of Tennessee Williams is often poetic, as is the language in the novels of Virginia Woolf. Here, for instance, is a passage from *Between the Acts*:

> Fly then follow, she hummed, the dappled herds in the cedar grove, who, sporting play, the red with the roe, the stag with the doe. Fly away. I grieving stay. Alone I linger, I pluck the bitter herb by the ruined wall, the churchyard wall, and press its sour, its sweet, its sour, long grey leaf, so twixt thumb and finger.

(1) The word *rhyme* has several meanings.

A *rhyme* can refer to a poem that has rhyming lines. It can mean, in general, the similarity in sound that certain words have. Specifically, it can mean end-rhyme. Hence, when we say *rhyming couplets* we mean two lines that end in the same sound:

> Say what strange motive, Goddess! could compel
> A well-bred lord to assault a gentle belle?
>
> Alexander Pope, "The Rape of the Lock"

(2) End rhyme means using similar sounds at the end of lines of poetry.

The sounds that rhyme are the accented syllables and all that follows. The rhyming, therefore, can involve just one syllable or two or three or even more, though the more syllables that are involved the more difficult the rhyming possibilities. End-rhymes usually involve one or two syllables and, occasionally, three:

hair — fair	mother — brother	readily — steadily
cold — bold	writer — fighter	imitate — intimate
blood — flood	beauty — duty	slippery — frippery
kill — thrill	flying — crying	flowering — towering

(3) Feminine rhymes are rhymes of two or more syllables in which the final syllable is unstressed.

All of the above examples, except those in the first column, are examples of feminine rhyme. In the second column there are *double feminine rhymes*, and in the third column there are *triple feminine rhymes*, the stressed syllable plus two.

(4) Masculine rhymes end in a stressed syllable.

Masculine rhymes include all single-syllable rhymes, as in the first column above, beginning with *hair—fair*. In masculine polysyllabic rhymes the unstressed syllables precede the final stressed syllable: *compel—dispel*.

TO GEORGE SAND
A RECOGNITION

Elizabeth Barrett Browning (1844)

True genius, but true woman! dost deny
The woman's nature with a manly scorn,
And break away the gauds and armlets worn
By weaker women in captivity?
Ah, vain denial! that revolted cry

Is sobbed in by a woman's voice forlorn, —
Thy woman's hair, my sister, all unshorn
Floats back dishevelled strength in agony,
Disproving thy man's name: and while before
The world thou burnest in a poet-fire,
We see thy woman-heart beat evermore
Through the large flame. Beat purer, heart, and higher,
Till God unsex thee on the heavenly shore
Where unincarnate spirits purely aspire!

(5) Off rhyme (near rhyme, slant rhyme) is the use of sounds that are close but not exactly the same.

Consider the following examples of off rhyme.

herd — beard (Shakespeare)
sound — wound (Wordsworth)
good — blood (Dryden)
love — prove (Marlowe)
throng — along (Dickinson)

Since pronunciation changes with time, it is possible that some of the off rhymes above once had the same sound.

In the following poem by Emily Dickinson the second and fourth lines of each stanza are off-rhymed:

Remorse — is Memory — awake —
Her parties all astir —
A Presence of Departed Acts —
At window — and at Door —

It's Past — set down before the Soul
And lighted with a Match —
Perusal — to facilitate —
And help Belief to stretch —

> Remorse is cureless — the Disease
> Not even God — can heal —
> For 'tis His institution — and
> The Adequate of Hell —

(6) Internal rhyme involves similar sounds within a given line of poetry.

Not all rhymes are end rhymes. Within a given line of poetry similar sounds may be used. The main devices involved are:

Alliteration: the repetition of sounds at the beginning of two or more words in the same line of poetry.

> Had we but world enough, and time,
> This coyness, lady, were no crime.
> We would sit down, and think which way
> To walk, and pass our long love's day.

Andrew Marvell

Assonance: the repetition of vowel sounds within a line of poetry or even throughout a group of lines or the whole poem.

> I wake and feel the fell of dark, not day.

G. M. Hopkins

Consonance: the repetition of consonant sounds, especially at the end of a word, within a line of poetry or throughout a group of lines or the whole poem.

> The Devil is dead, good people all!
> Who are the bearers that bear the pall?
>
> One of them thinks he has slain God too,
> With the self-same sword that Satan slew.

Mary Elizabeth Coleridge (1890)

Notice all the alliteration, assonance, consonance, and outright repetition of words in this poem by Gerard Manley Hopkins:

[I WAKE AND FEEL THE FELL OF DARK, NOT DAY.]

I wake and feel the fell of dark, not day.
What hours, O what black hours we have spent
This night! what sights you, heart, saw; ways you went!
And more must, in yet longer light's delay.

With witness I speak this. But where I say   5
Hours I mean years, mean life. And my lament
Is cries countless, cries like dead letters sent
To dearest him that lives alas! away.

I am gall, I am heartburn. God's most deep decree   10
Bitter would have me taste: my taste was me;
Bones built in me, flesh filled, blood brimmed the curse.

Selfyeast of spirit a dull dough sours. I see
The lost are like this, and their scourge to be
As I am mine, their sweating selves, but worse.

11e
Rhythm involves an arrangement of sounds with regular intervals and beats.

It is part of human nature to respond to rhythms. After all, they are inside of us as well as outside of us. We have a heartbeat. We breathe rhythmically. Even the simple act of walking has a rhythm to it. We have an inner clock that measures out time (our circadian rhythm). The world we live in is full of rhythms to which we respond: night and day, the seasons, the tides, the sounds that animals make, from the birds at dawn to crickets at night. The chirps of the snowy tree cricket are so precise that if you add the number forty to the number of chirps per fifteen-second intervals, you get the exact temperature in fahrenheit.

Rhythm is obvious in music and dance, but there are also natural rhythms in language. There are *stressed* and *unstressed* syllables. There is *pause* and *pitch* and the *length* of a phrase or clause. Ordinary speech in English tends to be *iambic*. An "iamb" is a metrical unit made up of two syllables, the first one unstressed, the second one stressed. The following ordinary sentence contains four iambs:

$$\breve{I} \; cám\text{e} \; t\breve{o} \; schóol \; al\breve{o}ne \; tod\breve{a}y.$$
$$1 \qquad 2 \qquad 3 \qquad 4$$

Though there are some natural rhythms in ordinary speech, there is not always a clear pattern. In literature we can manipulate language to create clearer patterns and more pleasing sounds. Rhythm can be varied to suit the material. It can be slower or faster. It can flow smoothly or it can be choppy and full of pauses. It can be a *rising rhythm* or a *falling rhythm*. There are subtleties and variations to suit all poetic occasions from love and death to awe-inspiring nature; from the mysteries of the universe to the microcosmic incidents in a moment as small as a raindrop.

(1) Pauses are used in a variety of ways in poetry.

The pause in poetry, as in music, is very important. It is a fundamental tool of the poet. There can be slight pauses and long pauses and anything in between. There are so many combinations of sounds that can be "poetic" that prosody can hardly be considered an exact science. However, three terms are often used in the discussion of pauses in poetry.

(A) CAESURA (INDICATED IN DIAGRAMMING BY //)

A clear pause or break that can occur anywhere within a line of poetry. Old English poetry, the main example of which is *Beowulf*, is written in lines that are divided into two parts by a strong caesura. This kind of pause remains a useful device. An effective use of the caesura can be found in the following poem by George Peele:

HOT SUN, COOL FIRE

Hot sun, cool fire, tempered with sweet air,
Black shade, fair nurse, shadow my white hair.
Shine, sun; burn, fire; breathe, air, and ease me;
Black shade, fair nurse, shroud me and please me.
Shadow, my sweet nurse, keep me from burning;   5
Make not my glad cause cause of mourning.
   Let not my beauty's fire
   Inflame unstaid desire,
   Nor pierce any bright eye
   That wandereth lightly.   10

(B) END-STOPPED LINES

Though the rules of grammar still apply in most poems, poetry is basically constructed by lines, and there is a natural tendency to pause at the end of each line when you read a poem. If the meaning or rhythm or construction of a line invites a full pause, the line is described as *end-stopped*. A series of full pauses has a clear effect on the overall rhythm. This anonymous poem was written in the early seventeenth century:

THE SILVER SWAN

The silver swan, who living had no note,
When death approached, unlocked her silent throat;
Leaning her breast against the reedy shore,
Thus sung her first and last, and sung no more:
"Farewell, all joys; Oh death, come close mine eyes;   5
More geese than swans now live, more fools than wise."

(C) RUN-ON LINES

When the meaning or construction of a line carries it quickly into the next line, allowing only a minimal pause, the effect on the overall rhythm is quite different. The run-on lines may contribute to the feeling of exhilaration in this poem by Robert Graves:

TO BE IN LOVE

To spring impetuously in air and remain
Treading on air for three heart-beats or four,
Thence to descend at leisure; or else to climb
A forward-tilted crag with no hand-holds;
Or, disembodied, to carry jasmine back
From a Queen's garden — this is being in love,
Armed with *agilitas* and *subtilitas*,
At which few famous lovers even guessed,
Though children may foreknow it, deep in dreams,
And ghosts may mourn it, haunting their own tombs,
And peacocks cry it, in default of speech.

(2) Cadence is a general term that refers to sequences of sound and arrangements of accents.

In free verse, cadence refers to a kind of rhythm that is not measurable in stressed and unstressed syllables but in sequences of sound, emphasis, and accent. Even in poetry free of conventional meter, there must be an element of music. In the following poem there may not be standard patterns of sound, but the sounds are certainly being arranged to provide a suitable cadence for the content:

BALL GAME
Richard Eberhart

Caught off first, he leaped to run to second, but
Then struggled back to first.
He left first because of a natural desire
To leap, to get on with the game.
When you jerk to run to second
You do not necessarily think of a home run.
You want to go on. You want to get to the next stage,
The entire soul is bent on second base.
The fact is that the mind flashes
Faster in action than the muscles can move.
Dramatic! Off first, taut, heading for second,
In a split second, total realization,
Heading for first. Head first! Legs follow fast.
You struggle back to first with victor effort
As, even, after a life of effort and chill,
One flashes back to the safety of childhood,
To that strange place where one had first begun.

(3) Scansion is a way of analyzing meter in poetry.

Scanning a poem means diagramming the lines according to stressed (ˊ) and unstressed (˘) syllables.

When I do count the clock that tells the time . . .

Shakespeare

Diagramming can help to clarify poetic structure.

(4) Meter is the pattern of stressed and unstressed syllables in a line or group of lines or whole poem.

Meter is measured in feet. A foot is usually a stressed syllable with one or more unstressed syllables. The most common meters in English are:

(A) IAMBIC (˘ ˊ)

Iambic meters are made of feet or units with an unstressed syllable followed by a stressed syllable (*iambs*). This is the most widely used meter in poetry written in English, perhaps because it seems natural in ordinary speech. These lines are from an anonymous seventeenth century poem:

> There is a lady sweet and kind,
> Was never face so pleased my mind;
> I did but see her passing by,
> And yet I love her till I die.

(B) ANAPESTIC (˘ ˘ ˊ)

Anapestic meters are made of units with two unstressed syllables followed by a stressed syllable (*anapests*).

> Oh, the flowers are blooming in England today,
> But her soldiers are dying in lands far away.

(C) TROCHAIC (´ ˘)

Trochaic meters are made of units with a stressed syllable followed by an unstressed syllable (*trochees*).

> Take me now in midnight darkness.
> Tell me how the morning's brightness
> Robs our love of peaceful lightness.

(D) DACTYLIC (´ ˘ ˘)

Dactylic meters are made of units with a stressed syllable followed by two unstressed syllables (*dactyls*).

> Cannon to right of them,
> Cannon to left of them,
> Cannon in front of them
>   Volleyed and thundered . . .

Tennyson: "The Charge of the Light Brigade"

(5) Some other terms are useful in the discussion of rhythm.

In addition to the words used to describe the four basic kinds of meter, there are a few other terms that you might find useful in discussions of the subject.

(A) MONOSYLLABIC RHYTHM (´)

A single stressed syllable does not meet the conventional definition of a metric foot since it is not accompanied by any unstressed syllables, but lines made up entirely of such sylla-bles do occur occasionally in poetry. They do not occur very often since they would sound like the unrelieved dripping of a faucet. They may be more suitable for chants and cheers, such as the one that begins: "Two, four, six, eight. . . ." On the other hand, some well-known poets have used such lines. Tennyson wrote, "Break, break, break . . ." And in T. S. Eliot's "The Waste Land" we find "Twit twit twit" and "Jug jug jug jug jug." In the following little poem considerable use is made of monosyllabic rhythm:

P.O.P.
Robert DeMaria

P.O.P.
Perfectly
Ordinary
People.
P.O.P.
pop, POP,
Pop, p.o.p.
popopopopop.
Population.

(B) SPONDAIC RHYTHM (´ ´)

A spondee does not meet the conventional definition of a metric foot, since it is made up of two stressed syllables and no un-stressed syllables. A line made up entirely of spondees is rare, but can occasionally be found. An example is Emily Dickinson's "Wild Nights! — Wild Nights!" (See Chapter 2.) Spondees are more often used to vary other meters.

(C) ACCENTUAL RHYTHM

In poems that are like songs the accents are very strong and can carry along a lot of miscellaneous unstressed syllables.

> Frankie she was a good woman, Johnny he was her man . . .

The cadence of free verse depends a good deal on accents.

(D) RISING RHYTHM

Iambic and anapestic meter are considered *rising*, since each foot ends in a stressed syllable.

(E) FALLING RHYTHM

Trochaic and dactylic meter are considered *falling*, since trochees and dactyls begin with a stressed syllable and fall away into unstressed syllables.

(6) The length of a line is measured in metrical units.

The length of a line of poetry can be described in terms of the number of metrical units (feet) used in that line. The conventional terminology is:

monometer (one unit)
dimeter (two units)
trimeter (three units)
tetrameter (four units)
pentameter (five units)
hexameter (six units)
heptameter (seven units)
octameter (eight units)

Rarely does a line of poetry have more than eight feet. There are certain practical and natural limitations, such as the way we breathe, and the fact that rhyme works better with lines of a reasonable length. Trimeter, tetrameter, and pentameter are the most commonly used line lengths.

(7) **Metrical line patterns are determined by the type and number of metrical units.**

A full description of a measured line of poetry includes the term that describes the units employed, as well as the term that describes the number of units employed. Many combinations are possible. Here are just a few examples:

(A) **IAMBIC TETRAMETER**

  ˘   ´   ˘   ´ ˘   ´ ˘   ´
Come live with me and be my love   (Marlowe)

(B) **IAMBIC PENTAMETER**

  ˘   ´ ˘ ´ ˘   ´ ˘   ´ ˘ ´
When I do count the clock that tells the time   (Shakespeare)

(C) **ANAPESTIC TRIMETER**

  ˘   ˘ ´ ˘ ˘   ´ ˘ ˘ ´
There was a young girl of Peru

  ˘   ˘   ´ ˘   ˘   ´ ˘ ˘ ´
Who had nothing whatever to do   (anonymous)

(D) **ANAPESTIC TETRAMETER**

  ˘   ˘   ´ ˘   ˘   ´ ˘ ˘ ´ ˘   ˘ ´
Oh, the flowers are blooming in England today   (anonymous)

(E) **TROCHAIC PENTAMETER**

  ´ ˘ ´ ˘ ´ ˘ ´ ˘   ´ ˘
Never, never, never, never, never!   (Shakespeare)

(F) DACTYLIC DIMETER

Cánnon to right of them,

Cánnon to left of them,   (Tennyson)

(8) Varying the pattern.

Poetry is a work of art, not a machine like a clock or a metronome. A poem that sticks perfectly to its basic meter is in
danger of sounding monotonous. Most poems, therefore, have
pleasant variations woven into their fabric. These variations
not only relieve the monotony of the meter, but they provide
poets with the flexibility they need to create a wide range of
sounds. A sudden spondee or anapest in a poem made basically
of iambic pentameter can introduce some interesting shades
and subtleties. This poem by Christopher Marlowe is written
basically in *iambic tetrameter,* but notice the occasional variations (for example, the monosyllabic stresses in lines three and
four and the trochee at the beginning of line six).

THE PASSIONATE SHEPHERD TO HIS LOVE
Christopher Marlowe (1599)

Come live with me and be my love,
And we will all the pleasures prove
That valleys, groves, hills, and fields,
Woods, or steepy mountain yields.

And we will sit upon the rocks,   5
Seeing the shepherds feed their flocks,
By shallow rivers to whose falls
Melodious birds sing madrigals.

And I will make thee beds of roses
And a thousand fragrant posies,   10
A cap of flowers, and a kirtle
Embroidered all with leaves of myrtle;

A gown made of the finest wool
Which from our pretty lambs we pull;
Fair lined slippers for the cold,   15
With buckles of the purest gold;

A belt of straw and ivy buds,
With coral clasps and amber studs:
And if these pleasures may thee move,
Come live with me, and be my love.   20

The shepherds' swains shall dance and sing
For thy delight each May morning:
If these delights thy mind may move,
Then live with me and be my love.

11f
Patterns and form are essential in literature.

The nature of literary form is complex and controversial. Scholarly wars have been fought over the definition of form, and whole schools of critical thought have been built on a way of defining it.

(1) *Form* and *genre* are sometimes used as synonyms.

Genre is a French word that means *genus, type,* or *kind*. It can be used very loosely to classify literary works that have various kinds of things in common. It can be used to refer to works that are grouped by content or by structure. Poetry can be considered a genre, but so can specific kinds of poetry, such as the lyric. The novel might be considered a genre, but so might the epistolary novel or the utopian novel. In this sense of the word, drama is a *form* of literature. Comedy, in turn, is a *form* of drama, and *farce* is a form of comedy. Some critics may object to using the word *form* this way, and some may object merely to the looseness with which it is used, but the real controversy has to do with mechanical versus organic form, especially in poetry.

(2) *Mechanical form* suggests that the content of a work can be separated from the techniques by which it is presented.

In such an approach *form* refers exclusively to those techniques, to structures and patterns. In poetry, for instance, form is seen as something "external," as a container into which the contents are poured. That form is usually created out of arrangements of rhyme and rhythm. Formalists believe that "form is everything," and that a poem can be judged strictly in terms of its language, style, and structure.

(3) *Organic form* is a concept preferred by a certain school of thought.

In this approach the form of a literary work is to be found in the whole work. It is that "internal" force that makes the work cohere, that which unifies it. Content, language, style, structure — all are interrelated. There is no separation between content and container. The artistic vision requires a fusion of all the ingredients. It is simpler to describe mechanical form than it is to describe organic form, but perhaps this is because mechanical form is simplistic. This is why some instructors prefer teaching the mechanical approach over the organic approach. Most modern scholars, however, seem brave enough to pursue all the implications of the concept of form as organic. One of these implications is that the grouping of works by genre and mechanics is not a very significant exercise and not a very valid way to understand a work of art. On the other hand, from our point of view, it might be useful to be aware, at least, of some of the conventional patterns and forms in literature, especially in poetry.

(4) There are certain conventional forms in fiction and drama.

There was a time when certain forces in society, especially in literary circles, kept poetry very conventional. Today, poetry has been liberated from these restraints, but, for the most part, fiction and drama have not. The marketplace may have a lot to do with it. There's not much money in poetry today and not much of an audience. The same cannot be said for fiction and drama. Million-dollar deals in mass-market publishing have become commonplace, and television has provided a huge and hungry audience for drama. A large audience tends to create conventions more easily, since there are substantial rewards for those who cater to the general taste, instead of exploring new ways of doing things. The only outlets for experimental work are usually small literary magazines. Such publications have proliferated, but they rarely achieve much circulation.

Formula writing has become widespread in television, film, and fiction. Certain forms dominate these fields. Situation comedies and adventure series, soaps and made-for-television movies have become rigid in format, content, and style. It is hardly necessary to describe the typical sit-com or soap opera. We are all sufficiently familiar with the forms. The same is true of mass-market paperback novels, which are carefully classified according to what the publishers call *genres*, such as romance, science-fiction, fantasy, adventure, mystery, and family saga.

Serious fiction and drama are more daring when it comes to form, but they are still influenced by certain conventions. Most short stories adhere to the conflict–development–resolution sequence. Most narratives are chronological. A few manipulate past and present or objective and subjective elements. Shorter fiction is usually written without major breaks or sections. Longer fiction may be divided into numbered parts. In the novel, the chapter is still the dominant subdivision.

Plays are divided into acts and scenes, usually three acts. Shakespeare preferred five, a convention of *his* time. One-act plays tend to adhere to unity of time and place and employ a single set and very few characters.

Of course, there are refreshing exceptions to these conventions, but they rarely attract sufficient attention to become widely known. This should not discourage the serious writer, whose real satisfaction must come from artistic success rather than financial reward. However, it is not a happy situation, and literary history is full of stories of great authors who spent their lives in misery and poverty only to be recognized posthumously. In an age of mass-communication and pandemic materialism the idealism necessary for honest artistic achievement becomes more and more difficult.

(5) There are certain conventional patterns in poetry.

When we talk about conventional patterns in poetry we are usually referring to mechanical form. Since contemporary poetry has become so dominated by free verse (free-form, open-form verse), there are some instructors who feel that it is not even worthwhile reviewing the conventional patterns. Some even feel that there is some risk of restraining or stifling the young poet. These extreme views, fortunately, do not prevent most workshops from discussing certain traditional patterns of rhyme and rhythm. Let us consider, then, some of the conventional ways in which the lines of a poem have been organized or grouped.

(A) THE STANZA

In measured poems a stanza is a grouping of lines that tends to have a well-defined form in terms of rhythm and usually rhyme. When a poem has more than one stanza, the pattern is usually repeated throughout. Stanzas can be as simple as the two-line couplet or as complex as the nine-line Spencerian stanza or the stanzaic sonnet of fourteen lines. The following terminology is used to describe the length of a stanza:

couplet (two lines)
tercet (three lines)
quatrain (four lines)
pentastich or cinquain (five lines)
sestet (six lines)
septet (seven lines)
octave (eight lines)

(B) COUPLETS, TERCETS, AND QUATRAINS

These groupings of lines have often been called the building blocks of poetry, since, more often than not, they serve as stanzas in longer poems, though they can stand alone as complete poems. Any meter can be used in these basic line groupings, but the rhyming possibilities are rather limited.

A couplet can only use *aa*. A tercet can use *aaa* or *aba*. Quatrains often use *abab*, but sometimes *abba* or some other configuration, especially if the rhyming runs on into the next stanza.

COUPLETS

Two-liners are often used in epitaphs, such as this one from Kipling's "Epitaphs of the War":

> If any question why we died,
> Tell them, because our fathers lied.

Aside from epitaphs there aren't too many two-line poems, but here is one by Ben Jonson called "To Fool or Knave":

> Thy praise or dispraise is to me alike;
> One doth not stroke me, nor the other strike.

The *heroic couplet* is two rhyming lines in iambic pentameter. It was once a popular form used in epic poetry and poetic drama, but it is not found very often in modern verse. There are plenty of examples in the work of Alexander Pope (1688–1744)—these often quoted lines from "An Essay on Criticism," for instance:

> A little learning is a dangerous thing;
> Drink deep, or taste not the Pierian spring:

TERCETS

Stanzas of three lines with a rhyming pattern that is sometimes linked to subsequent stanzas, as in *terza rima* ("third rhyme"), an Italian form that rhymes the middle line of each tercet with the first and third lines of the following tercet. One of the most famous examples in English literature is Shelley's "Ode to the West Wind," which begins:

> Oh wild West Wind, thou breath of Autumn's being,
> Thou, from whose unseen presence the leaves dead
> Are driven, like ghosts from an enchanter fleeing,

Another well-known poem written in tercets rhymes all three lines in each stanza (*aaa*) and uses iambic tetrameter. It is "Upon Julia's Clothes," by Robert Herrick (1591–1674):

UPON JULIA'S CLOTHES

> Whenas in silks my Julia goes,
> Then, then, methinks, how sweetly flows
> That liquefaction of her clothes.
>
> Next, when I cast mine eyes, and see
> That brave vibration, each way free,   5
> O, how that glittering taketh me!

Poems consisting of just one tercet are fairly rare, but Ben Jonson has given us this:

ON SPIES

> Spies, you are lights in state, but of base stuff,
> Who, when you've burnt yourselves down to the snuff,
> Stink and are thrown away. End fair enough.

QUATRAINS

The four-line stanza with a rhyme scheme is the workhorse of poetry. It is long enough to produce a complete and viable poem, but is more commonly used as a building block in longer poems. Quatrains lend themselves either to long lines or to lines that are brief and swift-moving. They are as appropriate for light verse as they are for serious themes. This example from Lord Byron is on the amusing side:

[WHEN A MAN HATH NO FREEDOM TO FIGHT FOR AT HOME]

When a man hath no freedom to fight for at home,
  Let him combat for that of his neighbors;
Let him think of the glories of Greece and of Rome,
  And get knocked on his head for his labors.

To do good to mankind is the chivalrous plan,
  And is always as nobly requited;
Then battle for freedom wherever you can,
  And, if not shot or hanged, you'll get knighted.

(C) MORE COMPLEX STANZAS

A brief mention here of some of the longer and more complex stanzas should be sufficient to indicate just how long and complex they can be:

Rhyme royal: seven lines of iambic pentameter (*ababbcc*)
Ottava rima: eight lines of iambic pentameter (*abababcc*)
Spencerian stanza: nine lines, eight of them iambic pentameter, one of them iambic hexameter (*ababbcbcc*)

(D) SONNETS, BALLADS, AND LIMERICKS

Some of our complete poetic forms have been around for a long time and are very conventional. Some of us forget, because we are living in a free-verse era, that for thousands of years and in cultures all over the world, poetry was full of conventions. Not only did tradition fix the forms of poetry, but it often determined the content and even the very wording.

The ancient Greeks brought formal poetry to a high level of sophistication that covered a wide range from the lyric to the epic to the poetic drama. The word *lyric*, in fact, comes from the Greek. Originally it meant a poem accompanied by a musical instrument, usually a lyre. Formalism was dominant throughout the development of English poetry. It has only been in the decades since World War I that there has been a widespread break with traditional forms, a natural reflection of the rebellion against *all* traditional forms, political, moral, and aesthetic. This modern artistic freedom is the main characteristic of contemporary poetry, but some of the sturdier conventional forms still survive, among them *sonnets, ballads,* and *limericks*.

SONNETS

The sonnet was imported to England in the sixteenth century from Italy, where it was developed during the Renaissance. It has fourteen lines and a rhyme scheme. The meter is usually iambic pentameter. The sonnet has survived for five hundred years because it is a useful form for the development of a single idea. The most famous collection of sonnets (154 of them) was written by Shakespeare, but almost every major poet has been drawn to the form, from Spenser to Donne to Edna St. Vincent Millay and more contemporary poets.

The Shakespearean sonnet, though it is a complete stanza in itself, has within it three quatrains in which alternate lines rhyme (*abab*) and a rhyming couplet that usually contains a concluding thought. The Petrarchan sonnet, which is not nearly as popular, is made of an octave (*abbaabba*) and a sestet (*cdcdcd*, or some other variation). The Petrarchan sonnet is also known as the Italian sonnet. Here is an example of each of these types of sonnets. Notice that the rhyme scheme in Donne's Petrarchan sonnet is *abbaabbacddcee*.

94
William Shakespeare (1564–1616)

They that have power to hurt and will do none,
That do not do the thing they most do show,
Who, moving others, are themselves as stone,
Unmoved, cold, and to temptation slow;
They rightly do inherit heaven's graces
And husband nature's riches from expense;
They are the lords and owners of their faces,
Others but stewards of their excellence.
The summer's flower is to the summer sweet,
Though to itself it only live and die,
But if that flower with base infection meet,
The basest weed outbraves his dignity:
For sweetest things turn sourest by their deeds;
Lilies that fester smell far worse than weeds.

10
John Donne (1572–1631)

Death, be not proud, though some have calléd thee
Mighty and dreadful, for thou are not so;
For those whom thou think'st thou dost overthrow
Die not, poor Death, nor yet canst thou kill me.

From rest and sleep, which but thy pictures be,
Much pleasure; then from thee much more must flow,
And soonest our best men with thee do go,
Rest of their bones, and soul's delivery.
Thou'art slave to fate, chance, kings, and desperate men,
And dost with poison, war, and sickness dwell,
And poppy'or charms can make us sleep as well
And better than thy stroke; why swell'st thou then?
One short sleep past, we wake eternally
And death shall be no more; Death, thou shalt die.

BALLADS

A ballad is a narrative poem easily remembered because of its simple stanza construction: four lines rhyming *abab* or *abcb*, with four accented syllables in the first and third lines and three in the second and fourth lines. Sometimes a refrain is added to each stanza. Ballads are often anonymous. Since they are handed down orally, there may be many variations of the same tale.

FRANKIE AND JOHNNY
Anonymous

Frankie and Johnny were lovers,
    Lordy, how they could love,
Swore to be true to each other,
    True as the stars up above,
        He was her man, but he done her wrong.   5

Frankie went down to the corner,
    To buy her a bucket of beer,

Frankie says "Mister Bartender,
    Has my lovin' Johnny been here?
        He is my man, but he's doing me wrong."   10

"I don't want to cause you no trouble
    Don't want to tell you no lie,
I saw your Johnny half-an-hour ago
    Making love to Nelly Bly.
        He is your man, but he's doing you wrong."   15

Frankie went down to the hotel
    Looked over the transom so high,
There she saw her lovin' Johnny
    Making love to Nelly Bly.
        He was her man; he was doing her wrong.   20

Frankie threw back her kimono,
    Pulled out her big forty-four;
Rooty-toot-toot: three times she shot
    Right through that hotel door,
        She shot her man, who was doing her wrong.   25

"Roll me over gently,
    Roll me over slow,
Roll me over on my right side,
    'Cause these bullets hurt me so,
        I was your man, but I done you wrong."   30

Bring all your rubber-tired hearses
    Bring all your rubber-tired hacks,
They're carrying poor Johnny to the burying ground
    And they ain't gonna bring him back,
        He was her man, but he done her wrong.   35

Frankie says to the sheriff,
    "What are they going to do?"

The sheriff he said to Frankie,
    "It's the 'lectric chair for you.
        He was your man, and he done you wrong."   40

"Put me in that dungeon,
    Put me in that cell,
Put me where the northeast wind
    Blows from the southeast corner of hell,
        I shot my man, 'cause he done me wrong."   45

LIMERICKS

Limerick is a county in Ireland, and legend has it that this light and amusing and sometimes naughty poetic form originated there. A limerick consists of five lines that rhyme *aabba*. There are three stresses in the first, second, and fifth lines, and there are two stresses in the third and fourth lines. Limericks are often anonymous.

> There was a young girl of Peru
> Who had nothing whatever to do,
>   So she sat on the stairs
>   And counted her hairs —
> Six thousand, four hundred, and two.

(E) OTHER FORMS

There are many other traditional forms, one of which is worth mentioning here, partly because it is used by Dylan Thomas in his widely appreciated poem, "Do Not Go Gentle into That Good Night." This poem is a *villanelle*, which consists of six stanzas — five triplets and a quatrain. There are only two rhymes: *aba, aba, aba, aba, aba, abaa*. The lines tend to have five stresses and to be iambic.

(F) BLANK VERSE

Any poetry written in unrhymed lines of iambic pentameter is called *blank verse*. These lines can be arranged in stanzas or they can go on indefinitely, as in poetic drama, where they have proven extremely effective, especially in Shakespeare's plays. Blank verse appeared in England in the sixteenth century. Though some minor authors first made use of it in drama, it was Christopher Marlowe, born the same year as Shakespeare, who first used it brilliantly. One of his most famous passages is from *Doctor Faustus:*

> Was this the face that launched a thousand ships,
> And burnt the topless towers of Ilium?
> Sweet Helen, make me immortal with a kiss.
> Her lips suck forth my soul: see where it flies.
> Come, Helen, come give me my soul again.
> Here will I dwell, for heaven is in those lips,
> And all is dross that is not Helena.
>
> (Act V, scene i)

(G) GRAPHIC FORMS

Poems designed for the eye can be considered along the same lines as those that have mechanical requirements, though they can also be considered with free verse because they are not subject to the usual conventions of rhyme and rhythm. Many poems have a visual dimension, but some poems depend *primarily* on the visual. The author actually draws a picture or design with his words, as in the case of this famous mouse's tale (tail) in *Alice's Adventures in Wonderland:*

Fury said to a
mouse, That he
met in the
house,
"Let us
both go
to law:
I will
prosecute
you. Come, I'll
take no denial;
We must
have a trial:
For really
this morning
I've nothing
to do."
Said the
mouse to the
cur, "Such a
trial,
dear Sir,
With no
jury or
judge,
would be
wasting
our breath."
"I'll be judge,
I'll be jury,"
Said
cunning
old Fury:
"I'll
try the
whole
cause,
and
condemn
you
to
death."

(6) Free verse has no rigid patterns of rhyme and rhythm.

Robert Frost said that free verse is "like playing tennis with the net down." The remark suggests that it is not only easier to write free verse but also unfair, not playing the game according to the rules. The formalists would applaud him; the believers in organic form would not. Furthermore, they might even object to the term *free verse* on the grounds that it suggests freedom from form. They tend to prefer the terms *free form* or *open form*.

The use of free verse in the twentieth century has a good deal to do with the search for a more natural way of using the English language. Poets such as Ezra Pound and William Carlos Williams objected to the artificiality and awkwardness created by the attempt to stay within traditional principles that we inherited from ancient Greece and Rome via literary giants such as Milton. A rapidly changing and democratic society such as America could not put up with the rigidity of formal poetry for long. Inevitably, American poetry found its own voice in a freer approach, a more natural language. The frontier country that embraced Huckleberry Finn could hardly feel at home with the rigid formalness of Milton.

Since all poetry has *some* form, "free form" is a bit misleading. By free verse we mean a way of making effective sounds without counting accents and syllables systematically. In addition, free-form verse does not depend on strict rhyming; it depends more on diction, cadence, and tone for its "music." The chief characteristic of free verse is "infinite variety," but the bottom line is a verbal creation that pleases the ear, the mind, and even the eye, whether it is achieved with free form or closed form.

With so much variety it is difficult to categorize free verse. The only approach that makes sense is to discuss each poem individually, to explore its language, its imagery, its cadence, and especially that central mystery that holds it all together and gives it unity and significance.

In the following poem what we have, primarily, is a very visual image. The boy standing on the road, wishing he could go home, sums up with great simplicity his reaction to the death of his father. The language is not merely appropriate, it is part of the whole effect, the stark simplicity. The cadence, too, is simple and child-like.

UPON LEARNING OF HIS FATHER'S DEATH
Fred Byrnes

A sandy-haired boy
in a flannel shirt
stands on a dirt road
with dust swirling
Hands in blue-jean pockets
fingering a fifty-cent piece
Wishing he could come home

Here is another free-form poem, this one about a mother. Notice how the title becomes part of the poem. There is no conventional structure here, no rhyme scheme or pattern of accents, though the general cadence of the first stanza seems echoed in the second stanza. It might have been written as prose, but something would have been lost. There is a visual dimension as the poem stands, and each line emphasizes something. The concise language sharpens the sustained image — the mother as protector and predator, as hawk and owl.

MY RIGHT EYE
Siv Cedering Fox

is a hawk
that circles all night
looking for the small mice
of dreams
to run out from under
my pillow.

My left eye is an owl
alert in its hollow
waiting for nightmares to come
on the wings
of bats.
In the morning

I am the predator
returning from my hunt,
the gatherer come back
to my nest.
My family is fed.
My eyes ache.

EXAMPLE 11a

WHAT LIPS MY LIPS HAVE KISSED
Edna St. Vincent Millay

What lips my lips have kissed, and where, and why,
I have forgotten, and what arms have lain
Under my head till morning; but the rain
Is full of ghosts tonight, that tap and sigh

Upon the glass and listen for reply,   5
And in my heart there stirs a quiet pain
For unremembered lads that not again
Will turn to me at midnight with a cry.
Nor knows what birds have vanished one by one,   10
Thus in the winter stands the lonely tree,
Yet knows its boughs more silent than before:
I cannot say what loves have come and gone;
I only know that summer sang in me
A little while, that in me sings no more.

EXAMPLE 11b

TRIANGLE OF LIGHT

Pamela Harrison

Perhaps it was nothing so much
as the tone of my mother's voice
that stopped me dead in the hall
as she talked softly to my brother,
in the kitchen, unaware — a tone
golden as the light that slants
beneath the trees late in August,
warming the gate, the path,
the gently sloping, green and gold field.

Even now, I see the shape of that long hall,
in whose deep recesses every possibility
waited to be realized, and the light
spilling in a triangle from the kitchen —

You must imagine the flooding gold
of that triangle of light, how it slid

across the threshold, heavy with its own
fullness, tilting like a wave cresting
to break into the shadows of the hall
where I was stranded, listening,
gulping knowledge like a burning cup.
Then imagine what
the Siamese twin must feel, the searing
fire along his breastbone where the knife
severs him from half he ever was or knew,
cleaving a wholeness he would spend his life
searching to complete.

Had you rounded the corner behind me then,
like a driver coming to rest behind a car
in whose rear window a plastic doll nods,
agreeing to everything, you might have sensed
my complicity, as something in me acceded —
no, affirmed the fitness of her choice: for *yes*,
I loved him, too, naturally, loved him
first and best, so that the moment passed,
breaking away. . . .

Sometimes it happens crossing a snowy yard
over whose smooth, chill expanses the evening
shadows lean, deeply blue, or, stepping
from some dim interior into the jarring
refractions of sunlight striking crisscross
off traffic: a moment you pause to remember
something, telling yourself you must remember
what was suddenly so present and so clear —

though, now, all you can recall
is the pressure of its importance, tangled
in the light, in the color, blue or gold.

EXERCISES

DISCUSSION

1. "What Lips My Lips Have Kissed" (Example 11a) by Edna St. Vincent Millay is a sonnet. Describe its pattern of rhyme and rhythm. Is it a Shakespearean or Petrarchan sonnet?

2. Comment on the imagery in this poem. Find specific examples of images and explain them.

3. What is this sonnet all about? How does it compare with the sonnets by Shakespeare and Donne?

4. Pamela Harrison's "Triangle of Light" (Example 11b) is less formal than Edna St. Vincent Millay's sonnet. Comment on its structure. Are there any patterns at all? Is it free verse?

5. Why is this poem called "Triangle of Light"? Discuss the imagery in the poem.

6. What happens in this poem? Is there a narrative element?

WRITING

1. Write a sonnet in either the Petrarchan or Shakespearean fashion.

2. Write a poem about some aspect of nature, using as many images as possible.

3. Write a poem in which you make *allusions* to at least *four* of the following: Venus, Prometheus, Job, Adam and Eve, the Apocalypse, Atlantis, Caesar, Napoleon, the Crusades, Babylon, Watergate, Woodstock, Disneyland, Hollywood, Dracula, Frankenstein.

4. Write a quatrain in iambic tetrameter that rhymes *abab*.

5. Complete a poem in *anapestic tetrameter* that begins:

   Oh, the flowers are blooming in summer today,
   But our soldiers are dying in lands far away.

6. Write a modern version of "The Passionate Shepherd to His Love" by Marlowe (11e). Start with the same opening line: "Come live with me and be my love." Use the same meter but your own content.

7. Write three limericks.

8. Write a ballad, with or without a refrain.

9. Write a free verse poem about something one of the following titles might suggest:

   Going to the Mall
   The Winter Solstice
   Children of the Night
   The Graveyard Shift at Seven Eleven
   Discovering Old Toys in Dark Places
   Falling in Love with Faraway Places
   Eyes that Smile and Lips that Lie

CHAPTER
TWELVE

THE MANUSCRIPT

Over the years, great works of literature have been written in many strange ways, in handwriting difficult to decipher, on scraps of paper of various sizes and color, on scrolls, in folios and notebooks. Before the standardization of spelling, there was a great deal of orthographical inconsistency. Shakespeare sometimes spelled the same word two or three different ways. Even his name comes down to us in a variety of spellings.

Individual eccentricities in the use of language and the preparation of manuscripts will probably always be with us, but certain technological advances have tended to stabilize the language and establish certain manuscript conventions. Movable type, the linotype machine, the typewriter, and the computer have all influenced the way we prepare and present written materials. Modern publishers expect manuscripts to be prepared in a way that is suitable for the publishing process. There are practical considerations, such as sufficient space for editorial and production notations. The exact manuscript form expected depends, to some extent, on the type of material involved.

12a
Fiction

If you have ever seen the manuscript of a piece of fiction after it has been through the mill at a publishing house, you will understand the logic of what is considered standard manuscript form. When the author's copy is returned, after the work has been edited, set, and printed, it is full of notations.

There are several kinds of editing involved in the processing of a manuscript. The *supervising editor* of a project usually edits for content and discusses possible changes with the author. Major changes of this sort take place before the manuscript goes into production. The author makes the negotiated changes and provides the publisher with a clean manuscript. Some authors will allow their editors a free hand in making changes; others will insist on approving all alterations.

Next comes the *copy editor* or *house editor*, who reviews the spelling, punctuation, grammar, and even certain purely factual matters, such as dates or geographical locations. These basic things are called matters of "style" (in a limited sense of the word). Since there is still no universal agreement on all matters of style, every publisher uses some standard style sheet, sometimes one developed in house, such as the *New York Times* style sheet. A widely used reference book is *The Chicago Manual of Style* (The University of Chicago Press).

The *production editor*'s job is to translate design decisions into notations for the printer and typesetter. Typographic instructions are made, involving such things as choices of type, line length, and indentation.

Usually, proofreading refers to the reviewing of galleys or a *proof* of the material that has been set in type. Since even the best typesetters make mistakes, both publisher and author review the galleys. Standard proofreaders' marks (see pages 266–267) are used for making corrections.

The main points to keep in mind about standard manuscript form for fiction are the following:

(1) Paper

Use standard 8½″ by 11″ white typing paper of a reasonable weight, usually a number 1 grade of 20 pound bond.

(2) Margins

Leave 1½″ at the top and left-hand side; 1″ at the bottom and right-hand side.

(3) Page numbers

Page numbers should be in Arabic numerals in the upper right-hand corner, about ½″ in and ½″ down from the corner.

(4) Indentation

Standard indentation is five spaces. Indent all paragraphs. Some designers prefer that first paragraphs and paragraphs following major headings (if any) be set flush left, as in this book.

(5) Titles

Titles of short stories or chapters of longer works should be placed three inches below the top of the page and should be typed in upper-case letters (capitals).

The marks of punctuation

⊙ Period

⋏ or ⅄ Comma

=/ or ⟋ Hyphen

:/ Colon

;/ Semicolon

⋁ Apostrophe

!/ Exclamation mark or
Exclamation point

?/ Question mark or
Interrogation point

/en/ or e̶n̶ En dash

/em/ or e̶m̶ One em dash

/2em/ or 2/e̶m̶ Two em dash

( ) or (|) Parentheses

Quotation marks
(double)

Quotation marks
(single)

The marks of typography

⌀ Delete or take out

⌀ Delete and close up

stet Let it stand "as is" or
disregard changes
marked

⋀ Caret. insert

∼ or ⊓ Transpose

↺ Turn over (letter or cut
upside down)

wf Wrong font

⊗ or ✕ Replace
broken or defective
letter

Insert space

⊂ Close up space

tr	Marginal symbol for transpose	✓	Equalize space
♂	Transfer circled matter to position shown by arrow	⊔	Indent one em or insert one em quad
⌐²	Two ems	*caps* or <u>Scott</u>	Capital letters
¶	Paragraph	S. C. or <u>Scott</u>	Small capitals
No ¶	No paragraph	C+S.C or <u>Scott</u>	Caps and small caps
⊏	Move to left	*rom*	Roman (change from italic to roman)
⊐	Move to right	*sp*	Spell out
⊐⊏	Center	?	Query to author
⊓	Move up	*out sc*	Out. see copy
⊔	Move down		No paragraph — run in
//	Align	*ld*	Insert 2 point lead
‖	Straighten or justify	⊥ or ⊥	Push down space
lc or *l.c.*	Lower case	✳	Asterisk
ital or <u>Scott</u>	Italic	V³	Superior figure or letter
bf or <u>Scott</u>	Boldface	^3	Inferior figure or letter

(6) Spacing

Use a double space between all lines. Between major parts of stories or chapters use four spaces.

(7) Corrections

Do not type over mistakes. Use a lift-off or white-out technique. Avoid hand-written corrections or insertions or marginal notes.

(8) Copies

Make a carbon copy as insurance against losing the manuscript, but, as soon as possible, make photo copies from the clean original. Avoid copying machines that leave smudges or lines.

Page 269 shows a diagram of standard manuscript form for fiction:

12b
Poetry

Since poetry has a typographical dimension, it is difficult to define a standard presentation. Poems depend heavily on line length and spacing. These are determined by the author, not by editors or printers. Freely structured poetry should be typed on 8½″ by 11″ white paper, and it should include the title of the poem and the author's name, either in the upper left-hand corner or at the end of the poem.

If the style of the poem permits, it is single-spaced, centered on the page, and usually uses a capital letter at the beginning of each line.

Use standard 8½″ x 11″   Page number here—   1
white paper.   can be omitted on title page.

Top margin 1½″

Standard indentation five spaces.

Title 3″ from top of page

TITLE IN UPPER CASE

Double double space after
title. Begin first paragraph
with or without inden-
tation. Subsequent para-
graphs indented five spaces.

Left-hand margin 1½″

Right-hand margin 1″

Double space the entire manuscript. Use double
double spacing to indicate breaks, parts, or subdivisions. Pica type is preferred to elite. Avoid
fancy typefaces such as italic. Use a good grade of
twenty pound bond. Do not use erasable bond.

Use mechanical correction, if possible. Avoid
handwritten corrections or insertions. Make a carbon only as insurance against losing the manuscript.
Make photocopies from the clean original. Avoid copy
machines that leave smudges or lines.

Bottom margin 1″

Untitled poems are usually referred to by their first line in brackets: [I Wake and Feel the Fell of Dark, not Day].

12c
Drama

A manuscript for a play written for the stage must take into account certain practical considerations. Plays are intended for production. Therefore:

(1) Characters

The names of the characters must be clearly indicated, so that the actors can see at a glance who speaks the lines. The names of the characters appear in caps at the left-hand margin and are followed by a colon. The rest of the script is indented.

(2) Dialogue

The dialogue must be clearly separated from all other notations. It begins immediately after the colon, unless there are some intervening stage directions. If the dialogue continues for more than one line, all subsequent lines are indented, using the standard paragraph indentation of five spaces.

(3) Stage directions

The stage directions must appear in a form that distinguishes them from the dialogue. They are italicized (underlined) and often placed in parentheses.

(4) Notations

Notations about how the character is to deliver certain lines (for example, *angrily, playfully*) can be distinguished from ordinary stage directions by being italicized and placed in parentheses after the character's name and before the colon.

There is obviously some flexibility in the above form, and you will find considerable variety in published playscripts. Some writers indent the characters' names and bring everything else back to the left-hand margin. Some use italics for stage directions, but not parentheses. In anthologies the publisher usually selects a format that is consistent throughout the collection.

In addition to using a clear manuscript form, the playwright must provide some introductory information: a *cast of characters* and an indication of *time* and *place* (scene). Some writers are very concise about this information; others are quite detailed. G. B. Shaw's introductory material, for instance, was often very elaborate.

Here is a brief example of the most commonly used playscript form. It is the beginning of a one-act play (or possibly a longer play) created merely as an illustration. You may want to try your hand at completing it.

INTIMATE STRANGERS

CHARACTERS

LAURA HOLMAN, *an attractive young woman, 21, from Boston.*
PAUL CONRAD, *a handsome, experienced man of thirty or so.*

TIME

The present, mid-summer

PLACE

A hotel room in the Berkshire Mountains of Massachusetts

(The stage grows light as someone draws open the curtains of the sliding glass doors that lead to a narrow terrace. The room is done in a typical modern resort style. It is neat and functional. Laura wakes up. She is scantily dressed and looks confused. When her eyes settle on Paul, who is silhouetted against the window, she is startled.)

PAUL: Good morning, Mrs. Conrad!

LAURA: *(holding her head and squinting her eyes because of the sunlight)*. Mrs. Conrad? *(She looks around, as though there might be another woman in the room.)* Who's Mrs. Conrad?

PAUL: *(smiling)*. You are, sweetheart. *(He advances toward the bed.)*

LAURA: *(holding a sheet to her breast and shrinking away)*. Now, wait a minute. Let me think. This is all a dream, right?

PAUL: *(as though he assumes she is joking)*. Right! And I hope we never wake up.

LAURA: *(frowning)*. I remember a lot of champagne bottles.

PAUL: We had a party.

LAURA: Who was there?

PAUL: Just me and you, darling. *(He sits on the bed.)*

LAURA: What was the occasion?

PAUL: The anniversary of our first meeting.

LAURA: But that was just a week ago at the Beacon. I remember that. I had had a big fight with my mother and step-father and told them I was moving out. I called Mary, my college roommate, and she said she'd put me up for a while. Then I guess I went to the Beacon for a drink. I was upset, naturally.

PAUL: There were tears in your eyes when I saw you sitting alone. I couldn't resist asking you what was wrong. We had a long talk. Later, you said you loved me. I felt the same way. It was all very sudden — love at first sight, I guess.

LAURA: *(beginning to remember).* That's what it felt like at the time.

PAUL: I called you up the next day and asked you to marry me.

LAURA: I thought it was a joke.

PAUL: But you said *yes.*

LAURA: You said something about spending the weekend together.

PAUL: Well, we did — I mean, we are. Only it's not an ordinary weekend; it's our honeymoon.

LAURA: *(shaking her head).* I must have really been out of it!

PAUL: You were very happy.

LAURA: It must have been the champagne.

PAUL: You mean, you don't remember?

LAURA: I do and I don't. The details are a little fuzzy. *(She looks at her left hand and sees a wedding ring there.)*

PAUL: We drove across the border and found a justice of the peace.

LAURA: A white house with green shutters?

PAUL: Yes.

LAURA: Next to a church and a graveyard?

PAUL: That's right!

LAURA: Oh, my God!

PAUL: You're not sorry, are you?

LAURA: No! Yes! I mean, I don't know. It's all sort of crazy. We hardly know each other.

PAUL: When you fall in love, nothing else is worth knowing.

LAURA: Why didn't we wait?

PAUL: If we had waited, you might have changed your mind. When we first met you told me how much you hated the way your head ruled your heart, and how you have never allowed yourself to fall in love.

LAURA: If I had been sober, I guess I'd never be here.

PAUL: *(moving closer and becoming amorous).* That's right. Now, aren't you glad we *are* here?

LAURA: *(holding him off).* Actually, I don't even know where we are, and — and, don't be offended, Paul, but I don't know anything about you. Where do you live? What do you do?

PAUL: What difference does it make? I'll take good care of you. We'll be very happy.

LAURA: *(charmed by his handsomeness and manner, but frightened by his evasiveness).* I need some coffee or something. I don't feel very well.

PAUL: I'm not surprised. We've been to the moon and back. This is the planet Earth, darling. Welcome back to reality.

(to be continued)

12d
Film and television

The standard manuscript form for film and television scripts is not quite the same as the manuscript form for a stage play. Here we are dealing with media that involve great flexibility and movement. The characters are not trapped on a live stage. Through electronic magic they can be moved anywhere and do anything. They are seen by the eyes of cameras, not the eyes of a live audience. They can be zoomed in, faded out, and frozen. Their movements can be speeded up and slowed down. They can take part in sweeping epics, battles, and natural disasters.

In order to deal with the practical requirements of film and television, the following manuscript form is recommended:

(1) Title

Use capital letters for the title. For scripts intended for submission a complete title page is necessary. It should include the title, author's name and address, or author's agent and address, and a brief indication of the type of script it is: an episode in a television series, an original screenplay, an adaptation of a novel or short story, and so on.

(2) Cast of characters

The cast of characters should be listed with a brief description of each character. There should be a heading for this list, and the heading and names of the characters should be capitalized. The descriptions should be in upper and lower case. Use a double space between characters.

(3) Master scenes

The line for master scenes begins at the left-hand margin and is entirely capitalized. Three elements are included: interior (INT.) or exterior (EXT.), location (WASHINGTON SQUARE PARK), and time (DAY or NIGHT). Use a dash between location and time.

Example:

EXT. WASHINGTON SQUARE PARK — DAY

A master scene is any scene that requires a set shift, even if it is from one room to another of the same house, or from outside the front door to inside the front door, or from outside of an automobile to inside of an automobile. Filming cannot be continuous when a new set is required, even though in the finished product there is an illusion of continuity.

(4) Stage directions

Stage directions include descriptions of action, places, and people. They are single-spaced and use upper and lower case. They begin at the left-hand margin. There is a double space before and after. Characters and camera notations are capitalized.

(5) Dialogue

Dialogue is centered, fifteen spaces from each margin, right and left. It is single-spaced. The speaker's name is centered and fully capitalized and followed by a double space. A passage of dialogue is also followed by a double space.

(6) Dialogue notations

Notations about how the words are spoken should be placed in parentheses one space under the character's name. Do not overuse such notations. Such notations, such as O.S. (off stage) or V.O. (voice over) are placed in parentheses beside the character's name.

(7) Camera notations

Camera notations are to be used only when absolutely necessary to describe the desired effect. Detailed camera notations are the business of the director, not the writer. They are fully capitalized. The most common notations are:

FADE IN: capitalized and followed by a colon, this notation begins at the left-hand margin and is used at the beginning of every script and at the beginning of each act, if there are several. It is followed by a double space.

FADE OUT: capitalized and used with a period at the very end of the script. It appears flush with the right-hand margin, and is preceded by a double space.

CUT TO: used with caps and colon, flush with the right-hand margin. It indicates a major shift in scene, not just minor set shifts. It is preceded by a double space and followed by a new master-scene line.

POV: indicates a shot from the point of view of one of the characters.

CLOSE UP: a close view of a portion of the shot, usually a face, perhaps just the eyes or hands or an object, such as a knife or a gun.

INSERT: used in master-scene lines in capitals for such items as a letter or newspaper story or clock. Inserts are isolated in the script because they are shot separately and inserted later.

ESTABLISHING SHOT: a form of insert, usually a stock shot of a location to let the viewer know where we are. For instance, a shot of the New York skyline, or the White House, or the Eiffel Tower in Paris. Used in master-scene lines.

Example:

EXT. ESTABLISHING SHOT OF NEW YORK SKYLINE — DAY

STOCK SHOT: any shot taken from the files and inserted to indicate place or action, such as an airliner taking off or landing, a train arriving or leaving. Used in master-scene lines.

MONTAGE: a series of rapid cuts showing a process or the passage of time or any series of related actions. For instance, a character thinking of her father might have a brief vision of the various stages of her childhood. Shot separately and inserted. Used in master-scene lines.

Example:

MONTAGE. MEMORIES OF CHILDHOOD

KIM riding a tricycle with her father nearby. KIM as a scout. KIM graduating from high school, her father in the audience, looking proud.

FULL SHOT (or WIDE SHOT): a full view of the set.

TWO SHOT: a close shot, usually just full enough for two people.

REVERSE SHOT: a shift in POV from one person to another, usually used in conversations between two people.

OVER THE SHOULDER SHOT: The camera's eye is behind the character and takes in the back of the character and beyond.

HIGH ANGLE: a shot that looks down at the action and has the effect of diminishing and distancing the characters and the action as though the POV were God-like.

LOW ANGLE: a shot from a POV that looks up at the action, so that the characters seem to loom and grow larger.

MOVING SHOT: a shot that follows a moving object, usually a person or a vehicle. The camera seems to stand still.

FOLLOWING SHOT: a shot that follows the action, but with a camera that moves along with the object.

EXAMPLE 12

APPOINTMENT IN SAMARRA

W. Somerset Maugham

There was a merchant in Bagdad who sent his servant to market to buy provisions, and in a little while the servant came back, white and trembling, and said, "Master, just now when I was in the market-place I was jostled by a woman in the crowd and when I turned I saw it was Death that jostled me. She looked at me and made a threatening gesture; now, lend me your horse, and I will ride away from this city and avoid my fate. I will go to Samarra and there Death will not find me." The merchant lent him his horse, and the servant mounted it, and he dug his spurs in its flanks and as fast as the horse could gallop he went. Then the merchant went down to the market-place and he saw Death standing in the crowd and he came to Death and said, "Why did you make a threatening gesture to my servant when you saw him this morning?" "That was not a threatening gesture," Death said. "It was only a start of surprise. I was astonished to see him in Bagdad, for I had an appointment with him tonight in Samarra."

The following adaptation of a short story by W. Somerset Maugham illustrates basic filmscript form:

APPOINTMENT IN SAMARRA

CHARACTERS

SERVANT, *a simple, uneducated man*
MASTER, *a wealthy merchant of Bagdad*
DEATH, *in the spectral form of an old woman*

FADE IN:

EXT. ESTABLISHING SCENE OF ANCIENT BAGDAD — DAY
A walled city of many mosques, narrow streets and crowds.

EXT. THE MARKETPLACE IN BAGDAD — DAY

A noisy series of stalls and shops where buyers bargain loudly with peddlers. FULL SHOT of the whole market. Then CLOSE UP of the SERVANT, who is shopping for fruit and vegetables at a stall where he must compete with many women. A woman behind him jostles him. He turns to her with an annoyed look, which turns quickly to a look of horror. What he sees is a skeleton-like face framed in a black shawl. It is DEATH in the form of an old woman. He runs away, pushing everyone aside.

INT. MASTER'S HOUSE IN BADGAD — DAY

The home of a wealthy man. Typical old Arab style. Arches and tiles and rugs. The MASTER is seated at the table, having a light lunch. Another servant, a woman, attends him. The SERVANT comes rushing in.

                    SERVANT
                  (breathless)

          Master! Master! You must help me. My
          life is in danger.

MASTER

Now, now, what is this all about?
Can't you see that I am eating?

SERVANT

Please, master, listen to me. I was
in the marketplace, getting the
provisions you asked for when I was
nudged by a ghostly creature who was
the very spectre of death. I am
afraid that she has come for me.
She made a threatening gesture at
me. I am sure I am going to die.
I must get away. I must escape
this fate.

MASTER

But if it is your fate, there is no
escaping it.

SERVANT

Yes, yes, I must try. I must flee
this city. I will go to Samarra,
where I am not known, where no one
will find me. Please, sir, lend me
your horse. Let me make my escape.

MASTER

If you insist, you may take the
horse, but I think perhaps you have
made a mistake. I will go myself
to the marketplace and find out
what this is all about. You are too

young to die. Perhaps the figure of
Death mistook you for someone else.

SERVANT

Oh, thank you, Master. Thank you!

He exits hastily.

EXT. STABLE OF MASTER'S HOUSE IN BAGDAD — DAY

SERVANT takes horse from stable and mounts. He rides off at a
gallop. MOVING SHOT lingers on his retreat.

EXT. MARKETPLACE IN BAGDAD — DAY

The MASTER makes his way through the crowd, pushing aside
lower class people, who show their humility when they see he is a
rich man. MEDIUM SHOT of MASTER looking here and there.
PAN of market stalls and crowd. CLOSE UP of MASTER spotting
the person he is looking for. He makes his way toward DEATH, the
old woman.

MASTER
(calling out)

You! You there!

DEATH turns to look at him. CLOSE UP of horrible face in a black
shawl.

DEATH

What is it, sir?

MASTER

My servant was here this morning and
said that you made a threatening

gesture towards him. I want to know
why.

DEATH

I'm sorry, sir. That was not a
threatening gesture. It was only
a start of surprise. I was astonished
to see him here in Bagdad, for I
had an appointment with him tonight
in Samarra.

FADE OUT.

CHAPTER
THIRTEEN

FUNDAMENTALS
OF WRITING

This chapter will help you with the most common problems in the fundamentals of writing. It has been put together with creative writing students in mind and is not intended as a comprehensive guide to college composition, which is usually a prerequisite for any more advanced work in writing.

13a
Grammar

In creative writing the most important rule to remember is that it is not ordinary *correctness* of language that counts, but aesthetic *effectiveness*. In short, whatever works for your story, poem, or play is what you should use. Language is the clay of the art of writing, and it can be molded into some strange and exotic forms. Keep an open mind, but don't forget the basic conventions of your language. Experiment at times, but don't be pointlessly ungrammatical.

(1) Sentence fragments

A sentence needs a subject and a predicate. The sentence has to be about someone or something (the subject), and something has to be said about that subject (the predicate). In general, avoid sentence fragments, unless you have a stylistic reason for using them. They often appear in dialogue, because certain characters talk that way. Some writers consciously use sentence fragments for emphasis. If you do use fragments, you should do so for a reason and not merely by accident.

Examples:

The best matador in Spain. [fragment]
Killed by a bull. [fragment]
The best matador in Spain was killed by a bull. [complete]
Since I was going to England. [fragment]
Since I was going to England I bought a map. [complete]
Being an only child. [fragment]
Being an only child is not easy. [complete]

(2) Fused sentences and the comma splice

Don't use a comma when a period is needed. Don't run two sentences together without an appropriate punctuation mark or conjunction. As in the case of the sentence fragment, there are literary exceptions. In a technique called "stream of consciousness," which is used to capture the thoughts of a character, punctuation is often ignored on the assumption that the mind's more primitive mode of expression is not concerned with such details (see Chapter 9).

Examples:

She decided to go to Chicago, the bus was leaving at eight. [comma splice; the comma should be a period]

The train to Paris was fast he would arrive before Maria. [fused sentence; it needs a period or a conjunction]

The train to Paris was so fast that he would arrive before Maria. [correct]

(3) Mixed construction

If a sentence begins with one type of construction and ends with a different type, it will contain a *mixed* or *shifted construction*.

Examples:

Because of my lack of ability is why I failed the course. [*correct:* Because of my lack of ability I failed the course; *or:* My lack of ability is why I failed the course.]

Shakespeare is a writer who, although he wanted fame and fortune, he did not sacrifice his art. [*correct:* Shakespeare is a writer who, although he wanted fame and fortune, did not sacrifice his art; *or:* Although Shakespeare wanted fame and fortune, he did not sacrifice his art.]

(4) Coordination

To coordinate two or more words, phrases, or clauses is to place them in a construction that lends equal weight to each element. They can be joined by coordinating conjunctions — *and, but, or, nor, for, so, yet* — as well as correlatives such as *either . . . or*. Coordinate elements are often separated by a comma or semicolon. *And which* and *and who* (*whom*) should not be used to coordinate unless a preceding *which* or *who* has been used. Avoid excessive or illogical coordination.

Examples:

I will go to *France* or *Italy*. [coordinate nouns]
He arrived in America *with high hopes* but *with no money*. [coordinate phrases]

If you have talent, and *if you work hard*, you will succeed. [coordinate clauses]

I gave my last dollar to an old man with a crippled leg, and whom I didn't even know. [*and whom* can only be used after a previous *whom*; *correct:* I gave my last dollar to an old man with a crippled leg, whom I had seen in the village, and whom I didn't even know.]

I went to London, and I went to Paris, and I went to Rome, and I had a very good time. [excessive coordination]

(5) Subordination

When two related ideas of unequal importance appear in a sentence, the relationship between them must be made clear by proper subordination. The *main clause* conveys the basic idea. One or more dependent elements add information. It is necessary to choose the proper subordinating conjunction in order to indicate the exact relationship involved. *Like* is not a subordinating conjunction and should not join two clauses.

Examples:

He returned the money *before anyone realized it was missing.* [The subordinate clause, in italics, indicates *when* the main action takes place.]

If I have enough money, I'll take a trip to London. [The subordinate clause indicates the *condition* under which the main action will take place.]

He climbed to the top of the mountain, *which gave him a good view of the sea.* [The subordinate clause indicates *relation*.]

He looked *like he had seen a ghost.* [incorrect use of *like,* which is not a conjunction; *correct:* He looked *as if he had seen a ghost.*]

(6) Modifiers

Any word, phrase, or clause that describes, limits, qualifies, or defines another element in the sentence is called a *modifier.* Adverbs and adjectives, for instance, are modifiers. One common error is to use an adverb when an adjective should be used, or an adjective when an adverb should be used. Another common error is to leave a modifier dangling, especially a participial phrase. Such phrases function as adjectives and must be clearly linked to a substantive (noun or pronoun). In the following example, the participial phrase should modify the missing subject (*he* or *she*) and not *the sun*. Avoid the habit of starting too many sentences with participial phrases, even if they do not dangle.

Examples:

He ran *swift* and *quiet* through the woods. [should be *swiftly* and *quietly*]

He could not play the violin very *good*. [should be *well*]

The roses smell *sweetly*. [should be *sweet*]

Coming home late at night, the sun began to rise. [dangling participle; *correct:* Coming home late at night, she saw the sun beginning to rise.]

(7) Case

Words can have different forms when they serve different functions in a sentence. *I* as the subject becomes *me* as an object and *my* as a possessive. The objective form is used after a preposition. *Who* is subjective and *whom* is objective. Nouns use an apostrophe in their possessive form. Pronouns do not.

Examples:

I think that *my* novel will make *me* famous. [subjective, possessive, objective]

Between *you* and *me* I think John is a thief. [objective after preposition]

To *whom* did you give the money? *Who* gave you your instructions? [*whom* is an object and *who* is a subject]

It's *John's* first story, but *its* plot is terrific. [correct use of possessive]

(8) Agreement

Agreement between a subject and a verb or between a noun and its pronoun means, in each case, that both items "agree" in (have the same) person and number. A singular subject takes a singular verb, even if a plural noun intervenes between the subject and verb. A plural subject takes a plural verb, even if there is an intervening singular noun between the subject and verb. A pronoun should agree in number and person with its antecedent regardless of what sort of elements are placed between it and its antecedent. If there are two subjects, one of which is plural, the other of which is singular, the verb agrees with the nearer one. Antecedents involving *kind of, sort of, type of* take singular pronouns, but the results are often so awkward that it might be better to avoid the construction. A collective noun can be either singular or plural, depending on the context.

Examples:

The bark of these trees *is* infested with bugs. [The verb *is* agrees with *bark* and not with the intervening plural *trees*.]

Amanda, together with a few others, finished *her* story before the deadline. [*Her* agrees with *Amanda* and not with the intervening plural.]

One or both stories are going to be published in the literary magazine. [When one subject is singular and the other plural, the verb agrees with whichever one is nearer.]

This sort of apples *is* good for applesauce. [correct, but awkward]

The committee is pleased with the decision. [collective noun as singular]

The committee are in serious disagreement. [collective noun as plural]

(9) Tense

Using the wrong tense means choosing that form of the verb that will place the action in the wrong period of time, either in an absolute sense or in relation to what is taking place in the rest of the sentence or paragraph. The six principle tenses are the following: *present* (I see); *past* (I saw); *future* (I shall see); *present perfect* (I have seen); *past perfect* (I had seen); *future perfect* (I shall have seen).

Avoid shifts in tense within a given passage or within the entire narrative. Most stories are told in the past tense, but in certain kinds of stories the present tense can prove effective. In any case, be consistent.

To indicate an action that took place in the past before another action that also took place in the past use the past perfect tense. To indicate an action in the future that will take place before another action in the future use the future perfect tense.

Examples:

I was visiting Amanda, and we were having a very serious discussion. All of a sudden, in walks Michael and ruins everything. [tense shift]

By the time he arrived *I had already hidden* the money. [past perfect]

I will start writing my book next week, but before then *I will have finished* all the necessary research. [future perfect]

13b
Punctuation

When we speak we naturally break up the flow of language with certain pauses or stops or more subtle indicators in order to make what we are saying as clear as possible. One might call these voice manipulations invisible punctuation marks. We all know what a question sounds like, and we know how to pause parenthetically. Since written language came after spoken language, this invisible punctuation had to be made visible. In English we have developed certain conventions of punctuation.

(1) Period

The period is commonly used to end a declarative sentence or even an imperative sentence. It is also used with some abbreviations, though, over the years, there has been more and more of a tendency to omit periods in abbreviations. For instance, we use *USA* instead of *U.S.A.*, and *NY* instead of *N.Y.* Periods are used with *Mr.* and *Mrs.*, but not with *Ms* and *Miss*. When in doubt consult a good dictionary.

(2) Comma

A comma indicates a slight pause within a sentence and is used in a wide variety of constructions. The following are the most common functions of the comma.

(a) A comma is used before the conjunction that joins two main clauses.

(b) A comma is used after an introductory dependent clause to separate it from the main clause.

(c) Commas are used to separate the parts of a series, unless conjunctions are used instead. They are not used with adjectives that are supplementary.

(d) Non-restrictive modifiers should be set off by commas. No commas should be used with restrictive modifiers.

(e) Commas should be used with appositives, parenthetical elements, and absolute phrases.

(f) Dates and geographical expressions should contain commas to separate their various parts.

(g) A comma usually precedes a quotation, though there are exceptions (see Chapter 8).

Examples:

You can try to make your living as a writer, or *you can prepare yourself for a more conventional career.* [two main clauses]

If I have enough time this summer, I plan to work on a novel. [introductory dependent clause]

Last week there were demonstrations *in England, in France,* and *in Germany.* [a series of phrases]

I stood under a *big* oak tree with a *little* old lady. [supplementary adjectives]

Angelica, *who has a wonderful sense of humor*, amused us all evening. [non-restrictive modifier]

The woman who amused us all evening was named Angelica. [restrictive modifier]

He went to Harvard, *one of the best universities in America*. [non-restrictive appositive]

When Laura was accepted at Harvard, she was, *naturally*, very pleased. [naturally is parenthetical]

She decided, *her novel having failed*, that she would go to graduate school. [absolute phrase]

On *April 2, 1988*, she arrived in *Boston, Massachusetts*. [dates and places]

Spinoza said, "Desire is the very essence of man." [quotation]

(3) Semicolon

A semicolon can often be used instead of a coordinating conjunction between independent clauses. A semicolon can also be used to separate a series of long or complicated elements within a sentence that are themselves subdivided by commas.

Examples:

Among Shakespeare's most impressive creations are Hamlet, a confused prince who thinks too much; King Lear, a proud old man who realizes his fault too late; and Lady Macbeth, an ambitious woman who drives her husband to murder. [a series, the parts of which contain commas]

(4) Apostrophe

An apostrophe is a mark used to show the omission of a letter or letters in a word or words forming contractions, or to show possession in nouns and indefinite pronouns. To show joint possession it is only necessary to use the apostrophe with the last owner named (for example, "John and Mary's house"). An apostrophe is not used in personal pronouns. It is used to form plurals of dates, numbers, or words being considered as words. It is used in certain phrases that express time or distance, though they do not really involve possession (for example, "a month's pay").

(5) Quotation marks

Quotation marks are used to enclose all direct quotations except those set apart in different type or distinguished by other mechanical means, such as special spacing. They indicate that the material was written by someone else and is only being reproduced. In fiction they indicate that one of the characters is speaking directly. Quotation marks are also used to enclose titles of shorter works, such as short stories, short plays, poems, paintings, or parts of books. To indicate a quotation within a quotation, use single quotation marks.

(6) Other punctuation marks

(a) *The question mark* is used for direct questions, but not in indirect questions.

(b) *An exclamation point* is used to show some strong emotion or surprise.

(c) *A dash* is used to indicate an interruption in thought. It is very useful in dialogue. Dashes can also be used to set off parenthetical elements.

(d) *Parentheses and brackets* are used to set off words, phrases, clauses, or even sentences that are inserted in a sentence by way of comment, explanation, or translation, but which are structurally independent of the sentence. In a parenthetical sentence within another sentence, the normal punctuation falls *outside* of the parentheses. In a separate parenthetical sentence the punctuation falls *inside* the parentheses. Brackets are used for editorial comments and translations. They are also used when a parenthetical remark falls within another parenthetical remark. Example: [Mary (who was Ted's lawyer) disagreed.]

(e) *Ellipses* (. . .) are used to indicate that within a quoted passage certain words have been omitted. If the omission takes place at the end of a sentence, a period is added (. . . .), but under no circumstances should there be more than four dots. In fiction, ellipses are sometimes used in passages of stream of consciousness to indicate a lack of continuity. This device should not be overused.

Examples:

Where did you get that money? [direct question]

He asked him where he got the money. [indirect question]

"Fantastic!" he said when he saw the view. [exclamation point for an emotional expression]

He said, "The murderer is — ," but before he could finish he died. [dash indicates interruption]

She bought that house — it is hard to believe — for less than forty thousand dollars. [parenthetical dashes]

Nil desperandum (never despair)! [foreign words in italics, translation in parentheses]

"Nothing appears more surprising . . . than the easiness with which the many are governed by the few." [Ellipses indicate that a phrase has been omitted from this sentence by David Hume.]

13c
Mechanics

(1) Capitals

In prose the first word of every sentence should be capitalized. This is also true of most poetry, but, in addition, the first letter of every line is usually capitalized. There are many exceptions, of course, especially in modern poetry.

Capitals are used in proper names, races, religions, states, cities, streets, societies, historical periods, days of the week, months, the names of courses (History 71), but not for the names of subjects (history). Capitals are used when a title that identifies the position someone holds precedes the name and is thought of as part of the name (for example, President Truman). This is also true of family relationships (Uncle John).

Capitals are used for the major words in all titles. Articles, prepositions, and conjunctions are not capitalized in titles, but the first and last words are always capitalized, no matter what they are. Anyone who has seen the poems of e.e. cummings knows that there are exceptions.

Capitals are used sometimes for emphasis. To attract special attention to a word one might capitalize the first letter or even the entire word. The proper noun "God" (in the Judeo–Christian tradition) and all the pronouns that refer to God are capitalized, but the common noun *god* is not capitalized.

The four directions are not capitalized unless they refer to specific regions of a country (the South, the West, the East, the North).

Examples:

Here's to my comrades, one and all,
Those who will live and those who will fall.

(anonymous)

[In conventional poetry the first letter of each line is capitalized.]

During the Korean War, President Truman ordered General McArthur home and relieved him of his command. [Capitalize names of wars and titles that are used as part of a name.]

Columbia University is located in New York City. Sheila took a course there in the Romantic Movement. [Capitalize names of institutions and cities and historical periods.]

Aldous Huxley wrote a novel called *After Many a Summer Dies the Swan*. [Capitalize major words in titles.]

The early Christians believed in God and rejected the pagan gods of other religions. [In the Judeo-Christian tradition *God* is a proper noun, and *gods*, meaning other deities, is a common noun.]

The only god she ever worshiped was Money. [A word can be capitalized at times for special emphasis.]

(2) Abbreviations

In formal writing some abbreviations are acceptable and some are not. Among the acceptable abbreviations are *Mr.*, *Mrs.*, *Dr.*; and *A.M.*, *P.M.*, *A.D.*, and *B.C.*, all of which are usually printed in small capitals; and *Y.M.C.A.* (and certain other organizations). Titles such as *Professor* and *President* should be written out, as should be the names of countries, states, cities, avenues, and streets.

Acronyms are words formed from the first letters of many words or from parts of those words without the benefit of periods. If an acronym is generally recognizable, it is acceptable in formal writing. Otherwise, the entire name of the object or organization should be used. Some of the acronyms that have been in general use for a long time are: *NASA*, *NATO*, *SAT*, and *HUD*.

(3) Numbers

Numbers should be written out if it is possible to do so in one or two words. If two words are required, they should be hyphenated. If a number requires more than two words, it should not be written out. Numerals should be used for numbering pages, for numbers in addresses, and for dates.

(4) Italics

Italics can be indicated in unprinted manuscripts by underlining. They are used for titles of publications, for names of ships, and for elements needing emphasis. Italics are also used for foreign words and expressions.

Examples:

He was reading *Pride and Prejudice* by Jane Austen and enjoying himself immensely on the maiden voyage of the *Titanic* in 1912. [Titles and names of ships are in italics. Dates are in numerals.]

As long as this is *my* house I will do in it what I please. [italics used to emphasize *my*]

It was a case of *de facto* segregation. [Foreign words and expressions are written in italics.]

13d
Spelling

Routine spelling questions can usually be handled with the help of a good dictionary and a few basic guidelines.

(1) Compound words

Compound words are made up of two or more words that serve as a single unit or modifier. Some of these are written as one word; some are hyphenated. Consult a good dictionary for specific cases. When they appear before a noun almost any words can be linked by hyphenation to form a single adjective, but the same words are not hyphenated when they appear after the noun.

Examples:

He was a well-known painter. [hyphenated before a noun]

As a painter he was well known. [no hyphenation after a noun]

The Marines established a beachhead with a do-or-die attitude. [hyphenated before a noun]

There were first-rate firemen and fire engines at the scene. [hyphenated before a noun]

(2) Final silent e

A final silent *e* is usually dropped when an ending beginning with another vowel is added (*dine, dining*). A final silent *e* is retained in certain words to distinguish them from words that have similar sounds or spellings (*dye, dyeing*). A final silent *e* is usually retained when an ending beginning with a consonant is added (*hate, hateful; shape, shapely*). The final *e* is not dropped in words ending in *ce* and *ge* when an ending beginning in *a* or *o* is added (*change, changeable; notice, noticeable*).

(3) Other spelling rules

(a) A final consonant is doubled when a suffix beginning with a vowel is added if the following conditions are involved: the consonant ends a stressed syllable or a word of one syllable, and the consonant is preceded by a single vowel. The word *begin* meets these conditions. When the suffix *-ing* is added, the consonant *n* is doubled and we get *beginning*. The word *talk* ends in a consonant, but the preceding letter is not a vowel. Therefore, when we add *-ing* we get *talking*.

(b) A final *l* should not be dropped before adding *ly* (*continual, continually*).

(c) Put *i* before *e* except after a *c* that is preceded by a vowel. After an *l*, *i* usually comes first (except *leisure*). After a *c*, *e* usually comes first, except in words ending in *ient* and *iency* (*receive, deceive, relief, science, efficient, proficiency, believe*).

(d) In a word ending in *y* preceded by a consonant, change the *y* to *i* when an ending beginning with anything except *i* is added to it (*lady, ladies*). For words ending in *ie*, drop

the *e* and change *i* to *y* before adding *ing* (*tie, tying; lie, lying*).
(e) Only three verbs end in ceed (*exceed, proceed, succeed*). Others that sound similar end in *cede*, except *supersede*.

13e
Diction

One of the most important ingredients in good writing is choosing exactly the right word for every situation. This is especially true for poetry.

(1) Word choice

We all have two kinds of vocabulary. One is *passive* and consists of all the words we can recognize when we read or listen to someone talk. The other is *active* and consists of all the words we are capable of using when we write or speak. When we write we must depend on the words that we have complete command of in order to guarantee precision and avoid unfortunate connotations. The *denotation* of a word is its literal meaning. Its *connotation* may be more subtle and may include certain feelings, ideas, and value judgments.

Examples:

[Preferred word choice in parentheses]

I want you to vote for Joe Boss, one of the greatest *politicians* (*statesmen*) in America. He has always been *truthful* (*sincere*) and *all tied up in his work* (*devoted to his public duties*).

This little *shack* (*house*) is for sale. It has an *outmoded* (*old-fashioned*) fireplace and *curious* (*quaint*) old windows. It has recently been *scraped and painted* (*redecorated*). It is located on a lovely *plot of earth* (*piece of land*) near an *overgrown* (*wooded*) area.

(2) Triteness (clichés)

The word *trite* comes from the Latin *tritus*, meaning *rubbed* or *worn out*. Trite expressions or clichés are expressions, often similes or metaphors, that have been used so often that they are worn out. They have lost their originality, their color, and their effectiveness. They should be *avoided like the plague* (for example), unless, of course, you are writing dialogue for a boring character who is inclined to use such expressions.

Examples:

Avoid like the plague	Nervous as a cat
Busy as a bee	Pretty as a picture
After all is said and done	Quick as lightning
At one fell swoop	Sleep like a log
Cheap as dirt	Trembling like a leaf
Clear as a bell	The early bird catches the
Dumb as an ox	worm.
Fat as a pig	Something is rotten in
Few and far between	Denmark.
Thin as a rail	In the final analysis
Method in his madness	Last but not least

(3) Jargon

The manner of speaking or writing peculiar to a certain occupation or profession is called *jargon*. The worlds of business, education, medicine, law, sports, and government generate a lot of jargon, a lot of specialized language, some of it evasive and euphemistic, some of it technical. The military long ago turned a *retreat* into a *strategic withdrawal*. Businessmen are fond of making verbs out of nouns such as *priority*, which becomes *prioritize*. In sports, *underdogs* are always out to *upset leading contenders*. Politicians talk about *human rights* and the *democratic process* and often consume a ton of language to tell us that *the future lies ahead*.

If you have characters who talk this way, then write realistic dialogue. Otherwise, try to avoid jargon.

(4) Slang (and other informal language)

The impulse to say things in an informal and colorful way seems to be natural and universal. Every language has its slang, as does every generation. Many of the expressions appear overnight like wild mushrooms, and some of them disappear just as quickly. The word *jazz* has stuck because it describes a kind of music, but expressions such as *jazz up* and *all that jazz* seem to be fading out.

Some slang is created by giving a new meaning to an old word. *Hock*, for instance, is old word that means "the joint of the hind leg of certain animals." About a hundred years ago it acquired the slang meaning "to pawn" or "to borrow money against some collateral." In more recent decades it came to mean "to shoplift," but that meaning is now disappearing. Other such words include: *cool, crazy, grass, acid, swell, haymaker* (a knockout punch). Some slang requires the combining of words in a new way: *goon* (from *gorilla* and *baboon*), *hangout, hangover, hotshot*. Some slang is sheer invention: *dork, scam, boondoggle*.

Colloquialisms are often informal abbreviations of formal words: *phone, comp, prof, math, auto, psych*. Illiteracies involve errors in grammar or spelling, but are often part of the every-day regional speech: *ain't, hain't, disremember, hisself, their-selfs, heared, sorta, kinda.*

Obviously, you will have to use informal language in dia-logue, but keep in mind that such language changes rapidly and can even identify the generation of the speaker. A jazz-age character might say, "We had a swell time at the roadhouse." A more contemporary character might say, "We partied all night at a club."

How much informal language you use, aside from dialogue, depends on your style. If you are attempting to write formal, classical prose, then you should probably avoid informal expres-sions or use them with caution.

(5) Accents

Many writers have attempted to capture regional accents in their works. The most famous, perhaps, is Mark Twain. *Huck-leberry Finn* is told in the first person by a poorly educated, but very amusing, boy of thirteen. The attempt to put on paper the actual sound of a dialect means abandoning grammar and all the conventions of spelling. It means trying to "sound out" the language. Some readers find this kind of writing hard to read. One way around this difficulty is to suggest the accent in a limited way and to use more normal language otherwise (see Chapter 8).

(6) Glossary (usage)

Listed here are a few samples of the problems in usage that might confront the writer. For more complete coverage see one of the standard reference books on usage, such as H. W. Fowler's *Dictionary of Modern English Usage* or Margaret Nicholson's *Dictionary of American–English Usage*.

accidently: An incorrect form of *accidentally.*

advice, advise: *Advice* is a noun. *Advise* is a verb.

affect, effect: *Affect* is a verb that means "to influence." As a noun *effect* means the "result." As a verb *effect* means "to bring about," as in: *Antibiotics effected a revolution in medicine.*

aggravate: Incorrectly used to mean "irritate." It means "to make worse."

allusion, illusion: An *allusion* is a reference to something. An *illusion* is a distorted idea of reality.

alot: Incorrect spelling of *a lot.*

already, all ready: *Already* means "before." *All ready* means "all prepared."

alright: Incorrect spelling of *all right.*

altogether, all together: *Altogether* means "entirely." *All together* means "all in a group."

among, between: *Between* is used with two objects. *Among* is used with three or more.

awhile, a while: Awhile is an adverb (*we stayed awhile*). *A while* is used after a preposition (*we stayed for a while*).

being as (that): Incorrect for *because.*

borrow off: Incorrect for *borrow from.*

bust: Informal for burst.

center around: Illogical for *center on.*

complement, compliment: A *complement* is something that completes. A *compliment* is praise.

consensus of opinion: Redundant. Consensus means "majority opinion."

disinterested: Means "impartial" not "uninterested."

eminent, imminent: *Eminent* means "famous." *Imminent* means "about to happen."

explicit, implicit: *Explicit* means "expressed openly." *Implicit* means "implied."

farther, further: *Farther* is usually used for distances. *Further* means "additional" in other contexts.

fewer, less: *Fewer* is used with things you can count in units. *Less* is used with general quantities (money, fuel).

fun: Should be used as a noun and not as an adjective.

go, goes: Should not be used for *say* (*says*).

hanged: *Hanged* means "executed." Otherwise use *hung.*

hanging out: Slang when it means "being somewhere without any special purpose."

hopefully: Incorrect when used to replace the verb *to hope* (*I hope, he hopes*). Correct when used as an adjective (He looked hopefully toward the sky.)

imply, infer: *Imply* means "to suggest." *Infer* means to "conclude."

irregardless: Incorrect for *regardless.*

lay: Incorrect when used instead of *lie* (I want to lie down).

liable to: Informal when used in place of *likely to.*

like: Incorrect when used as a conjunction instead of *as* or *as if.*

myself: Incorrect when substituted for *I* or *me.*

of: Incorrect when used instead of *have* (I could have done it).

okay: Informal. Also spelled *O.K.*

principal, principle: *Principal* means "main" or "chief." *Principle* is a noun that means "basic truth."

real: Informal when used as an adverb instead of *very.*

so: Incorrect as a substitute for *very* (She's always so tired).

stationary, stationery: Stationary means "not moving." *Stationery* is paper.

use to: Incorrect when used instead of *used to.*

-wise: A suffix used in a lot of jargon (*costwise, timewise,* comfortwise). Should be avoided in formal prose.

13f
Good writing is not just a matter of correct grammar and punctuation — it is a matter of effectiveness.

Here are some other fundamentals to consider.

(1) Logic

Good writing depends in part on precision, and being precise often means being logical. Avoid irrelevancies, hasty generalizations, and contradictions. Use your common sense.

Examples:

[all illogical]

He's probably a war criminal, because everybody in the village hates him and he's an old alcoholic, who reminds me of a horrible sergeant I had when I was in the army.

Although there are portions of the play that are extremely amusing, it is obviously a work of great significance.

I like Hardy's novels because I have always enjoyed reading them.

Television is a menace to society. Look at all the violence it has caused.

(2) Clarity

All writing should be clear, whether it is a description of how to fill out your income-tax forms or a novel that looks into the secrets of the human heart. Sometimes it is an overly complex style and a pompous vocabulary that leads to a lack of clarity. Sometimes a statement can be accidentally ambiguous.

Examples:

The cryptical involutions of this megalomaniac drew him into the crepuscular depths.

He met Miranda at the football game, which he thought was terrible.

(3) Emphasis

There are various ways to emphasize those elements in your writing that need special attention. There are simple mechanical devices, such as italics and capitalization. There is the repetition of key words or phrases. Also, there is the rhetorical question and the manipulation of word order. Sometimes, not revealing the full meaning of a sentence until the very end will create suspense. This device is known as a *periodic* sentence. If there is a series in a sentence, it can be arranged so that it builds from the weakest to the strongest element.

Examples:

All you need in life is love. [Periodic sentence. The meaning is not revealed until the final word.]

I believe in *work*, the doctrine of *work*, the religion of *work*. [using italics for emphasis]

Is there anything wrong with materialism? Is there anything wrong with wanting to be comfortable instead of uncomfortable? [rhetorical questions for emphasis]

"Reputation, reputation, reputation! O, I have lost my reputation! I have lost the immortal part of myself, and what remains is bestial. My reputation, Iago, my reputation!" [repetition for emphasis]

—Shakespeare: *Othello*

The movie was good; it was brilliant; it was the best movie I had seen all year. [a series that builds from mildest to strongest]

(4) Repetition

Though repetition can be used for emphasis, it can also be misused. The pointless repetition of certain words and phrases can mar your prose, and the excessive repetition of ideas can be boring. Redundancy sometimes means repetition in general, but certain expressions are labeled redundant because a part of them will express the whole meaning, which makes the rest of the expression superfluous. For example, consider "true facts" (what is true is a fact; what is a fact is true).

Examples:

Some writers are better writers than other writers, but sometimes the inferior writers have more commercial success than the superior writers. [excessive repetition]

In the book *Brave New World*, the author, Aldous Huxley, gives us a picture of the future world several hundred years from now. [redundancies: "the book," "the author," and "the future," should be omitted]

(5) Wordiness

Wordiness in prose can be a weakness, but in poetry it can be a disaster. Avoid circumlocutions (roundabout expressions), irrelevancies, and padding.

Examples:

In conclusion, I would like to say that it is, more or less, important, in my opinion, to create characters that are, in a sense, alive and have all the characteristics of living people. [wordy because of pointless qualifying phrases and repetition]

(6) Awkwardness

Awkwardness is something you can detect with your ear. Clumsy writing can be the result of any number of things, such as word choice, word order, sentence length, or a poor combination of sounds. Rhyming may be good for poetry but it is usually damaging to prose.

Examples:

The author, Thomas Hardy, of this story, in my opinion, gives very good details in it. [awkward because of word order]

The object of the game seems to me to be to see who can score the most points. [awkward repetition of sounds]

The slow sloop slid through the soft surf to the glistening shore. [awkward because of excessive alliteration]

(7) Variety

Without some variety in sentence length and pace, your prose can become as monotonous as a metronome.

Examples:

The soldier looked toward the mountain. The mountain looked mysterious. The clouds were very dark. Daylight was fading. The soldier turned back. The path was rough. Soon it was dark. [deadly repetition of the same sentence pattern]

EXERCISES

The fundamentals of writing can be improved in the following passages. Rewrite these passages, eliminating the weaknesses in grammar, punctuation, mechanics, spelling, diction, and effectiveness:

1. She was a child of the streets. Abandoned by her parents at the age of 10. She lived in the ruined rubble of collapsing

buildings in the south bronx. There were other wild or-phans in those ruins without parents. They herded together for survival and prayed on unsuspecting victims, and whom even pitied them thus being lured into a trap. Her name was Jennifer she could have been a star an actress or something on account of her beautiful looks, but no her life was wasted. They found her dead when she was only 12.

2. He thought of education like he thought of being fed by his mother when he was a small little child. She was always forcing food into his mouth, parting his teeth with the hard spoon, hurting him. Growing up his mother's voice haunted him, because she was always scolding him for this and that. So he could not open his mind to education and he rejected education and remained uneducated for a long time. One day when he was laying on his bed and starring out the window he saw a white seagull. Gliding on the wind, the freedom it epitomized stirred his heart and soul. He sud-denly knew what he had to do and everything was different from that point in time onward.

CHAPTER
FOURTEEN

WRITING AS A CAREER

There are many careers for people interested in writing. They include such jobs as newswriting and reporting, whether for print or broadcast journalism; editing and publishing; technical writing; advertising copywriting; and publicity writing. However, what we are mainly concerned with here is the difficult task of making a career of creative writing, which means, in most cases, freelancing.

Creative writing as a career is not easy, but it is possible. Many writers make money from writing fiction, poetry, plays, and scripts for the visual media or radio, but the percentage of freelance writers who can actually support themselves exclusively from writing is very low. A few, of course, become millionaires, but the odds aren't much better than the odds for winning the lottery. Most writers who are willing to gamble on freelancing are also sensible enough to have back-up jobs.

Many of them teach English. Some of them teach writing workshops. Others prefer "mindless" jobs that only require putting in time and do not interfere with what is going on in their heads. Alan Dugan, the Pulitzer Prize winning poet, once worked in a factory that made plastic anatomical parts for medical students. It used to be traditional for young writers to support themselves by holding a wide variety of odd jobs. They were laborers, truck drivers, waiters, dishwashers, fishermen, farmers, carpenters, and so on. If they became successful, they looked back rather fondly on these experiences, which they felt contributed to their awareness of the "real" world. More recently, young writers have tended to use the academic world as a haven. The expansion of writing programs has provided more jobs, and many universities have created graduate programs and liberal grants for writers, which has made it easier for young writers to survive, but some of the old-timers argue that knocking about in the outside world was better preparation and that the halls-of-ivy shelter has produced too many "academic" writers.

Whichever school of thought appeals to you, here are some of the practical things you ought to know about writing as a career:

14a
Writing is a craft.

There is a continuing dispute over whether or not writing can be taught. Certainly, genuis and talent cannot be taught, but craft is another matter. Whether writers are self-taught or educated in some formal way, they must learn that craft, even if, eventually, they do innovative and unconventional things in their literary efforts. Writers learn from what they read and from discussions of what they have written. Here are some useful books on the craft of writing and a very good guide to writing programs:

INTERVIEWS

Plimpton, George, ed. *Writers at Work*. New York: Viking Penguin Inc., ser. 1–8 (1958–88).

FICTION

Burroway, Janet. *Writing Fiction*. 2nd ed. Boston: Little, Brown and Company, 1987.

Forster, E. M. *Aspects of the Novel*. New York: Harcourt Brace Jovanovich, 1956. (Lectures delivered at Cambridge University in 1927.)

Gardner, John. *The Art of Fiction*. New York: Alfred A. Knopf, 1984.

Hills, Rust. *Writing in General and the Short Story in Particular*. New York: Bantam, 1979.

Minot, Stephen. *Three Genres*. 3rd ed. New York: Prentice-Hall, 1982. Covers fiction, poetry, and drama.

Surmelian, Leon. *Techniques of Fiction Writing: Measure and Madness*. New York: Doubleday, Anchor Books, 1969.

POETRY

Drake, Barbara. *Writing Poetry*. New York: Harcourt Brace Jovanovich, 1983.

Fussell, Paul. *Poetic Meter and Poetic Form*. rev. ed. New York: Random House, 1979.

Garret, George. *The Writer's Voice*. New York: Morrow, 1973.

Gibson, Walker. *Poems in the Making*. Boston: Houghton Mifflin, 1963.

Jerome, Judson. *On Being a Poet*. Cincinnati: Writer's Digest Books, 1984.

Nemerov, Howard. *Figures of Thought*. Boston: Godine, 1978.

Preminger, Alex, ed. *The Princeton Handbook of Poetic Terms*. Princeton: Princeton University Press, 1986.

Wallace, Robert. *Writing Poems*. 2nd ed. Boston: Little Brown and Company, 1987.

Williams, Miller. *Patterns of Poetry*. Louisiana State University Press, 1986.

DRAMA

Baker, George Pierce. *Dramatic Technique*. Boston: Houghton Mifflin Company, 1919.

Bentley, Eric. *Life of the Drama*. New York: Atheneum, 1964.

Cole, Toby, ed. *Playwrights on Playwriting*. New York: Dramabooks, Hill and Wang, 1961.

Egri, Lajos. *The Art of Dramatic Writing*. New York: Simon and Schuster, 1966.

FILM, RADIO, AND TELEVISION

Blum, Richard A. *Television Writing: From Concept to Contract*. New York: Hastings House, 1980.

Coopersmith, Jerome. *Professional Writer's Teleplay/Screenplay Format*. New York: Writers Guild of America, East, 1977.

Herman, Lewis. *A Practical Manual of Screen Playwriting*. Cleveland: World Publishing, 1963.

Hilliard, Robert L. *Writing for Television and Radio*. 3rd ed. New York: Hastings House, 1976.

Vale, Eugene. *Technique of Screenplay Writing*. New York: Grosset and Dunlap, 1972.

WRITING PROGRAMS

AWP Catalogue of Writing Programs (Norfolk: Associated Writing Programs, 4th ed. 1984). Descriptions of 279 writing programs in the U.S. and Canada, graduate and undergraduate, and of 18 writer's colonies and centers.

14b
Marketing your writing is the next step.

Once you have mastered the craft of writing sufficiently to produce a manuscript that has a chance of being accepted somewhere, the next job is to market it. This may be the most difficult part of trying to make a career out of freelance writing. Finding an agent who will represent you in the marketplace is half the battle. There is a separate note on agents later in this chapter. If you have to represent yourself, you must find out where the markets are and how to approach them.

The three most frequently consulted reference books on the literary marketplace are the following:

Fulton, Len, ed. *The International Directory of Little Magazines and Small Presses.* (Dustbooks, Box 100, Paradise, CA 95969). The 23rd edition (1987–88) lists 4,400 markets for writers. *The Wall Street Journal* has described this directory as "the bible of the business."

Literary Market Place (LMP). The Directory of American Book Publishing. (New York: R. R. Bowker Co.) Almost every library in the country subscribes to this reference book. It concentrates on all aspects of book publishing (not magazine markets). It has chapters on such things as book clubs, Associations,

Conferences, Courses, Awards, Contests, Grants. It describes practically every book publisher and then provides indexes according to fields of interest and subject matter.

Neff, Glenda Tennant, ed. *Writer's Market 1988*. (Cincinnati: Writer's Digest Books). It is subtitled *Where to Sell What You Write*. In addition to its extensive list of outlets it provides information about services, opportunities, agents, awards, contests, the business of freelancing, manuscript preparation, mailing, taxes, and rights.

Other useful reference books include:

Directory of Poetry Publishers. 2nd ed. 1986–87 (Dustbooks, Box 100, Paradise, CA 95969).

The 1986 Directory of Literary Magazines. (New York: CCLM, Coordinating Council of Literary Magazines, 666 Broadway, New York, NY 10012).

Judson, Jerome, ed. *Poet's Market 1987: Where and How to Publish Your Poetry*. (Cincinnati: Writer's Digest Books). Contains 1,500 listings and information on awards, contests, grants, conferences, colonies, workshops, organizations.

In addition to these reference books, there are many newsletters and guides issued by writers' organizations. (These organizations are listed later in this chapter.)

14c
Inquiries are often required before a publisher will look at a manuscript.

Some publishers will consider unsolicited material, others will not. Usually this is indicated in the directories where the publishers are described. Do not try to send your manuscript to those who have made it clear that they will not consider unsolicited manuscripts. Instead, write a letter of inquiry, in which you describe your project. This is usually not necessary in the case of small literary magazines, especially if you are sending out poetry. It is almost always necessary if you have a book to submit.

A letter of inquiry should be very brief, but it should include a description of the manuscript and a biographical note that mentions any earlier publications. If possible, you should get all this information into one page. Most of the directories listed above will indicate the names of editors. Always send your inquiry to a specific editor.

If you have a project, such as a screenplay, and you would like to reach a celebrity who you think might be interested, you might want to consult the following little reference book:

Levine, Michael. *The Address Book: How to Reach Anyone Who's Anyone*. New York: Putnam Publishing Group, Perigee Books, 1984.

14d
Agents can help you get your work published.

Finding an agent these days is very difficult. Most of the good ones are all booked up and will take a look at the work of a new writer only if it is recommended personally by one of their clients. At the other extreme there are agents who are not well connected and are not likely to be very effective representatives. Some agents charge for readings. Never pay an agent to read your manuscript. Most agencies take a 10 percent commission. A few go as high as 15 percent. Never send a manuscript to an agency unless you check them out first. The standard reference book is:

Literary Agents of North America. 3rd ed. (New York: Author Aid Associates, 340 E. 52 St., New York, NY 10022). This book describes every significant agency in the United States and Canada. It indicates the kind of material they are looking for, whether or not they look at unsolicited material, and whether or not they are interested in new writers.

If you are looking for an agent for a screenplay, the best source is the Agency List of the Writers Guild of America, Inc., which was founded in the 1930s as the Screenwriters Guild. It serves as a trade union, and it provides a registration service that will protect your material. There are two branches of this organization, East and West:

Writers Guild of America, East, Inc.
555 West 57 St.
New York, NY 10019

Writers Guild of America, West, Inc.
8955 Beverly Blvd.
Los Angeles, CA 90048

Their agency list is coded to indicate which ones will consider the work of new writers.

14e
Writers organizations can be good sources of information.

In addition to the Writers Guild of America there are many organizations that are dedicated to assisting writers in one way or another. Through them you can get information about markets, contests, awards, grants, copyrights, writing programs, writers' colonies, and agents. Most of them issue regular newsletters. Some of them publish useful directories. Not all of these organizations can be joined without certain conditions, but many of them will provide information to non-members.

For example, if you are enrolled in a writing program that has an institutional membership in the Associated Writing Programs (AWP), you are automatically a member. If you are not, you can join as an individual for a small fee. AWP provides many services for writers: a newsletter, a directory of writing programs, a placement service, and various awards.

Associated Writing Programs (AWP)
Old Dominion University
Norfolk, VA 23508

Poets & Writers, Inc. (P & W) issues a newsletter, *Coda*, which anyone can subscribe to. It contains a lot of valuable information about the craft, the market, new publications, and contests. P & W also publishes *A Directory of American Poets and Fiction Writers*, in which authors can list themselves with a description of their accomplishments and talents. This directory is designed to make it easier for program directors to find available writers who can give workshops or readings of their work. P & W also publishes a *Sponsors List*, which contains the names of organizations that are interested in hiring writers to give workshops and readings. Both P & W and PEN (see below) publish lists of grants and awards available to writers.

Poets & Writers, Inc.
72 Spring Street
New York, NY 10012

Additional organizations for writers are:

The Academy of American Poets
177 E. 87 St.
New York, NY 10128

The Authors League of America, Inc.
234 W. 44 St.
New York, NY 10036
(Includes The Authors Guild and the Dramatists Guild)

Coordinating Council of Literary Magazines (CCLM)
666 Broadway, 11th floor
New York, NY 10012

Mystery Writers of America, Inc.
236 W. 27 St.
New York, NY 10001

PEN American Center
Division of International PEN
568 Broadway
New York, NY 10012

Romance Writers of America
5206FM 190 West, Suite 208
Houston, TX 77069

Science Fiction Writers of America, Inc. (SFWA)
Box H
Wharton, NJ 07885

Western Writers of America, Inc.
1753 Victoria
Sheridan, WY 82807

14f
Contests, awards, and grants are available to give writers financial support.

There is considerable financial support available these days for aspiring writers. For those who choose the academic route, there are many graduate programs that offer MA, MFA, and PhD degrees. Almost all of them make available some kind of financial aid. Some of them are very generous and provide free tuition plus a stipend of from $3,000 to $7,500 a year in the form of grants, fellowships, or teaching assistantships. This assistance is described in the *AWP Catalogue of Writing Programs*. Further information can be had by writing to the program directors of specific programs. Public funds are also available to all writers through federal, state, and local agencies, such as the National Endowment for the Arts and the National Endowment for the Humanities and various State Councils on the Arts. The best source for financial assistance available to writers is:

Grants and Awards Available to American Writers. 15th ed. 1988/89 (A publication of PEN American Center, 568 Broadway, New York, NY 10012).

14g
Be informed about copyrights.

The best source for copyright information is the Copyright Office itself: Copyright Office, Library of Congress, Washington, D.C., 20559. They issue a number of circulars on the subject, beginning with R1 *Copyright Basics*, which tells you what kinds of works can be copyrighted and how to go about securing a copyright. Unpublished works as well as published works can be copyrighted. The appropriate forms can be requested from this office. Even before a copyright is registered in the Copyright Office, an author's rights are protected. All the author needs to do is indicate in the correct form on the manuscript a copyright notice: Copyright, 1990 Leslie Doe.

On January 1, 1978 the Copyright Act of 1976 (title 17 of the United States Code) went into effect. In general, it protects a work for the author's life plus fifty years. However, the law is complex and must be applied to many different kinds of works and circumstances. It is, therefore, advisable to get full information on the subject.

14h
Contracts protect an author.

Authors own the rights to their creation until they sign a contract giving away all or some of those rights, usually in exchange for a fee or royalty. All kinds of contracts can be written. The Authors Guild issues their recommended Standard Contract Form, which can be had by writing to that organization. In the case of poetry or short fiction published in a periodical the understanding, unless otherwise stated, is that the periodical has been given only the right to publish the work once in that publication. All other rights are reserved for the author. An agent will probably be able to negotiate a better contract than an individual can, and will take care of all the paperwork. If an agent is not involved, an individual can use a lawyer or handle the business personally. However, those writers who handle their own contracts should make sure they are well informed.

14i
Taxes

Writers are eligible to file a schedule C (for Business or Profession) with their 1040 form. This allows them to list all their deductible expenses, including agents' commissions, travel, research, entertainment, materials, supplies, and so on. In order to do this writers must keep accurate records, so that in the event of an audit they will be able to prove their deductions. The net loss or gain on a schedule C is subtracted from or added to one's adjusted gross income. There are, however, limitations on how many years a writer can claim a loss.

GLOSSARY OF
LITERARY TERMS

abstract: General and theoretical, without reference to specifics. Often applied to word choice. *Beauty* and *truth* are abstract.

absurd: Illogical or senseless. In literary works certain artistic effects can be achieved by using absurd elements.

accent: 1. The stress placed on a syllable in poetry. 2. A way of pronouncing a language that reveals a regional or foreign background.

act: A major subdivision of a play or opera.

action: The events that occur in any literary work. Action is presented through narration in fiction and poetry and through visual devices in drama and film. Dialogue and thoughts can also be considered part of the action.

adventure: Usually applied to works that concentrate on suspenseful happenings rather than subtleties of theme or depth of character.

alexandrine: A line of iambic hexameter (from French romances about Alexander the Great): "Beware the man who has no faith, no hope, no love."

allegory: A kind of literary work in which the characters stand for certain ideas. Bunyon's *The Pilgrim's Progress* is often cited as an example.

alliteration: The repetition of the initial sounds of certain words within a single line of poetry. "When I do count the clock that tells the time . . ." (Shakespeare)

allusion: A reference to a specific person, place, or thing, usually in a figure of speech: "Like Sisyphus he could have worked at his job forever without getting anywhere."

ambiguity: Having more than one meaning. When it is accidental ambiguity can be a flaw; when it is purposeful it can add richness to a passage.

anachronism: The placing of material in the wrong time period. Shakespeare, for instance, refers to a clock in *Julius Caesar*, though clocks were not yet invented in Caesar's time.

anagram: A rearrangement of the letters of one word to form another, as in *god — dog.*

analogy: A comparison, as in a simile or metaphor, in which one thing is like another thing. "Achieving success is like climbing a ladder. It requires a series of steps."

anapest: A metrical foot in poetry consisting of two unstressed syllables followed by a stressed syllable.

anecdote: A brief narrative, usually designed to make a point.

anticlimax: Any action that takes place after the climax or resolution of a literary work. It is either a dramatic letdown or totally unnecessary.

aphorism: A concise statement of some belief or truth. "Men are but children of a larger growth." (Dryden)

assonance: The recurrence of vowel sounds, often used in poetry. "The squat pen rests; snug as a gun." (Heaney)

ballad: A narrative poem or song, sometimes anonymous and belonging to folk art. In poetry the standard ballad stanza has four lines that rhyme *abcb*. There are four stresses in the first and third lines and three stresses in the second and fourth lines.

beat: A notation in scriptwriting meaning a pause in dialogue.

blank verse: Passages of iambic pentameter without end-rhyme.

cadence: The beat or rhythm of prose or free verse that is not conventionally structured or metrical.

caesura: A pause in a line of poetry because of meaning or syntax. "Beauty is truth, truth beauty." (Keats)

canto: A major subdivision of a long poem, as in Dante's *The Divine Comedy*.

character: 1. The traits or nature of a particular person. 2. A person, usually fictitious, who participates in the action of some work of literature.

classic: A literary work that has endured for a long time because of its impressive qualities and universal appeal.

classicism: In all the arts, including literature, an approach that involves formalism, discipline, restraint, and strong conventions, as opposed to romanticism, which is more subjective, unrestrained, and emotional.

cliché: A word or phrase that is worn out from overuse and loses much of its impact. "The ship of state."

cliff-hanger: An adventure full of suspense that leaves its hero or heroine in danger at the end of each chapter or episode, used frequently in film or magazine serials, and especially popular several decades ago.

climax: The moment of peak drama in a literary work. It often includes some sort of resolution of the conflict that has caused the drama.

coherence: Holding together. A coherent literary work is one in which all the parts are clearly put together.

colloquialism: A word or phrase more appropriate to informal conversation than to formal writing. Realistic dialogue cannot avoid colloquialisms.

comedy: A general event that is amusing, or, specifically, a play designed to amuse, as opposed to tragedy. Comedy can result from many sources, and can be farcical, satirical, slapstick, witty, situational, or even tragicomic.

conflict: In literature, characters or forces in opposition. There are social and psychological and political conflicts, as well as individual conflicts, internal and external. From conflict grows drama and suspense.

connotation: Extended meanings of words beyond their strict definition. Compare *politician* and *statesman*.

consonance: The similarity of consonant sounds, used especially in poetry.

continuity: A connected series of events that builds a plot. A technical term in scriptwriting that refers to the notations in a shooting script.

convention: An established practise in any area. There are many literary conventions, such as capitalizing each new line of a poem. In popular adventures, the triumph of good over evil might be considered a convention.

counterpoint: A musical term sometimes applied to literature to describe the simultaneous development of two or more sets of circumstances that have parallel elements.

couplet: A pair of lines of poetry, often rhyming and metrically similar.

crisis: A period of severe conflict during which significant changes take place, often the high point of a literary work.

criticism: In literature, the evaluation or analysis of a work. Sometimes the word is misunderstood as purely negative commentary.

cut: In scriptwriting a notation at the end of a scene. In editing, the shortening of a passage by omitting certain things.

dactyl: In poetry, a metrical unit made up of one stressed syllable followed by two unstressed syllables.

denotation: The literal meaning of a word, without additional connotations.

denouement: The final outcome or solution of a drama or narrative, in which all is explained.

description: That aspect of narration that tells you what things are like, usually as perceived by the five senses.

dialect: The particular way that a language is used by people of different regions or classes.

dialogue: The words spoken to each other by characters in any form of literature.

diction: The words chosen by an author. Diction is a major factor in tone and style.

dimeter: A line of poetry with only two metrical feet. "Roses are red."

dirge: A poem or song that mourns the dead.

dissonance: An unappealing combination of sounds; sometimes, however, used consciously and effectively.

documentary: A film of actual events, using a variety of sources. It can explore a subject in any field or dramatize episodes in history.

double entendre: From the French, meaning "double meaning." A conscious device often found in satire and comedy, but also in more serious works. For instance, Hamlet asks Ophelia, "Are you fair?" Naturally, she is puzzled by the double entendre. It is a reference to both honesty and beauty.

double rhyme: Words of two syllables that rhyme: *reaching, teaching*.

downstage: That part of the stage closest to the audience. Used in stage directions.

drama: Human events portrayed by actors on a stage with an audience in attendance.

dramatis personae: Characters in the play.

elegy: A poem for a funeral; a lamentation for the dead.

empathy: A sharing of other people's feelings. In literature a reader or member of the audience often feels what the characters in a book or on stage feel.

end rhyme: The similar sounds at the end of two or more lines of poetry.

end-stopped line: A line of poetry in which a pause comes at the end because of meaning or grammar.

English sonnet: Also known as the Shakespearean sonnet. Fourteen lines of iambic pentameter, rhyming *abab, cdcd, efef, gg.*

enjambment: A line of poetry that runs on in meaning to the next line: "My spirit is too weak — mortality
   Weighs heavily on me like unwilling sleep." (Keats)

epic: A long poem with larger than life characters and universal themes often drawn from legends. Homer's *Iliad* and *Odyssey,* for example.

epigram: A brief, witty saying, expressed usually in one sentence. "Two's company; three's a crowd."

epilogue: A brief statement added to a literary work after it has been essentially concluded.

epiphany: A revelation or sudden insight.

episode: A brief event in a longer narrative.

epistle: A formal and literary letter.

epistolary: An adjective used to describe novels made up exclusively of letters.

epitaph: A poem or inscription suitable for a tombstone, but not always put to that use.

epithet: A descriptive word added to a person's name: "Eric the Red."

essay: A short discussion of some theme or topic in prose. The word was first used by Montaigne to describe his personal thoughts and comments (1580).

eulogy: Formal praise, written or spoken, for someone who has died.

euphemism: A mild expression used in place of one that might be offensive: *passed away* instead of *died*.

euphony: A pleasing combination of sounds.

exposition: Any definition or explanation of something, either written or spoken.

expressionism: The use of distortions, symbols, and subjectivity in any of the arts.

fable: A simple story that makes a moral point and often uses animals as characters.

fairy tale: A story involving imaginary and magical creatures such as fairies, elves, and spirits.

fantasy: A story involving purely imaginary creatures in imaginary places.

farce: An obvious and exaggerated comedy that draws on loud and silly devices for its humor.

feminine rhyme: The rhyming of words with two or more syllables: *meeting—greeting*.

fiction: Any literary work that involves invented elements. More specifically, fiction refers to novels and short stories.

figure of speech: An expression that cannot be taken literally, often a simile, metaphor, or allusion. Non-literal comparisons:

"How sharper than a serpent's tooth it is/ To have a thankless child!" (Shakespeare)

first person: The point of view (*I, we*) from which much fiction and poetry is written.

flashback: Going back to an earlier time period than the period established for a literary work in order to insert a scene, often a memory or reverie.

flat character: A character without depth, sometimes a mere stereotype.

folklore: A body of traditions and legends expressed orally or in various kinds of literary works, usually anonymous, from proverbs and work songs to myths and ballads.

foot: A metrical unit consisting of two or more syllables, one of which is stressed.

foreshadowing: A clue or hint of things to come in a literary work with some kind of plot.

form: A clearly defined arrangement of the parts of a work. Some forms have become traditional, such as the sonnet or ballad; others are highly individual.

formula: A very conventional way of developing stories and plays, usually of a commercial nature and without much literary depth or originality. There are formulas for detective stories, westerns, situation comedies, romances, and other popular genres.

free verse: Verse without a fixed pattern of rhythm and rhyme, but with a pleasing cadence of some sort.

genre: A broad subdivision of literature, such as fiction, poetry, and drama, but also further divisions into more specific categories, such as lyric, romance, and docudrama.

hackneyed: Words and phrases that have become colorless from overuse are described as hackneyed or trite.

haiku: A Japanese verse form that usually uses three lines and a total of seventeen syllables and makes some kind of comment or comparison. There is some question about whether or not the form can be carried over into English.

heptameter: A line of poetry consisting of seven feet.

hero: 1. A hero or heroine, in general, is a person of courage and other admirable qualities. 2. In literature, the central character is often called the hero or heroine, no matter what qualities he or she possesses.

heroic couplet: In poetry, two lines of iambic pentameter that rhyme.

heroic stanza: A quatrain in iambic pentameter.

hexameter: A line of poetry consisting of six feet, or metrical units.

hubris: From the Greek, meaning arrogance or excessive pride, a serious tragic flaw.

humor: The comic appreciation of human foibles, absurdities, and amusing situations.

hyperbole: Obvious but literary exaggeration. Othello says to Desdemona that if he cannot love her, "Chaos is come again."

iamb: A metric foot of two syllables, the first of which is unstressed, and the second of which is stressed. The adjective is *iambic*.

idyll: A piece of poetry or prose in which the pastoral life and innocence are idealized.

image: A picture conjured up by a literary device such as a metaphor or simile or symbol. Images appeal to the senses and are essential to all imaginative literature.

impressionism: An approach to the arts, including literature, that stresses the subjective, the feelings of the author or of the characters.

incantation: The use of words to invoke supernatural powers, usually in the form of a chant.

interior monologue: The interior thoughts of a character, recorded in literature in a variety of styles from formal soliloquys to the poetic passages in Virginia Woolf and the cruder levels of thought in James Joyce.

internal rhyme: Similar sounds of two or more words within a single line of poetry.

invocation: An appeal to a supernatural being for help or guidance.

irony: Saying one thing but meaning something quite opposite. An ironic ending is one in which one thing is intended, but the opposite occurs, as in *Hamlet* when a poisoned drink intended for him is drunk instead by his mother.

Italian sonnet: Also known as the Petrarchan sonnet, it consists of fourteen lines, an octave and a sestet, rhyming *abbaabba* and *cdecde*.

jargon: The terminology of a particular activity, trade, or profession, such as sports, education, or law. When it is introduced pointlessly into standard English, it can weaken one's prose.

lament: Any literary expression of grief, such as an elegy.

lampoon: A criticism of characters, groups, or ideas through ridicule.

legend: A story of unknown origin handed down from generation to generation, and often about a colorful, heroic, or saintly figure.

limerick: A humorous and sometimes naughty form of verse, made up of five lines that rhyme *aabba*. The first, second and fifth line contain three stresses; the third and fourth lines contain two stresses.

lyric: A short poem that is subjective, musical, and full of feeling.

madrigal: A short, musical love poem that can be easily set to music, and often was in Italy, France, and England as early as the sixteenth century.

malapropism: The ridiculous misuse of words. A device often used in comedy. "I can't visit the country because I have an allegory to wild flowers."

melodrama: A play with implausibly exaggerated actions and emotions and not much depth or literary value.

metaphor: A non-literal comparison, a figure of speech: "His friend's betrayal was a dagger in his heart."

meter: Poetic measure, using units called *feet*, which are made up of combinations of stressed and unstressed syllables. Some poems are made of measured lines; others are free of meter but rely on cadence.

mixed metaphor: The illogical mixture of two or more metaphors within the same passage: "The rose of love is the altar at which he worshiped."

monologue: Something spoken by one person: a speech, a soliloquy, a narrative, a comic routine. An internal monologue tries to capture the thoughts of one person in some literary form.

motivation: The desires or other psychological conditions that cause the actions of characters. Motivations must be plausible if characters are to be believable.

myth: A traditional story of unknown origin that often contains a non-scientific explanation of some aspect of nature or the human condition. Myths of creation, for instance.

narration: An account of a series of events either in prose or poetry.

narrator: The one who tells the story, sometimes the author, sometimes one of the characters, sometimes an omniscient, anonymous speaker. See also *persona*.

naturalism: The approach to literature and other arts that tries to present human experience and the world as it actually is, without idealism or sentimentality.

novel: A coherent piece of fiction of a certain length, sometimes fixed at a minimum of about 50,000 words. Works shorter than that but longer than short stories are often called *novellas*.

ode: A formal, lyrical poem on a serious theme. See "Ode on a Grecian Urn," by John Keats.

octave: In poetry, a stanza of eight lines.

octameter: A line of poetry consisting of eight feet.

off-rhyme: A rhyme that involves sounds that are close but not precisely the same: *kiss—chess*.

omniscient: All-knowing. A frequently used point of view in literature.

onomatopoeia: The use of words that sound like what they mean: *crash, bang*.

ottava rima: A stanza of eight lines of iambic pentameter with a rhyme pattern of *abababcc*.

parable: A story designed to illustrate a moral principle or universal truth.

parody: A humorous imitation of a person, events, society, or ideas, intended to be satirical or critical.

pastoral: A literary work dealing with the simple rural life, especially its charm and innocence.

pathos: That which evokes pity, sorrow, or compassion.

pentameter: A line of poetry that consists of five feet.

persona: A narrator created to tell the reader what happens, not necessarily the author, even in works written in the first or third person. Even in the most personal works, a distinction must be made between the author's real voice and his or her literary voice.

personification: A literary device in which inanimate objects, animals, and abstractions are endowed with human qualities.

picaresque: A type of fiction made up loosely of the adventurous episodes in the life of a rascal or rogue.

plot: A carefully arranged series of events in a narrative work. The sequence is designed to lead to a certain effect, a revelation or emotional impact.

poetic license: The occasional violation of the conventional uses of language in order to achieve a special artistic effect. G. M. Hopkins, for instance, sometimes uses archaic diction.

point of view: The position of the narrator, who can be a participant or a non-participant in the action. If the narrator is a participant, the story is usually told in the first-person (I). If the narrator is not a participant, the story can be told in the second person, but that is rare and not advisable. The narrator will probably use the third-person. In that case, there are two major options: to see the action from the point of view of one of the characters, or to use an omniscient (all-knowing) point of view. In a long work, such as a novel, several different points of view might be involved.

prose: All forms of written expression except poetry, which has special requirements. Works of non-fiction as well as fiction are prose compositions.

prosody: The principles of poetic structure, including meter, rhyme, rhythm, and stanza forms.

protagonist: The main character in a literary work, no matter what his or her qualities are.

pun: An amusing play on words, such as this description of a poker game: "Chips that pass in the night."

quatrain: A stanza of four lines, or a complete poem if it consists of only one such stanza.

quintet: A stanza consisting of five lines.

realism: An approach to literature in which ordinary life is depicted with objective and photographic accuracy. Because this approach has so often focused on the harsh and sordid aspects of ordinary life, the word *realism* has taken on an additional connotation.

refrain: A portion of a poem that is repeated at certain intervals, often at the end of each stanza.

resolution: That portion of the final part of a literary work that ends the dramatic tension with some kind of solution of the problem or resolution of the conflict.

rhyme: Identical sounds in poetry, whether they occur within a line (internal rhyme) or at the end of certain lines (end rhyme).

rhyme royal: A rhyme scheme of *ababbcc* in a seven line stanza of iambic pentameter.

rhythm: A pattern of beats or accents either in conventional or unconventional forms. There is rhythm in prose as well as in poetry, though it may be impossible to scan.

romance: Once a term used to describe literary works with heroic characters and fanciful events; now used almost exclusively to describe a love story, sometimes of a superficial and commercial nature.

romanticism: An approach to literature marked by a freedom from classical rules and the expression of strong emotions, often subjectively.

round character: A fully developed, three-dimensional character that is utterly plausible, as opposed to flat characters that tend to be superficial and not altogether convincing.

saga: A long narrative about the adventures and achievements of an extraordinary or legendary character.

sarcasm: The use of harsh and wounding remarks with a touch of irony.

satire: A literary technique that uses ridicule, humor, and irony to point out the faults of an individual or a society or all of mankind.

scansion: The analysis of the meter and rhyme of a poem, using certain standard marks for stressed syllables, unstressed syllables, pauses, and rhyme patterns.

scenario: The sequence of events, including dialogue and characters, described in a script intended for film or television. A scenario can also be a hypothetical sequence of events, whether written down or not.

scene: A subdivision of an act in a play, a clearly defined unit of action in a longer work.

science fiction: A narrative that makes plausible use of scientific materials but remains within the realm of fiction. Often distinguished from fantasy, which includes fanciful and supernatural ingredients.

second person: In literature, an occasionally used point of view (*you*).

sentimentality: A preoccupation with exaggerated emotions that can weaken the quality of a literary work.

septet: A stanza of seven lines.

sestet: A stanza of six lines.

setting: The place where the action occurs in any literary work. The setting is formally named at the beginning of a play and any of its subdivisions (acts and scenes).

Shakespearean sonnet: See *English sonnet.*

short story: A short narrative, usually under 10,000 words, that deals with a single dramatic event or central conflict that is developed and then resolved.

simile: A figurative comparison that states that one thing is *like* (*as*) another, but not in a literal sense. "He was like a bull in a china shop."

slant rhyme: See *off rhyme.*

slice of life: A literary work that allows one to have a look at a segment of "real life" without much concern for plot. However, there is significance in the segment, often a commentary on a particular character or way of life.

soliloquy: A speech spoken aloud but intended as a representation of the character's thoughts.

sonnet: A poem consisting of fourteen lines of iambic pentameter and a rhyme scheme in which there might be slight variations. See also *English sonnet*.

Spencerian stanza: Eight lines of iambic pentameter followed by a line of iambic hexameter, rhyming ababbcbcc. The basic stanza of *The Faerie Queene* by Edmund Spenser.

spondee: In poetry, a metric unit consisting of two stressed syllables.

stanza: A subdivision of a poem with some kind of structure: couplet, quatrain, Spencerian stanza, and so on. A poem can consist of just one stanza.

stereotype: A simplistic and traditional view of things, a stock character, usually two-dimensional.

stock character: A figure with traditional characteristics but not much depth or individuality, such as the butler, the workaholic businessperson, the wide-eyed innocent.

stream of consciousness: A technique used in literature to capture human thoughts as they actually occur, however distorted and ungrammatical.

stress: Accent, emphasis. In poetry, the accent on a syllable.

structure: A logical pattern or plan in a literary work, such as the sequence of events in a story, the acts in a play, the rhyme and rhythm pattern of a poem.

style: The individual and characteristic manner of writing, influenced by the personality of the author and reflecting the author's attitudes.

subjectivity: The tendency to see the outside world from inside the characters. A preoccupation with the thoughts and feelings of the characters.

suspense: Uncertainty and anxiety about the outcome of a series of events.

suspension of disbelief: The willingness of the reader or audience to accept, for the moment, that fiction is fact, in order to experience literary works as though they were true.

symbol: Something specific that stands for something more abstract and complex. Moby Dick is a whale, but he stands for certain mysterious forces in the universe.

synopsis: A short summary of a longer work. A synopsis sometimes appears at the beginning of a novel when it is sent to an editor, and even more frequently at the beginning of a screenplay.

tags: In dialogue, the labels that indicate who is speaking: *he said, she said.*

tercet: A three-line stanza.

terza rima: A form of verse made up of tercets and a rhyme scheme in which the middle line of the tercet rhymes with the first and third lines of the following tercet: *aba, bcb, cdc.* The lines are iambic and eleven syllables long.

tetrameter: A poetic line of four feet.

theme: The central idea or impact of a literary work.

third person: The most common point of view used in fiction (*he, she, they*).

tone: The quality of a literary work that reveals the author's attitude: for example, satirical, sardonic, gloomy.

tragedy: Any literary drama about the downfall of a sympathetic hero or heroine, who often dies at the end. Classically, a tragic flaw is involved, but in modern times blame is sometimes shifted to society or circumstances.

tragic flaw: A defect in the character of an otherwise good or noble person. The defect leads to tragedy, as in the case of Macbeth and his "vaulting ambition."

tragic hero: Classically, a person of good qualities who makes an error in judgment because of a tragic flaw (such as pride or ambition). In Greek tragedy the hero was a person in a high position, often a king. The same is true, slightly modified, in Shakespeare (Hamlet, Lear, Macbeth). In modern times, a tragic hero is often a more ordinary person.

trimeter: A poetic line of three feet.

triplet: A three-line stanza.

triteness: Writing marked by worn-out phrases or ideas.

trochee: A metric unit in poetry (a foot) with a stressed syllable followed by an unstressed syllable.

unity: A quality that occurs in literature when all the parts are related by some central theme or artistic concept.

upstage: The back of the stage.

verse: Sometimes a single line of poetry, but more often merely a synonym for poetry in general.

villanelle: A poem consisting of five tercets and a quatrain with a rhyme scheme that uses only two rhymes: *aba, aba, aba, aba, aba, abaa*. The lines tend to have five stresses and to be iambic.

whodunit: An informal expression for a story or drama about crime. The suspense stems from the reader's curiosity about who committed the crime.

wit: A form of humor that depends largely on language and ideas rather than actions and situations.

COPYRIGHTS AND ACKNOWLEDGMENTS

INDEX

Page numbers in **boldface** following a title indicate an extract quoted as an example in the text.